Passing of the Giants of the Human Spirit

Passing of the Giants of the Human Spirit

The Rev. Herbert Daughtry

AFRICA WORLD PRESS

TRENTON | LONDON | CAPE TOWN | NAIROBI | ADDIS ABABA | ASMARA | IBADAN | NEW DELHI

AFRICA WORLD PRESS
541 West Ingham Avenue | Suite B
Trenton, New Jersey 08638

Book design: Dawid Kahts
Cover design: Ashraful Haque

Cataloging-in-Publication Data may be obtained from the Library of Congress.

ISBNs: 9781569027820 (HB)
         9781569027837 (PB)

What is the worst of woes that wait on age?
What stamps the wrinkle deeper on the brow?
To view each loved one blotted from life's page
And to be alone on earth as I am now.

—Lord Byron

Table of Contents

Introduction

The *Passing of the Giants of the Human Spirit* has a peculiar beginning rooted in anger, disappointment, grief, and more. A couple of the most painful memories—painful, even now, as I recall them—highlight my point.

A close friend of mine died. We had fought together on many fronts. I thought I should have been asked to participate in the funeral ceremony. Not only was I not invited, but I was completely ignored. At this special friend's funeral, I was left off the program. As the participants sat in the office of the deceased, a young minister, whom I knew not, stood as the presiding officer and commenced giving instructions. First, he asked me to leave.

As I departed from the office and tried to get in the sanctuary, I found that there were no seats. I remembered the countless hours, days, and nights I had spent with the deceased in the very office that I was told to vacate. The person who put me out probably hadn't been born, or was a child, during those days. I did not stay for the ceremony. I returned to my church in tears. I decided I would do my own eulogy for the deceased.

A similar situation occurred when my wife and I attended the funeral of a longtime friend, a special friend. Many times, he would unburden his soul to me. Often, he would come to my church for respite, solace, and inspiration. Depending on the celebrity status of the person, memorial services can be packed, with even reserved seats often taken by usurpers. Such was the case on this particular occasion.

I led my wife all over the place, looking for seats that were supposed to be reserved for us. In the rear of the church, we managed to secure seats. I went for a restroom break, and when I returned my seat was taken. I stood in the middle of the sanctuary. It seemed that all eyes were upon me. I felt small and humiliated. Again, I departed the ceremony. As I drove home, I tried to remember how many times this had happened, not to me only, but to many others. In fact, I wondered how many other people had had my experience.

I thought about the deceased. What would he do in such a situation? The answer came immediately, almost before the question was completed: He would smile, absorb the insults as if nothing had happened, be sympathetic to all concerns—he would stay above all the drama. I found myself smiling.

And then I knew what I would do: I would write.

I confess, I find some amusement in the drama: people suddenly put in charge, scurrying about, brimming over with self-aggrandizement, and sternly giving orders. I recall what a friend once told me upon his speedy recovery from a serious illness. I asked him what had happened to make him heal so quickly. He said, "When I thought about who would do my funeral, I told myself, 'I have to get well.'" It became a standing joke between us. But it revealed a startling truth.

Oftentimes, the participants in a funeral ceremony were resented or distrusted by the deceased. As I studied the people who had made the arrangements, the reason for their slights became evident. Also, the arrangements are made by the family or other designated persons, but they don't always know about the deceased's relationships or final wishes. They were left to guess. Their choices are made according to *their* personal values and relationships. If the deceased is a celebrity, then celebrity types commiserate with what the family perceives as the celebrity status of the deceased. The whole affair becomes status driven, from the selection of the mortician, to the coffin, to the flowers, to the cars and the venue. Much of the anxiety could have been relieved if the deceased had made their wishes known before their final hour. A discussion with the family, preparation of the funeral program placed into the will—or creating an addendum to the will—could alleviate the anxieties.

So what began as an exercise to vent or relieve pain, became a practice. Anyone with whom I've had the most casual relationships, or whom I've admired, I write about. I was denied participation in only a few of the funerals for the persons I've written about in the following articles, originally printed in *The Daily Challenge,* published by Thomas Watkins.

Writing these articles afforded me the opportunity to share my knowledge and/or feelings about the deceased. Some of these persons were nationally and internationally known. Others, while unknown to the world at large, were nonetheless special to me. Chronicling the passing of these persons also triggered other powerful memories that were central to my personal development and worldview. Such jolting of personal memories and lessons learned are part of the wisdom we all gain from the lives of the people we encounter on this journey of life, and so I included them in my reflections on the deceased.

In time, I came to realize I had a book on my hands that included the life and times of the deceased, but was in fact a book of living history. For I wrote while the forming history continued to unfold. I had on record a firsthand account of history, in addition to immortalizing the deceased, however obscure in life. I have found that in telling their stories, I was telling my own. In relating intimate details that may have been known by only the deceased and myself, I also have provided loved ones with a written keepsake. Of course, in some cases the deceased was famous and the subject of many biographies, but even so, my small contribution adds to the deceased's story.

Moreover, I leave a record of immense importance: If you feel someone or life has not treated you right, don't waste time and energy absorbed in self-pity or schemes of retaliation. Instead, turn the situation into substance for your own benefit. If a stumbling block has been put in your way, however it got there, make it a stepping stone. If you've been thrown a lemon, make lemonade. You'll be happier, healthier, purposeful, and productive.

This is the awesome power we have—our God-likeness—the capacity to bring something out of nothing, to take the worse and make the best, to turn pain into power. We, like God, are in charge of all creation. This is what is taught in the Holy Bible, and sages across history have confirmed it to be so. We are the masters of creation, circumstance, and events, the present and the future. That is, we are masters—if we believe it and act it.

The Makings of a Great Human Spirit

In this volume, I've explored giants of the human spirit, like Pope John Paul II, Judge Bruce Wright, Attorney Johnnie Cochran, Actor/Activist Ozzie Davis, Mr. Wilbur Levin, James Forman, Eloise Dicks, and Glenn Cunningham.

Over the years, I've known many other great men and women, some superficially and others in depth, such as Kwame Ture, revolutionary; Maurice Bishop, prime minister of Grenada; Michael Manley, prime minister of Jamaica; Joshua Nkomo, vice president of Zimbabwe (1987–1999), founder of Zimbabwe African Peoples Union (ZAPU), and grandfather of the African Liberation Movement; Dr. Martin Luther King, Jr., president of the Southern Christian Leadership Conference; Malcolm X, president of the Organization of Afro-American Unity; Dr. Betty Shabazz, professor of Medgar Evers College; Ella Baker, activist and mentor for many Student Nonviolent Coordinating Council (SNCC) leaders; Sonny Carson, activist; Leroy Applin, deacon of The House of the Lord Church; Shirley Chisholm, a US Congresswoman.

As I studied the lives of these great men and women, I wondered if there was a common substance or a common thread that ran through all of them. They were so different, and yet they were the same in many respects.

Below is the motif that I think resonate in all of them, and perhaps in all great people:

- **Expansiveness.** They embraced the world. They reached out to everyone. They were too big for any mold.
- **Sagacity.** They had a vast storehouse of knowledge and insight. Their interest seemed endless. They seemed to know something about everything. They were unsurpassed in their special calling.

- **A deep caring spirit.** They cared deeply and were particularly concerned about those deemed the least in society. They were not ashamed or afraid to be identified with the dispossessed.
- **Purpose.** They were committed to a cause or purpose bigger than themselves. They knew it and gave their life's blood toiling in the pursuit of their cause.
- **A love of life.** They all seemed to have had a zest for living, a love of life. They were willing to share life and sacrifice it for others.
- **Creativity.** They were creative pioneers, not afraid to break new ground, or to go where others feared to tread.
- **Courage.** They were uncompromising in their conviction. They spoke their minds. They held the line on what they believed.
- **Integrity.** They were honest and truthful. You felt you could trust them. They said what they believed and believed what they said.
- **Generosity.** They were generous with their time, talents, treasures, and resources.
- **Humility.** They were sincerely humble. They were easily accessible to all. They were comfortable with all kinds of folk. (A good way to determine the authenticity of any do-gooder or helper of the needy is asking, "Are they comfortable among the masses? Can they walk among kings and keep the common touch?")

I believe these qualities were common threads evident in the lives of all of the persons I have written about in this book.

Work was another theme that ran through their lives.

Good Work and the Quality of Life

From June through August 2007, I was touched by more deaths than in any similar time span in all of the seventy-eight years I'd lived at that point. Some of the deceased were notables. All were important to me. Among those who made their transition were:

- **Dave Brothers**—December 25, 1919–June 15, 2007
- **Mae Mallory**—June 9, 1927–July 2, 2007

- **Delores Cusberth**—September 10, 1921–July 23, 2007
- **Dennis J. Tinsley**—September 19,1953–July 25, 2007
- **The Rev. Joe L. Parker**—October 16, 1940–July 25, 2007
- **Max L. Roach**—January 10, 1924–August 16, 2007
- **Mzee Moyo**—August 11, 1943–August 16, 2007
- **Asa Hilliard**—August 22, 1933–August 16, 2007
- **Alberta B. Franklin** (cousin)—December 1, 1929–August 22, 2007

Becoming this acquainted with death in such a short time span made me examine life more closely, which quickly revealed the importance of work in the quality of our lives.

There is a Bible passage from the book of Ecclesiastes that says, "My heart took delight in all my work, and this was the reward for all my labor." I hope that all those who made their transition could read those words and say, "This Scripture applied to my life. Looking back across the years that I sojourned in the land of the living, I can truly say I am satisfied with my life's work."

To take delight in one's work is indeed a priceless remuneration.

Regardless of the type of work or where it fits on the social ladder, if you are happy in your work, you have achieved what few, relatively speaking, have achieved. Dr. Martin Luther King, Jr. said, "If a man is called to be a street sweeper, he should sweep streets even as Michelangelo painted, or Beethoven composed music, or Shakespeare wrote poetry. He should sweep streets so well that all the hosts of heaven and earth will pause so say, 'Here lived a great street sweeper who did his job well.'"

Most of us work at jobs we dislike or tolerate to make a living. We work to make a living, not to make a life. Therein is the major difference. To work because we have to is not to work because we want to. When we like what we do, we will always be working at it, even on what we call vacations. When we are away from our workplace, the workplace will still be in us. Because we like what we do, we derive satisfaction from thinking about it.

Let's be clear, I'm not talking about the workaholics. Workaholics are driven; they may or may not like what they are doing. Rather,

I'm talking about those who love their work, and work because of that love.

Also, there is the joy in a job well-done.

There is satisfaction in knowing you have done your best, and your best has resulted in a job well-done. There is satisfaction in knowing you have made a contribution to the human family or life, that you have put something back into the kitty or coffers of Mother Nature. What can be more pleasing than to look back on one's life and say, "My heart took delight in all my work."

The Apostle Paul, near the end of his life's journey said, "For I am now ready to be offered up, and the time of my departure is at hand, I have fought a good fight, I have finished my course, I have kept the faith: Henceforth, there is laid up for me a crown of righteousness, which the Lord, the righteous judge shall give me at that day: and not to me only, but unto all them also that love his appearing" (2 Timothy 4:6–8).

We should all strive to have that testimony at the end of our lives. The contemplation of having such a testimony ought to inspire us to live our lives in such a way that even the mortician will weep and offer a free funeral, that humans will grieve, and the angels in heaven will welcome us into the presence of God.

It's my hope that this book, this tribute to great human spirits who have left their mark on the world and the history of our time, will inspire others to such lifelong endeavors.

Author's Note

The articles in this book were originally published in *The Daily Challenge,* a Brooklyn-based weekly newspaper, from 2004 to 2016. These writings have *not* been updated because I wanted them to convey the insights and feelings I experienced when I wrote them. Also, inconsistencies in the use, or not, of courtesy, academic and professional titles throughout the text reflect the nature of the relationship I had with the deceased. Throughout these articles, I've interchangeably referred to friends by their well-earned titles and by the way I addressed them as a friend or associate. Lastly, the death of loved ones, friends, or associates often trigger memories—perhaps of a shared time period or neighborhood or event—that may only tangentially relate to the deceased. Nevertheless, those memories may hold substantial life lessons, and so I've included some of these in separate sidebars following my reflections on the deceased person.

Dedication

I want to dedicate this volume to Chairman Maurice Bishop of Grenada, friend, comrade, freedom fighter, on the 40th anniversary of his assassination along with the comrades who were assassinated with him; and the Grenadian people who always showed me love and appreciation, especially Dr. Carol McIntosh a member in our church, the house of the lord church from her student days, who saved my life by insisting that I see her classmate Dr. Bernard Rawlings when I was dying daily of a terrible disease. Dr. Rawlings miraculously performed a life saving surgery.

Stay up Grenada!
Forward ever Backward never!

Acknowledgements

This volume has been around for years as the passing of the last person indicates _____. It explains why some of my closest friends and comrades in the freedom struggle have not been included. They will be in Volume II. For years, the manuscript gathered dust on the shelf.

Finally, I asked Ms. Yvette Moore, who herself was writing her book, *Freedom Songs and Just Sketching* and Herb Boyd, for editorial assistance. Herb Boyd is a prolific literary giant who has authored many books and is the weekly columnist for the Amsterdam News. They did what was requested with great skill and encouragement. Still, it wasn't enough. There was work for me to do.

For whatever reason I neglected to fulfill my task. Back on the shelf went the manuscript. But Herb pushed and pulled and insisted the book would make a great contribution. Finally, I finished my assignment and submitted the manuscript to Kasshaun Checole, Publisher of Africa World Press. He had already published three of my books, *No Monopoly on Suffering, My Beloved Community, In My Lifetime: Towards the Presidency of Barack Obama.* Obviously, there was more work the publisher had to do to finalize the manuscript.

I want to especially thank my publisher, Mr. Checole for his patience, his expertise and for his readiness and willingness to publish another volume. Also, Sarah, my administrative assistant and my granddaughter-in-law who read and re-read, and assisted in the coordination of the work of all the participants as the book was evolving. Especially, I want to thank Herb Boyd. I can truly say that this book

11

would never have seen the light of day if Herb Boyd had not been involved. Plus he volunteered to write a prologue and participate in bringing his vast network and circulation experience to ensure the success of the volume - indeed this work is a Herb and Herb project – there will be others.

1

Business Leaders

Wilbur "Bill" Levin[1]

Sunrise: October 21, 1920, Brooklyn, New York
Sunset: April 12, 2005, Manhattan, New York

A Revered Rabbi

My wife and I joined other ministers and their spouses for the annual dinner at the home of one of the ministers of the Partnership of Faith, a group of multi-race, multi-faith leaders. It was an evening of food, laughter, and storytelling.

Then Rabbi Ronald Sobel, retired minister of Temple Emanuel-El in Manhattan, came over and greeted us in his usual jovial way. He inquired of family, health, and church. Then, somewhere in his conversation, as was our custom, he began to talk about a mutual old friend, Wilbur "Bill" Levin. He said he had officiated at Bill Levin's memorial.

My wife and I were startled speechless before saying, "Memorial!" in unison, after regaining our composure.

Rabbi Sobel proceeded to say that Bill Levin had died Tuesday, April 12, 2005, and the memorial had been Friday, April 15.

It was all we could do not to allow the sad news to dampen the joy of the evening. If Bill were here, we reasoned, he would be right in the midst of the joviality. He would want us to be happy.

I met Bill Levin around 1967. I was vice chairperson of Operation Breadbasket, the economic arm of Dr. Martin King Jr.'s Southern Christian Leadership Conference (SCLC). Dr. William A. Jones, pastor of Bethany Baptist Church in Brooklyn, New York, was the chairperson. I was leading a boycott against Martin's, a department store on Fulton Street, downtown Brooklyn, which has since closed along with E. J. Korvette and Mays department stores.

Bill Levin was president of Martin's. During the negotiation, Bill and I got into a heated exchange. Afterward, he came to me and said, "Rev., let's have lunch sometime." I said, "OK," thinking it would never happen.

It did happen. We had lunch not long after, and we continued to have lunch up to about six months before his death. From the time we had our first lunch, he attended nearly every major function we had.

Our frequent lunchtimes were delightful, informative, and sometimes argumentative. We both had strong opinions about everything. Sometimes we agreed, but frequently we disagreed. We were never hesitant about voicing our disagreement. Sometimes we would leave the restaurant arguing. Then before we parted, we would agree on the next date for lunch. We were determined not to let our differences spoil our friendship.

He used to say to me, "Herb, I like you, but I think your politics stink." My response was, "Well, Bill, I happened to feel the same way about you. I can understand your feeling that way about me. I guess if I were a wealthy president of a bank"—by then, he had now become president of a bank, a move he discussed with me—"I guess I'd feel the same way."

Bill was the personification of what, I guess, the English mean when they say, "a gentleman." He was always friendly to everybody. He loved to meet people. I think he rivaled the Rev. Jesse Jackson and me in knowing many different kinds of people. He was generous, kind, and caring. He always wanted to know who he could help or what cause he could support. I marveled at his range of knowledge, information, and his grasp of current events.

To me, Bill Levin was in the class with the people I call giants of the human spirit. He was a good man and a good friend. I will miss him very much.

Wilbert "Bill" Tatum[2]

Sunrise: January 23, 1933, Durham, North Carolina
Sunset: February 25, 2009, Dubrovnik, Croatia

Wilbert Arnold Tatum was born in Durham, North Carolina, on January 23, 1933, as one of thirteen children of Eugene and Mittie Novesta Tatum. Besides his daughter, Elinor, and his wife, Susan, he is survived by a brother, Herbert, and three sisters: Lorraine Graves, Edna Swann, and Kali Sichen.

After moving to New York, he became active in the community and was named assistant director for community relations for the Department of Buildings by Mayor John V. Lindsay in 1966. In 1970, he was Deputy Manhattan Borough president. A year later, he was able to bring together the investors who bought *The Amsterdam News*, one of the oldest and most influential African-American-owned newspapers in the nation.

Bill Tatum started out in journalism by writing for three small newspapers started by his father to provide information to black farmers. After serving in the Marine Corps from 1951 to 1954, he graduated from Lincoln University in Pennsylvania, and later received a master's degree from Occidental College in Los Angeles, California.

I can't remember when I first met him. I know it was in the late 1970s or early 80s. He was full of energy and was audacious, candid, and sometimes brusque or even abrasive. I was impressed with the brilliance of his mind. His thinking was quick and sharp. I always got the feeling he swiftly grasped the essence of an argument or conversation and patiently waited for the others to catch up or finish making their point, or sometimes he couldn't restrain himself and would abruptly interrupt the conversation as if to say, "Let's cut to the chase."

Across the years, there were countless ways we interacted in community meetings, workshops, demonstrations, rallies, etc. He was more than a journalist, a scholar; more than a reader and writer of books; more than a master of paper, pencils, and cameras, as laudatory as those professions are. He was also a fighter, a warrior, a "throw down the gauntlet," a "by any means necessary" man.

He was a wordsmith par excellence. His words could sometimes be like arrows or acid—sharp or burning—but they could also be gentle, soothing, encouraging, and challenging. Former New York City Mayor Ed Koch could attest to Bill Tatum's pugnacity. From February 1986 to September 1989, Tatum ran editorials entitled "Koch Must Go!" Week after week, and on the front page, he relentlessly slashed, burned, and jolted Ed Koch. And the articles were not empty rambling, but substantive, replete with facts, analyses, and relevant information.

His research was thorough and extensive. He was scholarly and widely read. He seemed to be interested in everything. His childish curiosity never left him. I used to marvel at the vastness of his knowledge and experience. He seemed to know something about everything.

- Tatum had a commitment to decency, fairness, and justice. His compassion for the impoverished, dispossessed, and oppressed was boundless and came through in his work and writings. Equal to his compassion for "the least of these" in society, and what seemed like a natural marriage, was his fiery passion for justice, equality, and human rights. He was a relentless foe of all the "isms"—racism, classism, chauvinism, anti-Semitism, and also homophobia. He captured the ideal Dr. King spoke of having "a tough mind and a tender heart."

Yes, he could be brash, feisty, "in your face" when someone or something rubbed him the wrong way. Percy Sutton tells the story of Tatum coming to work for him as an intern. Tatum was straining at the bit, eager to get to work. He became impatient. So he asked Percy, "What do you want me to do?" Sternly, Percy responded, "You watch me, that's what you do. That's your job—watch me." Tatum later said that was one of the most important lessons he learned: being in the presence of greatness, keenly observing, open to instructions and directions, inevitably osmosis will transpire.

Bill Tatum and I were members of Mayor David Dinkins's delegation to South Africa in 1991. It was during this journey that I got to know him better. Throughout the trip, he was the constant teacher and student, always engaged in lively conversation, comfortably interacting with the high and mighty and the humble and lowly. He personified Rudyard Kipling's poem: "If you can walk among kings and keep the common touch...then you'll be a man, my son."

He was a proud man who moved across the stage of life with confidence, class, and dignity. He was racially conscious—he was proud to be an African American—but he was cosmopolitan, too. The world was his stage. He embraced the human family. It seemed right that he should make his transition while traveling abroad. And that he should be with his wife, Susan Tatum. They were vacationing in Dubrovnik, Croatia. He was a strong family man. His daughter Elinor was the apple of his eye. He loved her dearly and was so proud of her. All of us parents know what he felt. The unspeakable joy, the profound pride we feel when our children do well, especially if they follow in our footsteps.

While he was a serious man, always seeming to have a lot on his mind, Tatum was not without humor. He could see the lighter side of life. He could write with wit and share a laugh with others. And like all people who are secure within themselves, he could laugh at himself.

I will always be grateful for his courageous, steadfast support for us during the upheaval in Crown Heights in 1991. The Rev. Al Sharpton, Attorney Alton Maddox, Sonny Carson, and I were condemned and vilified by an almost unanimous white press. Yes, and criticized by some black leaders and opinion-makers, too. Tatum refused to join the pack. He stood by us in his editorials. He extolled our leadership. It is interesting that, while an American Jewish Congress resolution claimed that I, along with others, "for opportunistic reasons," inflamed racial tension and hatred, the August 31, 1991 edition of the *Amsterdam News* called attention to the accurate, positive role we were playing. In that editorial, Bill Tatum wrote:

When leadership did emerge, it was essentially Black Leadership, and that leadership did what it could to contain the violence by engaging the youth in protest marches and prayer…. Much of the credit for this must go to Mayor Dinkins. But more, much more, credit must go to those who could communicate with the Black youngsters who had "had it up to here and didn't give a F--k what happened." Those who spoke and did communicate are some few Black Crown Heights community leaders. Then there were those who effectively led. They were the gentlemen who are now being blamed for the violence and the unrest: Al Sharpton, Alton Maddox, Colin Moore, C. Vernon Mason, Rev. Herbert Daughtry, and Sonny Carson. It is a false and unfair charge. It is quite likely that had it not been for these men, the city might well by now be up in flames.

What was said of Brutus, who was called the noblest of Romans in Shakespeare's *Julius Caesar*, would be applicable to Bill Tatum: "His life was gentle, and the elements so mixed in him that Nature might stand up and say to all the world, 'This was a man!'"

An Editor's Editor

It was 10:08 a.m. when the funeral ceremony for Bill Tatum commenced, and 12:02 p.m. when Rev. Sharpton completed his sermon. He spoke for twenty-five minutes.

It was like a recurring dream—or nightmare—except for some minor changes in the program and personalities: same place, Riverside Church; same occasion, funeral; same time, 10:00 a.m. But the person was different. March 2, 2009, it was Chuck Sutton. March 6th, it is Wilbert "Bill" Tatum. The weather had changed, too. Gone were the snow and wind, replaced by a comfortable overcast of forty degrees.

This time there were more cars jammed into the church's underground parking. Again, I followed the usual ritual. After parking, I went to the chapel, greeted the family—wife, Susan Tatum, and daughter, Elinor, both remarkably composed. I got the feeling that they, especially Elinor, had emptied their fountain of tears, and for the moment there was nothing left. They greeted everybody with smiles, embraces, handshakes, and "Thank you." Some of the same people who had attended the previous funerals were present: former New York City Mayor David Dinkins, Congressman Charlie Rangel, veteran NAACP leader Hazel Dukes, and other dignitaries, including Senator Charles Schumer, New York City mayor Michael Bloomberg, and NAACP national president Ben Jealous. Thoughtfully, the family had provided coffee and tea in the larger room adjacent to the chapel. People were seated quietly conversing while some were sobbing.

As I walked down the aisle, the sanctuary was already filled. News people were crowded down front, on both sides of the church; television cameras on the right side, still cameras on the left. Again, the procession began and the Rev. Brad Braxton, alongside Rev. Al Sharpton and followed by the coffin and the family, recited verses from the Bible. And again, having ascended the elevated podium, Rev. Braxton opened the ceremony with a welcome and remarks. He applauded Mr. Tatum as a journalist "in the knowledge business," who "by his pen, sought to empower those others tried to dispossess." He said, "If we didn't have Bill Tatum, I shudder to think of what the world would be." He quoted Dr. Martin Luther King Jr., saying, "Death is not a period, but a comma."

After Rev. Sharpton's invocation, there was a musical selection, "Vem Kan Segla," by Margareta Svensson, pianist and soloist. Charles Kohn and the Rev. Linda Tarry-Chard read Psalm 23 and John 14:1–6. An impressive list of speakers, some of them who had also spoken at Chuck Sutton's funeral, gave verbal flowers as beautiful as the natural flowers that surrounded the coffin. Governor David Paterson, the first speaker, compared the shoddy journalism of the *New York Post* with Bill Tatum's crusading journalism. "Thank God truth would rise again, every Thursday morning," he said, referencing *The Amsterdam News's* weekly publication day. Mayor Bloomberg praised Tatum for his courage and consistency.

David Dinkins was next. He went through his customary ritual of recognizing persons in the audience. I always feel grateful. He never fails to include me. On Tuesday, he paid me a high honor. After mentioning my name, he said, "The ceremony is official now." He said, "With the passing of Bill Tatum, another legend of Harlem has passed." He quoted W. E. Henley's poem, "Invictus," told the story of an old man who, having crossed a dangerous chasm, built a bridge. When asked why, the old man replied, "That others may cross over." David concluded by saying, "Bill Tatum built many bridges."

After Mayor Dinkins came silent reflections and reading of the obituary while organist William Randolph Jr. softly played the organ. The obituary was in the edition of the *Amsterdam News* that had been distributed as the attendees entered the sanctuary. On the front page was a thoughtful photo of Bill Tatum looking down, pencil in hand, as if editing a copy, with an edition of the newspaper close by. Inside, the editorial page was left blank. The musical selection, "I Did It My Way," sung by Kevin Anthony, seemed to have been especially written for Bill Tatum.

US Representative Charlie Rangel said, "How lucky I've been to have known and lived with Bill Tatum."

The granddaughter of Bill Tatum won the hearts of all. Standing on a box behind the podium next to her mother, she spoke of her grandfather's playfulness. "He was always making faces," she said. Then she expressed what gives us an important insight into Bill's approach to life. Quoting her grandfather, she said, "'It's all right to disagree with someone, but don't make it so bad that you lose friendship.'"

There were other speakers from various ethnic backgrounds who represented Tatum's wide associations. Former TV commentator Sydney Offitt said, "Bill had a passion for ideas." Victor Kovner, a noted New York City attorney who'd been a close adviser to Mayor Dinkins, spoke of Bill's "extraordinary integrity." In between the two speakers there was a musical selection by Ms. Svensson, "Send in the Clowns." Herb Boyd, author and columnist for the *Amsterdam News,* did an interesting thing. He said he asked the AM news staff to express their feelings about Mr. Tatum in one word. Some of the words were *genius, humorous, hope, guidance, patience, greatness, unflinching, straight-forward, tenacious, unforgettable, loveable, extraordinary, powerful,* and *fearless.* Herb said, "There was no subject he did not have a grasp on." Hazel Dukes of the NAACP said, "He adopted me as a little sister and was always there for me." Roz Abrams, TV commentator, read letters from President Barack

Obama, former president Bill Clinton, and Secretary of State Hillary Clinton, and recited the poem, "Around the Corner" by Charles Hanson Towne.

Elinor Tatum, still composed, tenderly and eloquently spoke of her father's love for her and others. "He had so many children. He loved them all, and he loved you," she said. "My father was around to help me with the paper and life. I didn't have a boyfriend, he didn't try to run over with the wheelchair." She said she was keeping him in the neighborhood and burying him on 2nd Avenue so that we might all be close to him.

Kevin Anthony sang a song I associated with Paul Robeson, "My Curly Headed Baby," and once again, Rev. Sharpton did the eulogy, this time wearing the colorful robes uniquely designed by the Riverside Church. Surely, everyone who had attended Chuck Sutton's funeral would be wondering what he would say this time. What would he do for an encore?

"*Faithfulness* is the word I think of when I remember Bill Tatum," he said.

Rev. Sharpton spoke of his long friendship with Bill Tatum—since he was a teenager. He cited the many times Mr. Tatum had to come to his rescue. He kept referring to the theme, "He was faithful." He told the story of visiting Bill's home and finding in the vestibule several homeless men who had come to see Mr. Tatum, too. And during the wake, homeless persons also came to the viewing. So deep was Mr. Tatum's concern, and so wide was his reach.

Rev. Sharpton said Bill never stopped fighting.

"Even in the wheelchair, he had a swagger." Rev. Sharpton referred to the *New York Post* cartoon and said, "Thank God Tatum was there to fight for us."

When he had come to the end, the audience was on its feet applauding.

Then the audience was silent as Diana Solomon-Glover sang, "Be Still My Soul." Rev. Braxton said the benediction and the recessional commenced with a recording of Paul Robeson singing "There is a Balm in Gilead."

After the coffin was placed in the hearse, inching through the wall-to-wall people, we returned to the dressing room. I said to Rev.

Al Sharpton, "Man you're something. You hit back-to-back home runs. Some of us have been preaching for years, and we haven't hit one home run."

The sun was shining fairly brightly as I drove down the Westside Highway. I kept thinking about the funeral, Bill Tatum, Paul Robeson, the events and personalities of history with whom I've been somehow associated. Somehow, New York City will not seem right without Bill Tatum's pen and presence. But we can console ourselves with the conviction, death is an imposter or a paper tiger. The scripture declares this: "Oh death, where is thy sting? O grave, where is thy victory?" Death does not make a final end. It is the pathway to the next stage in our eternal evolution. And for those of us who share the Christian faith, we believe we will meet again, and when we meet, we will know each other and there will be no more separation.

To the Tatum family: On behalf of my family, church, and the part of the community I represent, I extend our prayers and support. If you feel the need to cry, do so. But just know that Wilbert "Bill" Tatum lives. Rejoice in the time that he was with you. Be proud of his legacy. And keep the faith.

Percy E. Sutton

Sunrise: November 24, 1920, San Antonio, Texas
Sunset: December 26, 2009, New York, New York

Reflection on the Life and Times of Percy E. Sutton[3]
He Was There for All of Us

Today, January 13, 2010, I celebrate my 79th birthday. I can think of no better way to celebrate it than to initiate a series of articles of reflections on a man I believe was one of the finest human beings who ever lived anywhere at any time. While no words could ever fully express my love and admiration for the "Chairman," I hope and pray that I have, at least, expressed a measure of what I feel about Percy Ellis Sutton and his family.

Like a steadily flowing flood, tributes came from near and far, rich and poor, black and white, religious and non-religious, high and low, even from the president of the United States, and rightfully so. He deserved it all and more. Yet when all the words have been uttered and written, when all the tributes have been put at his feet, they wouldn't have told the whole story of this man named Percy Ellis Sutton. Indeed, you cannot fully understand and appreciate the person they called the "Chairman," apart from his family—father, Samuel; and mother, Lillian; siblings; relatives; especially his wife, Leatrice; son, Pierre "Pepe"; and daughter, Cheryl. How do you pay homage to a man who was bigger than life?

He truly actualized the Rudyard Kipling ideal: "He walked among kings and kept the common touch." He was so at home, comfortable, easygoing, no matter where he was or who he was with. In Brooklyn, I have walked with him through Bedford-Stuyvesant, Crown Heights, East New York, and I have observed him as he smiled and stopped to shake hands with everyone who approached him. Standing on the corners of Harlem, I witnessed the same friendliness. I have been with him in political circles, in business meetings, among the high and the mighty, and he was always the same. Yes, even among religious leaders, he did not change. Always, he was cordial, honest, candid, suave, articulate—strong as an oak and gentle as a summer breeze. He had a tough mind and a tender heart.

Percy made us feel special. He was so sensitive, so eager to bestow honor—to prefer others above himself. You might feel ever-so-small, but when you came into Percy's presence you left feeling like a giant, and you never forgot. You were right, Cheryl, when you said at the funeral, "People may forget what you say, and forget what you do, but they never forget how you made them feel." There was a deep gentleness about him that only the strongest and the most secure of men possess.

He was philanthropy personified. The name Percy Sutton was synonymous with charity. He didn't always give tax write-offs either. Some of his gifts, maybe even most, were given in private. It was not in his makeup to publicize his munificence. I don't think there is an activist, freedom fighter, or anyone trying to advance the cause of human rights and self-determination, who has not been the beneficiary of his moral and financial support. He was there for all of us. Nor did we have to send for him. More often than not, he would just show up, like the Lone Ranger of Western movies. He rode in when there was a need, and rode out not waiting for thanks and accolades.

Contrary to the popular notion regarding strength and toughness, Percy was strong and tough and yet profoundly humble. He was meek—let me hasten to add, meek like Moses of the Holy Bible, which describes Moses as meekest above all men. In fact, as I pondered the characteristics of Percy, they were strikingly similar to the qualities that I studied in Moses: perseverance, patience, courage, creativity, intelligent, persuasiveness, eloquence, vision, audacity, indomitability, leadership, compassion, skilled communicator, God-consciousness, and a mystical oneness with his people.

- How else can we explain why he was able to rise so high, starting so low? His father had been a slave who later sired fifteen children. Percy was the youngest. The old man taught his children well—discipline, hard work, commitment, fairness or the Golden Rule, the importance of education, and the love of family. Percy, as did all the children, thoroughly internalized the lessons. They became a family of achievers including scientists, doctors, lawyers, educators, union organizers, entrepreneurs, judges, elected officials, and public servants. How many of us could hold three jobs and go to school? He worked as a post office clerk, a subway conductor, and as a waiter at Lundy's Restaurant in Sheepshead Bay, Brooklyn, on the weekends. He arrived at law school at 9:30 each morning, and for three years, this grueling schedule continued until his graduation. Meanwhile, he and Leatrice were raising two children. He became an honest, competent attorney at law, establishing a law partnership with his brother Oliver.
- How else can you explain Percy's business success? Even here, the concern for his people manifested itself. It broke his heart that the Apollo Theater was decaying. Like Nehemiah in the Holy Bible, who was well-secure in his career and connections, yet he wept when word reached him that Jerusalem was in ruin.

He decided that, at whatever cost, he would rebuild the ancient city. Percy refurbished and revitalized the Apollo, revived Amateur Nights at the Apollo, and created *It's Showtime at the Apollo*, a syndicated TV show. In 1993, he established Apollo Theater Records, a record label and recording company.

- When he entered the media arena via radio, he told the world he wanted a radio station with a heart, where black people were free to communicate as they pleased. In 1972, he, along with his brother Oliver, Hal Jackson, Clarence B. Jones, and others purchased and operated New York City's first black-owned radio stations, WBLS and WLIB. Privately, he once told me that he was losing so much money on WLIB, but he kept it anyway, even while some of us were abusing it. Regarding print media, in 1971, with Clarence B. Jones, William Tatum, and John Edmonds, Percy acquired ownership of the *New York Amsterdam News,* and with his son, Pierre, founded the weekly newspaper the *New York Courier.*

- How else can we explain his courage and commitment to the civil rights movement? He boarded the Freedom Ride buses and headed southward, where brave men and women were killed, maimed, and jailed for defiantly riding on a bus seated next to a white person, or sitting in the white section of the bus. Like Alfred Tennyson's *Charge of the Light Brigade*, "they rode into the jaws of death." Fourteen times he was arrested, and he was incarcerated at the despicable Parchman Farm Penitentiary in Mississippi.

- How else can we explain his success in the political jungle? He became one of the most powerful politicians in New York City. He was an elected New York State assemblyman, was an organizer and founding member of the New York State Black and Puerto Rican Legislative Caucus in New York State Assembly, and he served as Manhattan Borough president for eleven years. In 1977, he made a historic run for mayor of New York City. I was among the first to endorse him. Percy's influence was felt nationally and internationally.

- How else can we explain how he became a Tuskegee Airman—a Black Eagle—zooming through the sky, doing battle far above the clouds? The Black Eagles never lost a bomber. The white pilots who resisted their participation eventually fought to have their skill, dexterity, and bravery escort them on their bombing raids.

Yes, he was like Moses. He was a statesman, a judge, a lawgiver, a teacher, an organizer, a motivator, and a liberator. Without controversy, we as a people could not have gotten this far in our journey without Percy. While we have not reached the Promised Land—we are still in the wilderness—we have been freed from some of the chains of the past. Like the old preacher said, "We ain't where we want to be, and we ain't where we gonna be, but thank God we ain't where we used to be." Thanks, in no small measure, to Percy Ellis Sutton.

Reflecting on the Life and Times of Percy E. Sutton[4]

I cannot recall when I first met him. It seemed that we've been around each other since the beginning of my ministry in 1958. I cannot think of a single issue of importance that Percy was not present in some way. In 1976, when Crown Heights was in a seething caldron of conflicting interests, one of the most hotly contested issues was the community boundary line between Crown Heights and Bedford Stuyvesant. People of African ancestry in Crown Heights wanted the boundary line to remain along Atlantic Avenue, where it had always been.

The Hasidim, an ultra orthodox segment of Jews, wanted the boundary to be moved back to Eastern Parkway. The Hasidim, which was almost exclusively located in Crown Heights, strategized that by moving the boundary line, there would be less people of African ancestry with which to contend, thus enhancing their numerical strength, which they reasoned would give them more power. When the issue was brought to the Board of Estimates—the final decision-making body at that time which consisted of Borough presidents and mayoral appointees Percy Sutton and Paul O'Dwyer—in the face of jeering crowds and powerful Hasidim supporters, Percy voted with the black community. We still lost. I remember staying up, along with other ministers, half the night with then Mayor Abraham Beame to convince him not to reverse his decision, but to stay with the original boundary lines. Our opportunities fell on deaf ears.

In the same year of 1976, when America was celebrating its two hundredth anniversary, a friend named Chester Williams brought me an idea: "Let us, people of African ancestry, remember our four hundred years of travail, including the transatlantic slave trade." We called it a Quadra-Continental. Percy was asked to join us as we marched along Flatbush Avenue to Empire Boulevard to Prospect Park, where we planned to have a program and picnic. He was then Manhattan Borough president. There were many people who criticized our effort. They said we were unpatriotic and wanted to do our own thing. They said, "That's what's wrong with black folks."

Percy joined us anyway. He had one condition that I will never forget, and which I confess I have used often. His condition was that he did not want to stay around once he completed his task.

"I will be glad to march with you and do whatever you ask me," he said. "But when my assignment is done, I need to leave immediately. If I stay around, people will bombard me with requests for help, and if I cannot deliver, they will be disappointed, and I will be frustrated."

Percy was with us when we went to jail on the South African issue. When Randall Robinson, then chair of Trans-Africa, former Congressman Walter Fauntroy, and historian and civil right scholar Mary Frances Berry were arrested for protesting the apartheid system at the South African Embassy in Washington, DC, in 1984, it ignited a Free South Africa Movement. There were pervasive arrests across the country as countless angry protesters, including well-known celebrities of every stratum, went to jail[5].

During the 1980s, I chaired the National Black United Front (NBUF). Current City Councilman Charles Barron was then my chief of staff, and I asked him to assist in coordinating the Free South Africa civil disobedience in New York. New York's most prestigious personalities, including former Mayor Dinkins, Congressman Charles Rangel, in fact all the top politicians lined up to go to jail, as did Ozzie Davis, Ruby Dee, and other notable artists and athletes.

Percy made an extraordinary request. He wanted to go to jail at a time when he could take his family with him. When that day arrived,

Percy Sutton with his children submitted to the arrest. I was inspired to do the same. My wife and I and all of our children were arrested. During these times and in other situations, too numerous to mention here, Percy was always courtly, courteous, and confident.

Percy was a frequent visitor of our church. It seemed when he was deeply disturbed about something and needed some trusted person and place to bear his soul, he found his way to our church. Just to mention five of the most memorable visits come to mind.

- In 1977, when he was running for the mayoral office, we had a fundraiser for him at our church. I invited some of the New York Jets to attend the program. (I was the unofficial chaplain with the New York Jets football team for five years.) A substantial amount of money was raised—at least for us. When we presented the money to him, his face lit up. In his precise, articulate voice, he said, "Good Lord, these young people have raised all of this money. I am so inspired." I can still see his face beaming with gratitude and joy.
- There was another occasion that he attended which was not so pleasant. It was early Sunday morning, and as we sat in my office, he was almost in tears as he rehearsed how black leaders castigated and demeaned each other on WLIB. In a crackling, tremulous voice, he said, "I'm hurt. I wanted a radio for our people, and they have turned it into a battleground. I feel like shutting it down." Of course, he did not close it down. WLIB still exists.[6]
- There was another time that he came to march with us. There was nothing unusual about it; he had marched with us many times before. This time, it was on Martin Luther King Jr.'s birthday. We wanted to march from the church to city hall. When we got to Brooklyn Bridge, we were prevented from taking the roadway. Police insisted we march along the pedestrian route. Tension erupted as we argued with the police and continuous police enforcement crowded the area. I remember Percy standing with us, calm and unruffled. He provided protection and leadership. No one was hurt. One person was jailed, but this was because of other issues.

- Another memory I recall was just a few years ago, when Percy was at the church for a Kwanzaa program featuring Dr. Maulana Karenga, founder of the Afrocentric celebration. We sat together as we listened to the eloquent speech of Dr. Karenga. I remember feeling that my church family and I were so blessed to have these two giants in the Freedom Struggle in our church. I had the overwhelming feeling of unity and being wrapped in the mantle of history.

- Finally, and perhaps the most memorable, surely the most melancholy, was a visit that he made some years ago. I think he was just out of the hospital, or some confinement, due to illness. Refusing the elevator chair, he came up the stairs slowly with a walking cane. When he reached the sanctuary, he moved over to a seat in the corner of the church, in a section closest to the landing. He sat quietly to himself. You wouldn't know when he arrived. There was no fanfare because he was such a part of our church. He wanted space, and we provided it for him. He was very attentive as the worship proceeded. After the worship service, my wife and I conversed with him.

He said, "I had to be in the House of the Lord this morning. I drove myself. They didn't want me to come, but I insisted. So when no one would drive me, I drove myself."

My wife and I were speechless. We walked with him back down the steps, out to the street where his car was parked, and watched as he drove away all by himself.

The last time I saw him was at the funeral of his nephew Chuck Sutton. It was at Riverside Church, too. Percy was slumped over in a wheelchair, but his eyes were still clear, and his mind was lucid. I bent over and whispered to him, "Mister Chairman, how good it is to see you, always." He responded, his voice barely above a whisper, "You're so special. You've come all the way from New Jersey just to be with us. You're so special."

What a remarkable man, I thought. Even in his bereavement and bodily debilitation, he was still trying to honor me and lift my spirit.

What better way to attempt to sum up the life of this giant than to repeat his words: "You're special." That is the way he viewed all of us, whatever station in life we held, whatever the complexion, political ideology, religious creed, we were special. What can we say other than, "Mister Chairman, what you said about us, you're the same, and that goes double."

A paragraph in his obituary captures the man: "A loving family man, a savvy politician, a mentor, a sage, a man who spoke truth to power, a man who gave to others, a man who treated all the same, a consummate orator, a weaver of tales, a man who made you feel special like a long lost friend, even after a few minutes together; the family patriarch who made you feel like he was yours and yours alone; a good father, a good husband, and an elegant gentle soul. Summing the life of such an iconic person is nearly impossible."

Thank God for the hope that death does not make a final end. Beyond the grave, there is another reality, and the Bible teaches it is a reality whose beauty is beyond human description. In that new reality we shall meet again, and there will be no more parting of the ways.

Goodnight Mr. Chairman, old warrior, beloved friend. I will see you in that new reality, one morning soon.

When Old Friends Gathered at the Viewing[7]

It was a bitterly cold morning as we drove across the George Washington Bridge to Riverside Church. I wondered how many funerals I have attended at this world-famous edifice. I remembered the last time was for the funeral of Chuck Sutton, the nephew of Percy Sutton. It was 9:00 a.m. when we pulled up to the church. About thirty well-wishers had already lined up in front of the church. They were bundled up from head to toe with coats, scarves, blankets, ear-muffins, hats, and only God knows what else. They greeted me with broad smiles and enthusiastic hello's as I walked down the line, shaking hands with each one.

When I entered the church, I was led to a large waiting hall next to the gym. From there, I was guided to the chapel. There were three areas in the mammoth church that had been arranged to accommodate the people. As you enter, to the right was the large hall (to which I already referred), where there were hot beverages served. Next to the hall was the chapel.

There was the huge ornate sanctuary where the ceremony would take place. In the chapel, Percy Sutton lay in a casket opened to the family, VIPs, and close friends. Green wristbands and reception tickets were given to the appropriate persons.

When we entered the chapel, there were only a few people in the rear. Among them was Percy Sutton's nephew Chuck (Another nephew named Chuck? I thought Chuck Sutton died first.) For ten minutes, we shared memories. "I was with my uncle the night before he passed. He was still concerned about us." I shared with him how often Percy visited my church. Then I was given a piece of information which answered a question my wife and I had pondered for a long time. I mentioned the occasion of Percy's coming by himself after it seemed as though he had been hospitalized. The nephew said, "Yes, he had fallen and broken his hip." I said, "Oh, that's the answer."

For a few minutes, my wife and I had the chairman to ourselves. He was dressed in a navy-blue suit with a slight pinstripe. His tie, clasped at the neck of his white shirt, was a mixture of blue and red dots. He looked as he always did—well-groomed. His face was peaceful with a faint smile, as if to say, "I have done my job. I finished my course. I've kept the faith, and now I go to meet my Maker."

I stared long at the body before me. I wanted to bend over and embrace him as I was accustomed, and whisper in his ear what I've always said to him: "Man, we love you. You've done so much for us. We honor you and thank you for everything." I restrained myself and settled for a touch of his tie. I walked back to my seat.

The first VIP to enter was former Mayor David Dinkins, preceded by his wife, Joyce. He walked down the short aisle, sadly shaking his head. I affectionately greeted him. I always thought we had a special relationship. David and I looked knowingly into the eyes of each other. We could only shake our heads. He whispered as he walked toward the casket, "And then there were three." It was a reference to Congressman Charlie Rangel, Basil Paterson, and himself. They had been called the Gang of Four.

I think that name for the four was first used among African Americans in New York City in 1985. We had formed a Coalition for A Just New York in an attempt to empower New Yorkers, particularly so-called minorities. When the mayoral race commenced, some members had selected Herman Badillo as the mayoral candidate, and Al Vann for Brooklyn Borough president. Many of us knew nothing of this plan. At the eleventh hour, we gathered at Astor Place to vote our choices. Herman Farrell, who was then assemblyman and Manhattan Borough Democratic County leader, threw his hat in the race. After a long and heated debate through the night, the majority of the assemblage voted for Herman Farrell. It fractured the organization and opened wounds that were years in healing. There were those who believed that Herman Farrell's entrance into the race was the doing of Paterson, Dinkins, and Rangel.

They wanted to get even with Badillo for not supporting the mayoral quest of Percy Sutton in 1977. They were called the Harlem Gang of Four. Obviously, the fourth person was Herman Farrell (not Percy Sutton). No such thing had taken place. The mistake was, that is made so often, a deal had been formulated without the participation of the larger body.

Basil Paterson, long-time Democratic power player and the father of the present governor, face lit up, as did mine, once we saw each other. It had been a long time since we had seen each other. I think it was during the last Transport Workers Union (TWU) strike in 2006. We met at a hotel room with the TWU President Roger Toussaint, his staff, and advisors to strategize regarding the strike and the city's response.

We exchanged old battles and talked about our children. Basil pulled Clarence Jones into the conversation and rehearsed the history of Sisters Against South African Apartheid (SASAA). He remembered that my wife was bemoaning the treatment of black South Africans and complained that no one was doing anything. I said to my wife, "Why don't you do something?" After a moment of anger, she took up my challenge. Thus was born SASAA and all of the great work that it did.

Clarence Jones had been Dr. Martin Luther King's attorney and confidante. He was a partner of Percy on various business ventures. I introduced my wife to him.

"This is my hero," I said. "He was with Doctor King from the beginning to the end. He has been a consistent source of great encouragement and inspiration to me."

"You have always been consistent through the years," Jones replied. "I know how Percy felt about you, and how you felt about him. I know because Percy often talked about you."

I gave him another embrace. It pleased me greatly to hear someone I admired, and who knew Percy, say what I always felt and believed about Percy's feelings toward me. Now it was confirmed.

Dr. Roscoe Brown—one of the Black Eagles, Tuskegee Airmen, the African American fighter pilots famous for their exploits during World War II— moved toward the coffin slower than most of the mourners. Roscoe owned the distinction of being the first pilot to shoot down a German jet. We discussed the New York Yankee Council, a group that he, Judge Laura Blackburn, and I, with the New York Yankee President George Steinbrenner, formed. It came as a result of derogatory remarks made by one of the executives of that New York baseball franchise. We sought and received a meeting with Mr. Steinbrenner encouraging him to become more responsive to the black community in general, and the Bronx in particular. Out of this meeting was born the New York Yankee Council, funded by Mr. Steinbrenner. Roscoe, who was also president of Bronx Community College, became president of the Council following the presidency of Bob Williams. I asked him about the next meeting. I said, "Now that the Yankees have won the World Series, they ought to make available more funds." He replied, "The meeting will take place."

I always liked Dr. Brown. His support was always consistent even on the most controversial issues. One of my touching recollections of Dr. Brown happened over thirty years ago. I was becoming a vegan, and my body reflected the change. My face had begun to look gaunt and sallow. I had the appearance of a very sick man. Roscoe gingerly came to me, choosing his words very carefully, and said, "We have been observing you, and you're not looking well. I have been delegated to approach you and ask you how you are doing, and if there is anything we can do for you." I was so moved. I said, "I love you very much. I appreciate your concern, but I am becoming a vegetarian, thus I am going through changes. But I will be all right shortly." Dr. Brown smiled. A conspicuous relief enveloped him.

More Memories and Reflections[8]

When I looked up, New York Governor David Paterson and Rev. Al Sharpton were heading towards the coffin. I approached the governor with a hello and an embrace. I said to him, "How are you doing, man? I want you to know that we are praying for you all the time." He smiled and said, "Hi Reverend. You have a birthday coming up soon?" I replied, "Man! How do you remember that? All of the stuff on your head, how do you remember my birthday?" Then I recall, at the Democratic Convention in 2009, he remembered my daughter Leah's birthday and sent her flowers. I was startled then, and even more so now. I wanted to ask him how he planned to participate in the funeral and be in Albany by 1:00 p.m. for the annual State of the State Address. I later turned on the television, and there he was, sternly announcing a new day in Albany in which ethics would be high on the agenda.

Charlie Rangel stood long at the coffin. He seemed more devastated than all the rest. As he passed me, I hesitated to disturb his thoughts. He looked up and said, "Hi, Reverend," shaking his head. "How's the family? How are you doing?" I replied, "I'm doing well, under the circumstances. These are challenging times." He nodded and moved away. I always liked Charlie Rangel. To me, he has always been a gentleman in the best sense of that word, and the consummate elected official.

The Rev. Jesse Jackson, along with his daughter Santita seemed to appear out of nowhere. That's probably the way Jesse wanted it. As always, his head seemed to be above the crowd. He seemed to be all-surveying and all-knowing. Without fanfare, we greeted each other. I think we have a mutual admiration society. No matter how long the distance since our communication, we always knew our affection for each other was intact.

"How are you doing? How's the family?" I asked.

"Everybody's fine. How are you?" he replied.

"Everybody's okay," I said.

As he walked away, I thought, he will always be my hero. I will always be grateful for the years that we spent struggling and traveling together. I learned so much from him. I remembered when he did the eulogy for Jackie Robinson in this same church in 1972. I could still hear the smooth, melodious voice of Roberta Flack singing, "I told Jesus he could change my name…"

There was an incident in the 1984 presidential campaign that came to mind. Jesse, or his staff, had made some moves that deeply disturbed me. After a long day of campaigning, I cornered him in his hotel room. In the strongest language I could command, I criticized him. He was so hurt and startled that he called Percy that same night. The next day, Percy called me and said, "Jesse called me last night or early this morning. What did you say to him? He said you accused him of giving away our campaign. You need to go back and talk to him. He's under a lot of pressure. He needs us." I humbly replied, "Yes, Mister Chairman. I will call him immediately." Which I did. The chairman had spoken. Who could do otherwise?

As Jesse moved further down the aisle, I looked back at Percy and smiled, and said to myself, "Yes, Mister Chairman."

Hazel Dukes, national board member of the NAACP, and a veteran activist, was an early arrival. We waved at each other, seeming to share the sorrow of a mutual loss. I wondered how many times we have been sharing the pain of tragedy, death, violence. So many, many funerals we have attended. So many, many times we have been on the frontlines of so many, many battles.

I waved at John Edmonds across the aisle. He was a member of the conglomerate that participated with Sutton on various enterprises. He is a big man with a big round face, all of which seemed to heighten and enlarge his sorrow. He radiated a pain that was huge. We exchanged no words. We simply nodded. We knew what each felt.

Eric Eve was there. After embracing, we discussed his new job as New York City deputy comptroller. He had been a vice president of Citibank. Eric was a little boy running around the house with his brother and sister when I first saw him. I had organized a couple of buses filled to capacity to support his father, Arthur Eve, in his run for the mayoral seat in Buffalo, New York. I spent the last week of the campaign living with the Eves in their home, daily campaigning with Arthur. I was there the night Arthur celebrated winning the Democratic primary. Afterwards, we went to a soul food restaurant called Gigi. Eric was always pleasant, mannerly, and had been very helpful to many community leaders and organizations. He thought that the time had come for him to move on to another job. However, he assured me that all the right people were in the right places.

The Final Farewell[9]

Suddenly, a heavy hush came over the room. You knew, even without being told or looking around, that the family was entering the chapel. Slowly, they came down the aisle, led by Percy Sutton's son, Pepe. Immediately, I noticed something different. It was his clean-shaved head. Even so ,that pronounced change could not divert attention away from the heavy burden he was bearing. His arms were around his mother's shoulders. She was literally hanging on to him.

They paused before the coffin, nodded to each other, and then went to their front seats. Still intertwined, they sat, bodies slightly in a stoop, and received a line of sorrowing mourners. I often wondered if this tradition was helpful, especially when mourners—practically strangers, and/or had no, little, or a strained relationship with the deceased. Some even asked, in words or looks, "Do you know who I am? Or, "Do you remember me? Your grandmama's third cousin married your grandpa John Henry…remember?" Or some people want to engage in conversation repeating hackneyed, worn-out phrases, all the while trying to look you in the eyes to make sure you know who they are and what they are saying. I always wondered if it doesn't add to the burden of the bereaved—another something with which they are obligated to respond.

I remember the biblical story of Job. Everybody has read or heard about the suffering of Job. His three friends came to comfort him. They sat for three days and nights never saying a word. Then when they spoke, they said all the wrong things. Finally, Job, weighed down with grief, summoned enough indignation to say, "Miserable comforters are ye all. Would to God you have kept your mouth shut."

After pondering these thoughts, when the line was exhausted, I took a chance, haltingly, and I went to Mrs. Sutton and Pepe. I knelt, looked into her eyes. I don't know if I've ever seen a human body in more contorted pain. She is of small stature, but seemed even smaller now, as if the pain inside was drawing her into a knot—perhaps that's how she felt. Our eyes met, neither of us said a word—but we knew. We felt! We shared! There was no need for word noise. I turned toward Pepe—the same interaction. I'm not sure if he even recognized me. I wasn't about to try to find out. Later, as we prepared to enter the sanctuary, we faced each other again. This time he said, "Thanks for being here, and for all you have done." I nodded and mumbled, "For me, there's nowhere else to be." I said to myself, "That is exactly what his father would have said, and the way he would have said it."

It was time to march into the sanctuary. The mortician gave directions: "Please back away. Let the family be closer before we close the casket. The ministers will say prayers, and this is the way we will line up. Program participants will go first, and then the casket, followed by the ministers. Then the staff followed by the VIPs."

There followed a sad spectacle of selfish projection. Instructions were ignored. People still jockeyed for space. "Please stand back. Please let the program participants pass. Please let the family though. Please let the casket out," the mortician repeated. After a herculean effort, success was achieved.

What took place in the smaller chapel with the family and VIPs was happening in the sanctuary. Reserved seats meant nothing. Uninvited occupants claimed seats and refused to move. "Please move and make room for the family," said first the usher, and then the security, all to no avail. They harassed an overextended staff—some, inexperienced, were doing the best they could. But the task was much too large. The church was packed with human bodies, a few people standing (mostly security), all seemingly on the move, uncertain which way was trying to follow mixed signals. When the big doors to the sanctuary were shut, crowds stood outside holding up green wristbands. Others claimed to be family members.

After observing the scene for a while, I decided I'd had enough. I've seen it all, from the greeting hall to the chapel and in the sanctuary. Most of all, I had a moment with the family. They were bearing it all with remarkable dignity, strength, and extraordinary courtesy that I am sure pleased Percy, who was somewhere watching. Always, I feel bound to commend the family and funeral arrangers in these high-profiled cases. What an awesome task it is to satisfy all concerns and interests. They usually do a great job. The mistakes, which are generally few, are understandable.

And I had a moment with old struggles, and with the body of Percy Sutton. There was nothing left but speeches and prayers by people I knew so well and pretty much knew what they would say. I had been with all of them at other funerals. Better, I thought, to let someone have my seat. And most of all, I wanted to be alone. I guess I'm one of those rare old dogs who prefer to bear his pain alone— to crawl up under the house and hurt and weep. The deeper the pain, the deeper the desire to be alone. Of course, when I have had to live through the grief of transitioned loved ones, I have submitted myself to the traditions and sincerely thanked all of the supporters and sympathizers.

Moving On[10]

Lost in memories, I returned home from Percy Sutton's memorial services and made myself comfortable. Then the telephone calls came. Would I agree to do an interview with a couple of television stations, on the subject of the term "Negro" being included in the US Census questionnaire? I said yes. I would do the interview with TV 11, in front of the Riverside Church.

It was around 5:00 p.m. when Monica Morales of TV 11, and the cameraman, drove up. She asked about the use of the word "Negro" in the Census questionnaire, and I responded:

There is a cruel irony about this term being used and becoming public on the same day of the funeral of a man who did so much for so many, especially for people of African ancestry. He tried to empower minorities economically and politically. He understood the importance of culture. And here we are talking about Negroes today. We, people of African ancestry, decided a long time ago we no longer wanted to be called niggers, Negras, Negroes, or Colored. Every individual and/or people has a right to define themselves, and the world should accept the definition. We are a people of African ancestry, with a magnificent history, whose ancestors made great contributions to civilization. Our pigmentation is black. We resurrected the majesty and the beauty of blackness.

I am suspicious of the reference Negro. *Is it an attempt to turn back the clock, to return to Jim Crow, to segregation? How far back? Back to slavery? But we are not going back. Percy Sutton and others have brought us this far."*

After the interview, fighting the strong wind blowing across the Hudson River, I made my way to the car.

I sat for a while, surveying the huge, overpowering church which silently engulfed everything. All the people who were here a moment ago were gone. There was an eerie stillness. All the strivings of the human family, the driving ambitions, the shining trophies, the applause and adulation of the crowd, the loves and hates, the sound of music, the vaulted status, the pomp and circumstance, and the crowns of kings and queens will, at some point, be silent, still, dead, gone forever —at least, on this side of history. The melancholy musing of the psalmist on this subject then came to my mind. He said:

I was silent and still; I held my peace to no avail; my distress grew worse; my heart became hot within me. While I mused, the fire burned; then I spoke with my tongue: "Lord, let me know my end, and what is the measure of my days; let me know how fleeting my life is. You have made my days a few handbreadths, and my lifetime is as nothing in your sight. Surely everyone stands as a mere breath.... And now, O Lord, what do I wait for? My hope is in you." (Psalm 39:2–5, 7)

As I pondered about these matters, the question was, "In light of the ephemeral nature of all things human, what kind of human beings should we be?" The answer is, like Percy Ellis Sutton: live and leave a legacy of self-giving. Strive to make the human family better. And then enter the next life, joyfully confident that good things await.

It was well after 5 p.m. The traffic was building, and cars were speeding up and down the highway. Faces behind the steering wheels stared straight ahead. I wondered what was on their minds. Are they

happy or sad? Do they know what is important in life? Do they know that Percy is dead? But like the moving vehicles, we move on.
Life moves on. If we are to maintain our sanity and direction, we must move with it.
Maybe that is the meaning and the reason for funeral ceremonies. In a gathering of loved ones and sympathizers, we are encouraged to move on with life. At some point in history, the human family found benefit in having ceremonies when loved ones departed. Alas, we mourn the passing of loved ones, keep memories alive, build monuments, write books, and live better lives. One day, we too shall pass away, and hopefully, we can leave a legacy like Percy Sutton.

On the Quadra-Centennial[11]

After having completed recent articles of the *Passing of the Giants of the Human Spirit*, I came across relevant pictures and articles germane to the persons in question. The persons were Percy E. Sutton and Dr. Imari Abubakari Obadele, dated Saturday, December 3, 1977, and February 16–March 1, 1980.

I was so overwhelmed as many precious memories came flooding into my mind. I thought I would share them with you. Regarding Percy Sutton, I mentioned earlier that he had attended a march, and then a program in Prospect Park.

In 1976, America was celebrating its two hundred years of independence. Dr. Chester Williams came up with the idea that black people should be celebrating four hundred years. An article in the *Victory Newspaper* in May 1976 captures and answers the reason for a Quadra-Centennial:

Ideas, some say, exist in space separate and apart, awaiting the right conditions to become manifest in man's consciousness.

Contemporary American Blacks, gyrating in a whirlpool of confusion, seem unable to pull the reins that will halt the spinning which carries us to destruction. Silent we stand as others determine our destiny through programs borne of neglect, condescension, or arrogant superiority. They are smug in the belief that our opposition will be sparse, short-lived or half-hearted. This thought pattern is carried over in the nation's bicentennial celebration; its outlets and directions predetermined. Adhering to the history books profile of its elect, America recognizes, selects, and extols Blacks whose struggles are consistent with its own self-image. Knowing this image to be at times neglectful, an idea emerged that perhaps the time has finally arrived for Blacks to present their own picture, determine their own celebrities, and make their own party. Hence, The Quadra-Centennial. We on the committee desire to make known that the first Blacks on American shores were not slaves, and that indeed after nearly 400 years as residents we need not consider ourselves intruders. In celebrating, we wish to recognize the contributions, efforts, hopes and disappointments of our 400-year ongoing struggle. We are amassing resources from all areas: education, medicine, religion, etc., to depict a panoramic view of the heroes, their dreams, achievements, downfalls, and hurts—the struggle and euphoria!

On July 4th, there will be a parade down Brooklyn's Eastern Parkway, a silent honoring of the men and women of our past, present and future. In Prospect Park's Long Meadow, the parade will terminate, and the theme will be depicted via displays, booths, performances, and skits.

Presently, you will hear of the Quadra-Centennial through the mass media. But to be fully successful, we need your participation. Won't you join in our celebration of our heritage within America?

Another reference to Percy E. Sutton is an article in the *Amsterdam News,* dated December 3, 1977, regarding a program I had organized that was the first annual celebration of the Commission on African Solidarity. Mr. Sutton was the Manhattan Borough president. He gave me a proclamation declaring November 19th as "Reverend Daughtry's Day in Manhattan." Also attending the affair was Judge William E. Booth, president of the American Committee on Africa, and the youth double-Dutch group from our church called the Jumping Joints, which was headed by my daughter, Sharon Daughtry. Significantly, the Jumping Joints were one of the first double-Dutch teams in America. They won many championships. Double-Dutch has become quite famous all over the world. In the article I wrote at the time, I criticized black businesses, foundations, leaders, and educators for not recognizing the artistic genius of these kids. To me, what I saw in these kids' coordination, agility, and creativity was poetic genius in motion. I knew that eventually it was going to become popular. I knew whites would capture it and make it serve their interests.

And also, entertaining was the Daughtry Singers, another youth group from our church, which included Sandra Nix, Victoria Robinson, and Leah Daughtry. We honored Dr. Callistus Ndlovu, chief representative of the Zimbabwe African People's Union, and His Excellency Mr. Davis Thomas, ambassador of Liberia, His Excellency Dr. Thomas Tlou, Ambassador of Botswana, and Ambassador Plenipotentiary of the Republic of Guinea in Africa.

Endnotes

1   This is a version of an article that originally appeared in *The Daily Challenge* newspaper, published in Brooklyn, New York, by Mr. Thomas Watkins, publisher.

2   This is a version of articles that originally appeared in *The Daily Challenge* newspaper, published in Brooklyn, New York, Mr. Thomas Watkins, publisher.

3   This is a version of an article that originally appeared in the January 13, 2010, *The Daily Challenge* newspaper, published in Brooklyn, New York, Mr. Thomas Watkins, publisher.

4   This is a version of an article that originally appeared in the January 15–18, 2010, Weekend Edition of *The Daily Challenge* newspaper, published in Brooklyn, New York, Mr. Thomas Watkins, publisher.

5   This campaign was similar to the jail going at 1 Police Plaza in 1991 in the aftermath of the killing of Amadou Diallo. In fact, it was from our South African experience that I conveyed to Rev. Sharpton the idea of doing similar daily arrests. We were returning to New York from Albany where we had participated in a protest against the Rockefeller Drug Law. I thought at the time that the people were angry enough to submit to continuous arrest. Rev. Sharpton agreed. He chose 1 Police Plaza.

6   WLIB and WBLS were sold in 2012, to YMF Media LLC, a group that includes Earvin "Magic" Johnson, and again in 2014, to Emmis Communications based in Indianapolis, Indiana.

7   This is a version of an article that originally appeared in the January 20, 2010, *The Daily Challenge* newspaper, published in Brooklyn, New York, by Mr. Thomas Watkins, publisher.

8   This is a version of an article that originally appeared in the January 27, 2010, *The Daily Challenge*, published in Brooklyn, New York. Mr. Thomas Watkins, publisher.

9   This is a version of an article that originally appeared in the January 29–32, 2010, Weekend Edition of *The Daily Challenge*, published in Brooklyn, New York. Mr. Thomas Watkins, publisher.

10   This is a version of an article that originally appeared in the February 3, 2010 edition of *The Daily Challenge*, published in Brooklyn, New York. Mr. Thomas Watkins, publisher.

11   This is a version of an article that originally appeared in the February 13–15, 2010, Weekend Edition of *The Daily Challenge*, published in Brooklyn, New York. Mr. Thomas Watkins, publisher.

2

Civil Rights Leaders & Activists

Mrs. Eloise Dix

Sunrise: Unknown
Sunset: Aug 24, 2004, New York City

So Long, Old Warrior...Well Done!

When I arrived at Mrs. Eloise Dix's home, Ollie McLean was sitting by the bed, Mr. Dix (Nana) was seated in an adjoining room. Mrs. Dix was lying on a special bed. Mr. Dix came over and embraced me.

"I'm so glad to see you. I know she is happy, too," he said, pointing to his wife.

When Mrs. Dix saw me, she came alive. She held out her arms, and I bent over, kissed and embraced her. She started talking about the African Burial Ground. She talked incessantly, covering a number of issues. Then she asked for food.

After sitting for a while, when I thought she was about to doze off, I decided it was time to leave. So I prayed with them, then departed with everybody's expression of gratitude ringing in my ears.

The next time I saw Mrs. Dix was August 31, 2004, at St. James Presbyterian Church. She was straight and strong in the simple cas-

45

ket, just as she had been when she moved among the living on this side of history. She was like chiseled granite, lying there so still, so peaceful, so regal, and so beautiful, still the warrior, still the conqueror.

They say she died on August 24th. I say that she made her transition. She has gone from life to life. We shall no more see her physical presence, but her spirit will always be with us.

There is an old military ballad that says, "Old soldiers never die. They just fade away." Well, old strugglers never die either, nor do they fade away. We don't let them. We keep them alive in our memory, in our songs, in our literature. We build monuments to them, and we name streets after them.

The Pilgrimage

One of my most memorable recollections of Mrs. Dix is the four days we spent on the re-interment pilgrimage to the African Burial Ground in lower Manhattan, where more than 20,000 Africans were buried over five acres during the 17th and 18th centuries. Their remains were discovered during construction excavation for a new federal building, and a struggle began to demand these ancestors were treated with the dignity and respect they were denied in life.

Mrs. Dix was a leader in that struggle. The pilgrimage marked a victory in that struggle and a return to the African Burial Ground of the 419 remains that had been removed to Howard University for repose and research.

When an agreement on internment was finally reached with the US General Service Administration (GSA), the four-day symbolic journey charting a part of the Underground Railroad was organized by Dr. Howard Dodson, executive director of the Schomburg Center for Research in Black Culture. The journey started September 30, 2003, at Howard University in Washington, DC, with stops in several cities along the way for ceremonies, and culminated October 4, 2003, in New York City, where we then reburied the remains at the burial ground. Four small coffins bearing the bodies of a man, woman, boy and girl, symbolically representing all of our dead ancestors, had been carried all of the way.

All along the journey, I observed Mrs. Dix with her husband of fifty-three years, walking across the busy streets of the cities where we stopped—Baltimore, Maryland; Wilmington, Delaware; Philadelphia, Pennsylvania; and Newark, New Jersey—riding on the bus, eating in the restaurants. In each city's ceremony, Mrs. Dix made her way to the podium and was eloquent as she passionately spoke of history, Freedom Struggles, and dignity for our ancestors. I marveled at her strength, perseverance, and royal bearing. Her words of wisdom and inspiration regarding our African Origin and accomplishments will always ring in my heart.

The African Burial Ground

In 1991, an African cemetery was discovered that roughly encompassed Wall Street to Foley Square, during excavation to construct a federal building in the area. I was one of the first to go down into the gravesite to see the bones. Words cannot express the emotions that overwhelmed me.

Over a decade of conflict ensued regarding what should happen to the remains and who should be in control. Eventually, we reached a four-point agreement that included:

1. A burial park where the bones would be reinterred
2. A memorial artistic expression inside 290 Broadway (one of the buildings that were under construction when the bones were discovered)
3. Architectural design in Foley Square
4. A museum.

There were those who tried to exclude Mr. and Mrs. Dix and others. But the leadership of city council member Charles Barron, Mrs. Ollie McLean, and Ms. Juanita Thomas, and the support of the community, prevented the exclusion. And as the African Burial Ground gained prominence, the same kind of offenders who have always had tension with community people struggling for empowerment or participation again laid claim to all the activities surrounding the re-interment.

I often wonder about commitment. If there was no money, no contract, no pat on the head from benefactors, who would be around, or who would carry the struggle? And here is the shocker: There would have been no black executive director at the Schomburg Center if community people, led by council member Charles Barron, hadn't demonstrated to demand a black executive director. A white one had already been appointed. And as too often happens, once our brothers or sisters secure the jobs, they act as if they had some special quality that landed them in the position. Then, to further exacerbate the situation, they distance themselves from the very people who made the sacrifice or paved the way to make it all possible.

Go Down Death

In her waning hours, I would call Mrs. Dix occasionally. She would say how tired she was. She was ready to go. After the funeral, I spoke to her husband, Nana. He said, in her last hours, she spoke to her aide and her grandson. Then she turned to him and said, "I'm going home." Tearfully, it brought to my mind James Weldon Johnson's poetic sermon, "Go down Death": *Weep not, weep not, she is not dead.* She has only just gone home.

Day before yesterday morning,[1]
God was looking down from His great high heaven,
Looking down on all His children
And His eyes fell on (Sister Caroline) Sister Dix
Tossing on her bed of pain.
And God's big heart; was touched with pity,
With the everlasting pity.
And God sat back on His throne,
And He commanded that tall, bright angel standing at His right hand;
Call me Death!
And that tall bright angel cried with a voice
That broke like a clap of thunder.
Call Death!—Call Death!
And the echo sounded down the sheets of heaven
Till it reached a way back in that shadowy place,
Where Death waits with his pale, white horses.
And Death heard the summons;

And he leaped on his fastest horse,
Pale as a sheet in the moonlight.
Up the golden street, Death galloped,
And the hooves of his horses struck fire from the gold,
But they didn't make no sound.
Up Death rode to the Great White Throne,
And waited for God's command.
And God said Go down, Death,
Go down to Bronx, New York
Find Sister Eloise Dix.
She's borne the burden and heat of the day,
She's labored long in my vineyard,
And she's tired
She's weary.
Go down, Death, and bring her to me.
And death didn't say a word,
But he loosed the reins on his pale, white horse,
And he clamped his spurs into his bloodless sides,
And out and down he rode.
Through heaven's pearly gates,
Past suns and moons and stars,
on Death rode,
Leaving the lightning's flash behind,
Straight down he came.
While we were watching round her bed,
She turned her eyes and looked away,
She saw what we couldn't see,
She saw Old Death. She saw Old Death
Coming like a falling star.
But Death didn't frighten Sister Dix.
She looked to him like a welcomed friend.
And she whispered to us: I'm going home,
And she smiled and dosed her eyes.
And death took her up like a baby,
And she lay in his icy arms,
But she didn't feel no chill.
And death began to ride again—
Up beyond the evening star,
Into the glitter light of glory,
On to the Great White Throne.
And there he laid Sister Dix

On the loving breast of Jesus
And Jesus took his own hand and wiped away her tears,
And he smoothed the furrows from her face,
And the angels sang a little song,
And Jesus rocked her in his arms
And kept a-saying: Take your rest,
Take your rest.
Weep not, weep not,
Sister Dix is not dead,
she's resting in the bosom of Jesus.
Let us remember Mrs. Eloise Dix always as the gallant warrior
she was who loved her people and lived to set them free. May her
memory inspire us to go and do likewise.

James Forman[2]

Sunrise: October 4, 1928, Chicago, Illinois
Sunset: January 10, 2005, Washington, DC

A Formidable Revolutionary

James Forman, former executive secretary of the Student Nonviolent Coordinating Committee (SNCC) died January 10, 2005, at seventy-six. He was one of the most influential leaders during the years of the Civil Rights Movement.

The news opened a floodgate of memories of an era when young men and women put their lives on the line for a cause bigger than themselves. In my mind, it forced a comparison between those days of the Civil Rights, Black Power, and African liberation movements, when young people heard a drumbeat beckoning them to daring deeds of self-giving, with the youth of today, who all too often hear another kind of beat that moves them to self-indulgence and self-aggrandizement.

Those youths of yesteryear left the comfort, security, and in some instances, luxury, of kith and kin and went off to the battle-grounds of the South—Mississippi, Alabama, Georgia, North and South Carolina, etc. Some of them never returned home. James Chaney, Andrew Goodman, and Michael Schwerner, whose mothers still weep, are a few whose names we know, but there were too many others known only to loved ones and fellow strugglers who were killed, beaten, and jailed.

There was the Mississippi Freedom Project, when thousands of young people, mostly black and white students, went to Mississippi on a voter education/registration venture. There were the marches, demonstrations, boycotts, pray-ins, wade-ins, eat-ins, freedom rides, civil disobedience—whatever tactic they conceived to challenge the racist laws and customs of the South. They knew they were risking life, limb, material goods, family, and reputation. They were up against forces that seemed to come straight from the pit of hell. But they braved it all, and so turned the nation around and moved us further along the road to freedom. Wish God their kind were with us today. Where have you gone, Kwame Ture, Robert Lee Jackson, Fannie Lou Hamer, Ella Baker, and Dr. Martin Luther King Jr.? We long to see your kind again.

There are stalwarts from those days who are still around. They remind us that those days did exist, and the gallant people, young and old, were living creatures, not heroes fashioned from dreamy stuff.

They lived and they gave their all. There is Julian Bond,[3] Bob Moses, Marion Barry,[4] Eleanor Holmes Norton, John Lewis, Walter E. Fauntroy, and Andrew Young, all still alive and making their marks on the canvas of history. They were there. They remember. They tell the story, and the stories they tell us of heroism, sacrifice, and bravery challenge us today, and call to mind H.W. Longfellow's poem:

Lives of great men all remind us,
we can make our lives sublime,
and departing, leave behind us
footprints on the sands of time.

I first met Forman in 1969. It was after he had disrupted the communion service at Riverside Church in New York City, and demanded reparations. During the service, he stood up and made a speech recounting the history of racism and the exploitation of African people, and demanded reparations from Christian churches and synagogues. He made the connection that churches and synagogues had participated in reaping the benefits from slavery, and therefore owed a debt to people of African ancestry.

He was in an office at 475 Riverside Drive, "The God Box," as the building is affectionately called. I went to see him with Dr. Calvin Marshal, pastor of Varick Memorial African Methodist Episcopal Zion Church. Rev. Marshal and I were deeply involved in the struggle for community control of schools particularly in Ocean Hill, Brownsville. Dr. Marshal was co-chair of a multi-racial, multi-religious group of religious leaders called the "Clergy Vigil," which set out to impose "a moral guardianship over the public school system." When we walked into the room, Forman barely looked up from his writing. He greeted us cordially, but his mind was fixed on what he was doing. I had the feeling he was in many places.

Maybe he was reflecting on what he had done at Riverside Church, or plotting his next move, or pondering the strategies they had employed during the Civil Rights, Black Power movements. Who knows, but he was with us while elsewhere. His audacious act of disruption at the Riverside Church had generated a tumultuous reaction of criticism and compliments across the country.

His hair was bushy. His handsome bronze face was tired but radiant. His body conveyed the feeling of caged energy. There was no doubt in my mind that he was a man of strength, integrity, enormous courage, and singular humility.

We began conversing:

"How're you doing?" we asked.

"All right. Okay."

"How is…," he asked about specific people.

"They're doing fine," we answered.

"Do you need anything?" we asked.

"No, I'm all right."

All during this time, he was writing. Occasionally, he would pause and look up for a moment. It was clear that his mind, while engaged in conversation, was on other things.[5]

We didn't spend a long time with Forman, and the time went by so swiftly. All of us had things to do, "promises to keep and miles to go before we sleep." I wish I could have spent the day with him. In fact, I wish I would have joined him in the reparations movement at that time. But there were other struggles that I had prioritized and committed myself to: Clergy Vigil and the struggle for community control of public schools; Youth in Action and the work youth advancement; Operation Breadbasket, the economic justice arm of Dr. King's SCLC; the Black Intellectual Independent Political Movement and political empowerment; Clergy and Lay Persons Concerned About Vietnam, and the anti-war movement. Then there was the Black Power movement that had raised black consciousness to another level and engendered tensions all over the place.[6] And on top of all of these were my pastoral obligations and ecclesiastical duties.

Now, Forman is gone but not forgotten. He is forever enshrined in the hall of fame of human rights strugglers. His heroism will be there for all to read.

Congressman John Lewis in a profoundly moving account tells of Forman's last hours.

"I knew James Forman for more than forty years," he said. "In that time, he was a brother, a friend and a colleague. We sang all of his favorite spirituals and freedom songs, recited speeches, and cared for him. We were there when he took his last breath."

Black Manifesto[7]

James Forman didn't stop his demand for reparations at the Riverside Church. He continued to show up at various religious places and meetings. On April 26, 1969, at a conference sponsored by the National Black Economic Conference in Detroit, Michigan, Forman issued his Black Manifesto, which later became a pamphlet of the same title that put forth his ideas regarding reparations.

The introduction was titled, "Total Control as the Only Solution to the Economic Problems of Black People." In the opening paragraph, he stated, "We have come from all over the country, burning with anger and despair, not only with the miserable economic plight of our people, but fully aware that the racism on which the Western world was built dominates our lives. There can be no separation of the problems of racism from the problems of our economic, political, and cultural degradation. To any black man, this is clear."

After touching on many subjects—including history, capitalism, socialism, racism, violence, revolution, and of course, reparations—he concluded with, "Our seizure of power at this conference is based on a program, and our program is contained in the following manifesto."

In the opening paragraph of the Black Manifesto, Forman stated:

We, the black people assembled in Detroit, Michigan, for the National Black Economic Conference, are fully aware that we have been forced to come together because racist White America has exploited our resources, our minds, our bodies, and our labor. For centuries, we have been forced to live as colonized people inside the United States, victimized by the most vicious, racist system in the world. We have helped to build the most industrial country in the world. We are therefore demanding of the White Christian churches and Jewish synagogues, which are part and parcel of the system of capitalism, that they begin to pay reparations to black people in this country. We are demanding five hundred million dollars from the white Christian churches and Jewish synagogues.

Forman had a ten-point program as to how the money would be distributed:

- Establishment of a Southern land bank to help our brothers and sisters who had to leave their land because of racist pressure, for people who want to establish cooperative farms but have no funds.
- The establishment of four major publishing and printing industries in the United States.
- The establishment of four advanced scientific and futuristic audiovisual networks.
- Research/skills center.
- The establishment of a training center for teaching skills in community organizing, etc.
- Support for the National Welfare Rights organization.
- Support for a national Black labor strike force.
- Establishment of an International Black Appeal (IBA).
- Establishment of a Black University.

- The Interreligious Foundation of Community Organizations (IFCO) is the umbrella agency to allocate all unused funds in a planning budget to implement the demands of the conference.

Clearly, James Forman was in the mainstream of black struggles for freedom. These struggles in opposition to some have never been confined to one tactic. As the historian Lerone Bennett Jr. observed a long time ago, the monster we fight is so immense that we need all the strategies, skills, and thinking we can get. I once coined a phrase when I chaired the National Black United Front: "Let us never 'absolutize' a methodology."

In the past several weeks, reparations hit the news again in reports that, while seeking a contract from the city of Chicago, JP Morgan Chase & Company had lied about its connection to slavery. When confronted with the truth, that bank admitted that it had profited from the slave trade. The company issued the following statement:

> Recently, JP Morgan Chase completed extensive research examining our company's history for any links to slavery to meet a commitment to the city of Chicago. Today, we are reporting that this research found that between 1831 and 1865, two of our predecessor banks—Citizens Bank and Canal Bank in Louisiana—accepted approximately 13,000 enslaved individuals as collateral on loans, and took ownership of approximately 1,250 of them when the plantation owners defaulted on the loan.

JP Morgan Chase & Co. was forced to make this admission because the city of Chicago has a disclosure ordinance that requires companies doing business with the city of Chicago to reveal whether they profited from slavery.

When JP Morgan Chase & Co. attempted to secure city contracts and was denied, the company then made the confession. The company offered $5 million dollars in scholarships for students in Louisiana—an offer which was immediately rejected by reparation advocates.

The issue of reparations was front and center again in New York City when the December 12th Movement, Millions for Reparations, and City Council members Charles Barron and Bill Perkins convened a press conference at City Hall on February 9, 2005, to demand reparations-related legislation.[8] After the press conference, we marched to the office of JP Morgan Chase & Co., where we held a rally and made speeches. City Hall hearings on the issue of reparations was set for 9:00 a.m. on February 17, 2005.

Thanks to James Forman and many others before him, and those in the present and those to come, the issue of reparation will not die, although it may, from time to time, seem to gain momentum and then lose steam. Those of us who are in the movement, however, believe that we shall win a significant victory. In fact, we believe we have already won: We have raised consciousness, expounded on history, and changed posture from that of beggars to demanders of a debt, and some corporations have been willing to at least pay something.

James Forman came our way and continued to raise the issue of reparations in particular, and many other issues besides.

Robert "Sonny" Carson[9] aka Mwlina Imiri Abubadika

Sunrise: May 22, 1936, South Carolina
Sunset: December 20, 2002, New York, New York

The Education of Sonny Carson

It was forty-five summers ago in 1960, when I first saw Robert "Sonny" Carson. How vividly I remember his ebony face shining in the sun. His voice was strident, rough, and forcible. He was angry. He castigated white people as he rehearsed the history of racism. He repeatedly used the term "honky" for white people.

The crowd in the park on Fulton Street clapped and cheered at almost every sentence he uttered. I stood enthralled by the speaker. I appreciated his brutal candor. I liked the strength, courage, and intelligence he radiated. It was obvious to me that he was a tough, no-nonsense, determined man. He personified the new strong, proud, bold, intelligent Black man that was emerging at that time—that would years later give birth to Black power, African Liberation Day, Black consciousness, Black pride, and Black theology, and which coincided with the African liberation movement on the continent.

I vowed to myself that I would search him out. I had the feeling, even then, that in some mysterious way our destinies were meant to interact. All of us have met people who, as wind-driven leaves across our paths, made no impact on us. On the other hand, all of us have encountered people where we instinctively knew the meeting would have deep and lasting consequences.

The next day, I found him in a small office of the Congress of Racial Equality (CORE). I walked in, announced I was looking for Sonny Carson, and was directed to his desk. I introduced myself:

"I am a minister and have only been in the ministry for several years. I pastor a small storefront church. I saw you speak yesterday, and I liked what I heard. I wonder how we could work together."

He looked up sternly, and in a gruff voice said, "I don't like no preachers."

"I don't like them either, but what has that got to do with anything? I come to talk about working together on behalf of our people."

In cracking laughter—which I would hear frequently in subsequent years when he was challenged—he nodded, and our conversation began. I had pierced the granite facade. Immediately, I could see that behind that exterior was a deeply sensitive compassionate interior.

Crack No Laughing Matter

Across the years, we had many memorable experiences—like the time we took over a multi-dwelling building on Washington Avenue.

Although there were families living in the building, it seemed abandoned. Sonny had a CORE office on the first floor. I started a church on the fourth floor. In this arrangement, the liberalism of Sonny Carson is manifested. He was not wedded to any religious persuasion; he was committed to the advancement of black people and was prepared to accept and work with anyone or institution who shared his commitment.

Then the owners of the building decided to remove the tenants. We were equally determined that we would not let them. We gathered the tenant families and told them they might have to fight to stay in the building, so whatever they had, they had better find it.

One family informed me they had only an old weapon. Later, we all had a belly laugh about that. I should have learned my lesson. Years later, police fired more than twenty shots at Luis Baez and killed the twenty-nine-year-old with mental illness. While organizing the angry crowd, I told them to meet us in the park that night and bring everything they had. The people placed a liberal interpretation upon my command.

It was a tension-filled night. After a lengthy standoff, the issue regarding the building was finally resolved without incident.

During the anti-poverty years, Sonny encouraged and supported my run for chair of Youth in Action (YIA). I was elected a vice chairman, and teamed with Sonny in trying to allocate resources to the grassroots people whom Sonny was always most concerned about.

When *The Education of Sonny Carson* movie was being filmed, Sonny gave me the script. I disliked the words of the preacher eulogizing a little boy in the movie, so I rewrote the script. During the same time, Sonny was on trial for manslaughter, and he asked me to be the treasurer of his fundraising campaign.

Youth development and raising the consciousness and pride of Black people were of paramount importance to Sonny. All of the above interests came to fruition in the School of Common Sense, housed in a church once occupied by First Baptist of Crown Heights, purchased by the late Jim Cuffe.[10] Sonny started a committee to honor black heroes, to pay homage to our ancestors, to educate and to engender pride. The renaming of some Brooklyn streets after great men and women of African ancestry bears his fingerprint.

Moreover, when the scourge of dope spread across our community, Sonny did something about it. He organized Black Men's Movement Against Crack. I always admired his let's-do-something-about-it spirit. When he saw a need, when black people were threatened or needed help, he did not say, "Why doesn't somebody do something about it?" He rolled up his sleeves and went to work.

Just as he organized a delegation to welcome home the long-exiled Herman Ferguson when he returned from Guyana, Sonny brought home to Brooklyn the unclaimed bodies of brothers who had been killed in the 1971 Attica prison rebellion, and arranged respectful funerals for them. Who would have thought of doing such a thing besides Sonny Carson?

It was Sonny who first raised the issue of Tawana Brawley. He called me one day, and in his usual gruff, demanding way, he asked, "Did you hear what happened?"

"I don't know. What are you talking about?"

"White men raped and sodomized a sixteen-year-old black girl in Poughkeepsie, New York. Let's go up there."

"When?" I asked, knowing the answer, but hoping I was wrong.

"Now!" he shouted back.

Just like that, we ended up in a church in Poughkeepsie, talking and organizing around the Tawana Brawley issue.

It was Sonny Carson who I first heard shouting, "No justice, No peace." Sonny's concerns were not confined to Brooklyn and New York City. He was very much active in the peace movement. At one of the largest anti-Vietnam War rallies, Sonny organized a large delegation to join the rally. It was held at Dag Hammarskjold Plaza, and one of the main speakers was Dr. Martin Luther King, Jr.

But at the top of his international interest was Africa. He traveled frequently and extensively across the continent. Although seldom given the credit, he fought hard to prevent further desecration of the African Burial Ground in lower Manhattan, and to erect a monument on the site. He wanted to take the bones back to Africa.

African Bones

Often, I visited the hospital where he lay in a coma. The last night I was with him, I did my usual prayer and whispered, "So long, old warrior." Before the break of day, he was gone. I was consoled by the fact that I was with him until the end. We had spent years and done so many things together. It was as if God wanted me to be there—an old friend to bid farewell.

It was hard to believe when I heard the news, yet somehow I knew it was coming. When people die who had been our rock, who seem always to have been there, unmovable, unbreakable, unshakable, we just cannot bring ourselves to believe they are truly gone.

Of course, they are gone in the flesh, but the spirit will never leave us. Brooklyn does not seem the same without him. In a real sense, he was one of the best of Black Brooklyn: tough, uncompromising, ingenious, courageous, creative, tenacious, resourceful, brilliant, combative, diverse, and comprehensive.

Occasionally, I still expect to hear his voice when I pick up the phone, or to see him entering the church (always without an appointment) and hear him say, "Rev., did you hear about…? We got to do something about it. Meet me there," or "I'll pick you up." I do not ever remember saying no.

Yes, we still miss him, but his spirit lives on, and as Marcus Garvey said, "Look for me in the whirlwind." We will say to the world, we will look for Robert "Sonny" Carson in the streets of Brooklyn and wherever our people need help, even in the whirlwind of social change.

To the eternal credit of Atim and all the disciples of Sonny Carson, his memory has been kept alive through various activities. On Sunday, June 19, 2005, between 3:00 and 9:00 p.m., there was a memorial for Sonny Carson, at the Restoration Building on Fulton Street. We had another opportunity to pay our respects and remember the giant who dwelt among us.

Coretta Scott King[11]

Sunrise: April 27, 1927, Heiberger, Alabama
Sunset: January 30, 2006, Rosarito, Mexico

Losing Another History Maker

It was January 31, 6:15 a.m. My wife and I were driving down FDR Drive when we heard the radio reporter say, *"I interrupt this program with a special announcement: Mrs. Coretta Scott King is dead…."* As he continued, emotions overwhelmed my mind. It was difficult to grasp the rest of the information.

I heard my wife say, "It seems like everybody's gone—Betty Shabazz, Rosa Parks, Mawina…" She continued a stream of names, and her voice became inaudible. As we drove through the morning

mist, my mind went back to Morehouse College, 1968, and the funeral services for Dr. Martin Luther King Jr. After private services
at Ebenezer Baptist Church, there was a procession led by the mule-
drawn wagon carrying the coffin of Dr. King. His followers, dressed
in overalls, clasped hands and lined up on both sides of the caisson
for the journey to Morehouse College for the public funeral.

Mrs. King walked up the outside stairs where I was standing.
She was leaning on the arms of two men—Reverends Ralph Abernathy and Andy Young, I believe. Our eyes met, and I was transfixed. I had seen her eyes before, but this time it was different. She
seemed to be viewing something that the rest of us could not see.
There was deep, deep pain, but there was something else, too. An
all-embracing compassion, incredible strength, undeviating purpose
and determination. A profound knowing. I guess she was saying, *"I
am painfully aware of this moment, but prodigious responsibilities
await me. I must be ready, and I will be ready."*

The old hymn, "There Is Balm in Gilead," with its comfort and
challenge, filled the campus air. The venerable and aging Dr. Benjamin Mays[12] delivered his powerfully moving eulogy, and the ceremony was over. As I was trying to absorb it all, Mal Goode, the
veteran ABC television newscaster interrupted my musing with a
request for an interview. He asked my opinion regarding the funeral ceremony, particularly all of the dignitaries that were present. I
remember saying, "I am overwhelmingly impressed with all of the
proceedings. I was moved by the creative way in which they included the mule-drawn coffin. It was so appropriate for and consistent
with Dr. King's life and values. But what people do in the future will
validate or invalidate all their verbal and symbolic expressions."

When I returned home, actor Ralph Carter of the TV show *Good
Times*, about six years old then, approached me as I walked up the
steps to my church, and shouted, "I saw you on the Martin Luther
King Jr. Show!" History has proven how right I was in the readings
of Mrs. King's eyes. How true is the saying, "The eyes are the window of the soul." She was one of a kind. To cite the famous Shakespearean quote from Hamlet, she had endured "the whips and scorns
of time, the slings and arrows of outrageous fortune and a thousand
natural shocks that the flesh is heir to." While moving ahead and

making lasting contributions for the good of humankind, she had to live in the dehumanizing segregation system.

Mrs. King lived with constant threat when her husband was alive. I know a little bit about that. There was a time when my family, even children, had to wear bulletproof vests when going to a rally or meeting. She had to live with her husband's many arrests and the uncertainty of his safety while in jail. She had to endure the physical attacks on her husband. He was stabbed in Harlem. His head was bloodied from a rock thrown during a march in Chicago. She even experienced the bombing of her home.

There was the illegal malicious war waged by J. Edgar Hoover, then director of the FBI,[13] in an unparalleled attempt to destroy the character and reputation of her husband. With its COINTELPRO,[14] the FBI took steps to destroy the character and reputation of black leaders and attempted to put so much pressure on them that they would commit suicide, go insane, or be crushed emotionally and mentally. And finally, Mrs. King had to endure the assassination of her husband. And after that, she had to bear the awful burden of protecting, promoting, and perpetuating Dr. King's legacy. There were many wolves in sheep's clothes that were eager to exploit the memory for personal gain. Let us admit the painful truth. She wasn't always the beneficiary of love and praise. She had her detractors and times of rejection and verbal abuse.

I was at the 1984 Democratic Convention, when Black people's frustration reached a point that manifested itself in boos for Mrs. King and the Rev. Andy Young.

Gallantly, the Rev. Jesse Jackson came to their defense. It was a low point in our struggle, comparable to the boos that greeted Dr. King years before in Chicago. We are ashamed of ourselves now, but they understood—and they never stopped loving us.

How ephemeris is the adulation of the crowd. Those who cry, "Crown him!" one week, will be among the crowd that cry, "Crucify him!" next week. Those of us who are leaders, or want to be leaders, should always remember to wear the praises of the crowd as a loose garment—always ready to divest ourselves of the adoration while keeping our eye on the prize. True warriors of, and for, the people understand that the jeers of the masses express the pain and frustration of being long denied legitimate rights. All leaders can become the conspicuous or subtle, direct or indirect, object of the anger of the very people they are called to lead, and even after having done it so effectively.

Any one of the above developments would have crushed the stoutest heart, or at the least driven them to retreat or withdraw from the struggle. But not Mrs. King, Not this beautiful, brilliant woman of African ancestry. It seems she only mourned for a moment. A few days after Dr. King's funeral, she went to Memphis to continue giving support to the sanitation workers that her husband had started.

However, she mourned—and God only knows the depth of her mourning—she sallied forth to meet towering challenges. She kept the self-seekers at bay. She took control of her husband's affairs, deepening and expanding his vision by adding her own talent, wisdom, and vision. In so doing, her future was inextricably woven into her husband's legacy, and what they had been in life, they would continue to be in the future work. The two become one flesh, each having their particular gifts and personalities, but marvelously married into oneness.

The King Memorial Center is a monumental achievement. I used to participate at the center during the early annual memorials. In fact, New York City councilman Charles Barron reminded me the other day that when he was my chief-of-staff, I sent him to Atlanta to assist Mrs. King and others in organizing the twentieth anniversary of the March on Washington, and a national holiday for Dr. King for the King Memorial Ceremony in 1982. Event organizers included Stevie Wonder and the Rev. C.T. Vivian, a close associate of Dr. King.

Countless telephone calls, letters, and invitations—obligations of every description demanded her attention. She seemed to be everywhere. Noble causes beckoned her, and she bravely and graciously answered the requests. Unstintingly, she gave her prestigious presence and support to myriad causes and movements—civil rights, human rights, women rights, children's rights, environmental protection, voter registration, Peace and Nuclear Disarmament, and the list goes on.

One of my most cherished memories is her participation in the June 1982 Disarmament Rally & March in New York City's Central Park. The program started at the United Nations and concluded at Central Park with over a million people gathered from around the world. It was the first time that that number of people had assembled anywhere in the United States. Mrs. King was accessible and cordial to all. She shared her experience and wisdom. I introduced my children to her, and she gave them her undivided attention. She was so unassuming, so easy to talk to, and so radiant as the sun lovingly shined upon her face. I treasure some photos that captured Mrs. King and me at the Central Park rally. In one picture, I am making some notes as we discussed our families, the national holiday, the King's Center, the twentieth anniversary of the March on Washington, and the success of the Disarmament Rally & March. In another photo, she is looking off in the distance.

It reminded me of the look I saw in Atlanta, except in Atlanta, the look revealed sadness, wisdom, and strength. In this picture, the eyes, while still knowing and compassionate, are filled with serenity and happiness.

She was able to walk among kings and queens and keep the common touch, to paraphrase Rudyard Kipling. She was always humble, always there for the people, like her husband. In addition to awesome movement tasks, responsibility, and obligations, she was still a mother with four little children to take care of: Yolanda, Martin III, Dexter, and Bernice. How could she have managed it all? We are overwhelmed with awe when we ponder the incredible balancing act that she performed with such grace, humility, brilliance, dignity, serenity, skill, dexterity, and confidence.

What was the source of her strength? What inspired her to carry on? On the surface, it would seem that her background didn't prepare her for the rough and tumble, gritty, grimy business inherent in the struggle against injustice and bigotry. Somebody has said, "Never put on your Sunday suit and go to a revolution." I would add, "Don't allow yourself to be blindly naive and get in the struggle for social change."

She was middle class, sheltered, and artistically gifted. While she was in Boston at the conservatory of music, having received a music scholarship, she met her husband. But paradoxically, it was that very background that provided the source of her strength and being. More specifically, it was the church, the black church, the old ship of Zion, that was the rock from which she was hewn, the anchor that held her secure. Deeper still, it was her faith in the God of this church that sustained her, made her triumphant, and finally, called her home bearing immortal palms.

This church, the Black church, had always been the womb that birthed, the nursery that nurtured, and the environment that raised to adulthood our heroes and heroines—indeed, people of African ancestry. It was the God of this church who gave us Harriet Tubman, Sojourner Truth, Ida B. Wells, Ella Baker, Fannie Lou Hamer, Betty Shabazz, Queen Mother Moore, and Rosa Parks; and before them, Queen Nzinga and Nanny of the Maroons. It was the same God who gave us Frederick Douglass, Denmark Vesey, Bishop Henry McNeil Turner, and the Reverends Henry Highland Garnet, Dr. Alexander Crummell, Richard Allen, Absalom Jones, Edward Blyden, Adam Clayton Powell, Jr., and Dr. Martin Luther King, Jr.

And it was the same God who gave us Coretta Scott King. She learned early on to internalize and hold fast the promises of scripture—that God would never leave her nor forsake her. Just as the scriptures say in Isaiah 40:28–31: "Hast thou not known? Hast thou not heard that the everlasting God, the Lord, the Creator of the ends of the earth, fainteth not, neither is weary? There is no searching for his understanding. He giveth power to the faint; and to them that have no might, he increaseth strength. Even the youths shall faint and be weary, and the young men shall utterly fall. But they that wait upon the Lord shall renew their strength; they shall mount up with wings as eagles; they shall run, and not be weary, and they shall walk and not faint." Her strength was the strength of a hundred because her heart was pure.

Precious Lord

She knew, and as a child embraced to the core of her being, the old hymns of the church. And in this connection, I think of the song her husband loved:

Precious Lord, take my hand,
Lead me on, let me stand,
I am tired, I am weak, I am worn.
Through the storm, through the night,
Lead me on to the light.
Take my hand, precious Lord,
Lead me home.

But there were other hymns equally encouraging and inspiring:

There Is a Balm in Gilead
To heal the broken heart
There is balm in Gilead
To make the wounded whole
Sometimes I feel discouraged
I think my work is vain
But then the Holy Spirit
Revives my soul again There is balm in Gilead.

On Christ the Solid Rock I stand
All other ground is sinking sand.
When darkness veils its lovely face,
I rest on his unfailing grace.
And every high and stormy, my anchor holds within the veil.
His oath, his covenant, his blood
Supports me in the whelming floods
When all around my soul gives way,
He then is all my hope and stay.

I Ain't No Ways Tired
I've come too far from where I started
Nobody told me the road would be easy
But I don't believe God brought me this far to leave me.

She embraced the music of the movement, grappling with it while singing its songs as her very own, including the preeminent song of the Civil Rights Movement: "We shall overcome. Deep in my heart, I do believe we shall overcome, some day."

The best description that I know to characterize this extraordinary woman, this rare gem of a lady, is she was a superstar. Let me explain. When I was an unofficial chaplain with the New York

Jets, I asked myself, "What makes a superstar?" In professional football, as in all professional sports, all of the players are good at their positions, otherwise they would not be professionals. But there emerges from the crowd a superstar. Why? I came to the conclusion that superstars play hurt. Superstars can perform at their best even when they are in pain. In fact, it would seem sometimes that they grow stronger and more skillful while they are enduring pain. Players without that unique quality may be as skillful, but they cannot match the superstar capacity for pain. When we study the history of our people, we have been a people who have been able to not only survive but to make progress while being subjected to the cruelest acts. While we were hurting, we were succeeding.

That's why I call Mrs. King a superstar. She was able to perform hurt. She was able to make lasting contributions to the progress of the human family. She was able to see clearly with tears in her eyes, to walk steadily while burdened with disappointment, betrayal, intolerance, and loneliness. She was able, with bloodied hands, to build a monument of lasting achievement. She was a superstar.

When I used that description on a television program, the person who was interviewing me responded, "Missus King would never think of herself that way." I replied, "You're right. But that is another reason she is a superstar. Superstars think that it is the norm to perform hurt. They do not ask for, nor reach for, pity or sympathy while they are hurting. They do what they have to do because they are superstars." [15]

David Brothers[16]

Sunrise: December 25, 1919, New York City
Sunset: June 25, 2007, Virginia Beach, Virginia

Remembering Dave Brothers

David Brothers was funeralized at The House of the Lord Church in Brooklyn, on Sunday, July 2, 2007, after our congregation's worship services. Dave was born on December 25, 1919, in New York City. He died after months of failing health, on June 25, 2007, in Virginia Beach, Virginia. He had been involved in many civil rights organizations, and was known as a revolutionary pan-

Africanist freedom fighter. He chaired the New York Chapter of the Black Panther Party and was a longtime friend of Kwame Ture, formerly Stokely Carmichael, chairman of the Student Nonviolent Coordinating Committee (SNCC). Dave's famous saying was, "Light the fire! Organize the people!"

The proceedings began at 5:00 p.m., with a two-hour viewing, and the church was packed, primarily with veteran activists and their supporters. People came from as far away as California. There were representatives from SNCC, the Black Panther Party, the December 12th Movement, the National Black United Front, the Patrice Lumumba Coalition, and of course, the All African People's Revolutionary Party (AAPRP), of which Dave was a member until his death. There were solidarity messages from across the world, including the Nation of Islam and the American Indian Movement.

Dave was laid to rest in white African apparel. As the scores of viewers filed by the casket, they voiced their amazement at the youthfulness of his appearance. "He looked to be about fifty," one viewer said. Family members sat on the front seats. They wept silently as they gazed at the body in the open casket.

The first part of the ceremony followed the traditional religious pattern: Invocation, Scripture readings—Old and New Testament—by Senior Minister Renaldo Watkis and Minister Afiya Dawson. Condolences were read by Sister Inez Barron, a member of our church who has since been elected to the New York State Assembly, and later the New York City Council. A resolution, specially prepared by members of The House of the Lord Church (Dave was an honorary member for many years), was read by Dr. Karen Smith Daughtry. After which she sang a powerful rendition of "Wind Beneath My Wings" that moved the church to its feet and applause.

I delivered the eulogy. I spoke of our longtime friendship, and Dave's dedication to the freedom of our people. We showed photos and video footage from our monthly Activist Sunday Service when Dave, along with Jitu Weusi and Viola Plummer, were honored at the church.

The second half of the ceremony was presided over by Jama Lumumba and Chaka Cousins, chair of the AAPRP New York chapter.

There were many speakers who gave solidarity messages. I concluded the ceremony with a benediction and recessional.

After the memorial, family and friends again gathered downstairs in the church's Fellowship Hall for a meal, ending the week much as we had started with Iyanla Vansant and her kin.

The repast for Dave was like a family reunion as old friends and strugglers, many of whom had not seen each other for years, shared experiences in the intervening seasons. Among the speakers were Mr. and Mrs. Herman Ferguson, Elombe Brath, Viola Plummer, and Jitu Weusi. Also present were Professor James Small; Michael Thelwell, co-author of Kwame Ture's autobiography, *Ready for Revolution*; New York councilman Charles Barron; attorneys Michael and Evelyn Warren; and many others.

On Monday morning, the ceremony concluded with an internment at the Calverton Cemetery in Long Island. With family members, friends, and members of the AAPRP, I did the burial ceremony, which included scripture readings, words of comfort, and a challenge. Dave was a veteran, so before the final prayer, as a bugle played "Taps," two sailors came forward, folded the American flag in the unique military fashion, and gave it to his daughter, Donna Freedman. I offered the final prayer: "Ashes to ashes, dust to dust. Looking for the resurrection to come at which time God will gather all of His servants. There will be no more sickness, no more death, no more parting of the ways."

So we left Dave Brothers's body, but his spirit went with us and will forever be with us, inspiring us and challenging us to be all that we can be and do all that we can do to build a better world, especially for people of African ancestry.

A Eulogy for Dave Brothers

We gather here today to celebrate and remember a revolutionary, freedom fighter, statesman, family man, comrade, and friend. Honor requires, and duty demands, that we remember, reflect, and rededicate ourselves to the commitment, values, and principles that governed his life.

I have been digging deep in my memory to exhume the time of our first meeting. I have not succeeded. Once in a while, we meet people who, it seems, we have known all our lives. So it is with David Brothers. He was a rare specimen of God's creation. He was strong enough to be humble. He was courageous enough to be sensitive. He was tough enough to be compassionate. He was secure enough to entertain opposing values. He was grounded enough to be flexible. He was balanced enough to be humorous.

He was a member, an honorary member, of our church. His attendance was consistent. Almost every Sunday he was there. He would persevere through his discomfort and inconvenience. He would push his way up the front stairs to the pew where he usually sat. He was very much a part of our worship. Eyes flashing, body moving, hands upward, he thoroughly enjoyed himself. He was one with our spiritual experience. Till the end, he was generous and consistent. For years, he was a faithful listener and supporter of our weekly Sunday 10:30 a.m. broadcast on WWRL-AM 1600. Often, he would call to commend me on a particular broadcast.

Whenever Kwame was in town, David would bring him to the church. We spent many hours discussing and debating the conditions of the world, especially as they related to people of African ancestry. When the debate became heated, Dave acted as referee. He would never take sides or engage in the argument. He would sit engrossed and moderate. He was kind, considerate, loyal, empathetic, and caring. He was my friend, faithful and just to me. When I hurt, he hurt. When my back was against the wall, when I was besieged, beaten and betrayed, especially when I was under attack from our comrades and fellow strugglers, he was always there. We can endure the arrows from enemies. We know they are coming, and so we prepare ourselves. But the arrows from our friends, comrades are almost unbearable. Many strugglers have not been able to survive the wounds received in the house of friends.

Brother Dave was always there for me. When the attacks intensified, he seemed somehow to know. He would call. In a raspy, reassuring, forceful voice, he would say, "Light the Fire. Don't worry about what people are saying about you. Stay strong. You are on the right side of the issue. You are fighting a good fight." He was consistent; what he said about me privately, he said to others privately and publicly. Then he would reinforce his encouragement with a message from Kwame. He would say, "I talked to Kwame. He sends his greetings. He wants you to stay strong."

There are no words in any language to say how much that meant to me. You have to understand, I was a founding member and the first chairman of the National Black United Front (NBUF). I resigned after eight years as leader. The NBUF was the most effective grassroots pan-Africanist organization of that time. African leaders had always dreamed of a black united front. We argued about it. We had different views on its composition. I, a preacher, a believer in Jesus Christ as Lord and Savior, a pastor of a Pentecostal church (usually the most conservative, at times the most reactionary, in Christendom), had become the head of the National Black United Front. There were many who wouldn't accept it. There were many—maybe most in the nationalist community who viewed Christianity as the white man's religion—"his trick bag." Christianity taught blacks to be docile and passive to whites.

It was always disturbing, sometimes amusing, to me that these ranking radicals, cultural purist, socialist ideologists, and intellectual know-it-alls didn't know—or refused to divulge that they knew—the African origin and early influence Africans exercised in the formulation and dissemination of the Bible's content.

As I went about the work of trying to unite people of African Ancestry, irrespective of their political and religious views—I was constantly criticized, no matter what I did. But there were some veterans of the movement who were always encouraging (e.g., Dr. Maulana Karenga, Dr. Oba T. Shaka, Amiri Baraka, Haki Madhubuti, Afeni Shakur, and most members of the Black Panther Party, Khalid Muhammad, Jitu Weusi, Kwame Ture, and Dave Brothers.)

Dave was somebody special to me. Down to the very end, when he moved to Virginia, we would still converse occasionally. It became most difficult to always understand, but we persisted in conversation. I will miss him very much, and so will countless others. Because of him, many of us were productive in our leadership. Dave never sought the limelight. He was pleased to see others out front. At this funeral, when my wife sang "Wind Beneath My Wings," it was the most appropriate song. Especially the verse that says, "You were content to let me shine. You always walked a step behind…" Here was a man who never sought the spotlight. He never pushed to get out front or to be the leader. He was satisfied to stay behind the scene and help others take the lead.

I conclude with the words from Shakespeare: "The elements in him were so mixed, well might nature stand up and say, 'Here was a man!'"

Dave Brothers's Obituary

I want to share with you a portion of Dave Brothers' obituary:

Reflections of a Revolutionary Pan-Africanist Freedom Fighter

Born eighty-seven years ago, David Brothers has had a history of relentless, uncompromising struggle for the People. He has a rich and glorious history of serving the masses of African People. David was known and respected as a leading organizer for the All-African People's Revolutionary Party (A-APRP).

A proponent of democratic rights, social justice, and improvement in the quality of life for African People, David was exposed to nationalist, pan-Africanist, and socialist political thought as a child. His mother was a member of the Honorable Marcus Garvey's Universal Negro Improvement Association. During the years of the depression in the United States when Africans were suffering horrendously from the ravages of capitalism, David was impacted by the work of Father Divine, who sought to provide some of the basics needed for survival such as food, clothes, work, and shelter.

David mobilized support for Paul Robeson when he was being terrorized, victimized, and white-balled by the US Congress House on the Un-American Activities Committee. He always championed the struggle of African People, understanding the dire necessity to work for social justice. He participated in the mobilization of mass support for Marian Anderson when she was banned from performing at Constitutional Hall in Washington, DC, by the Daughters of the American Revolution for being African, and even participated in the mobilization efforts to elect Adam Clayton Powell, Jr. to the US Congress, from Harlem. David would also work for the election of socialist and communist candidates for electoral office, such as Ben Davis.

Never wavering in his commitment to African People, he was active in the nationalist movement in New York and supported the work of the Student Non-Violent Coordinating Committee. David went on to join the Black Panther Party for Self-Defense in New York, becoming its chairman, where he stood firm against imperialism and the countless terrorist onslaughts of the FBI-CIA. With the destruction of the Black Panther Party, David intensified his readings and work.

David Brothers was a Revolutionary pan-Africanist of the first order. A tireless worker, he was guided by Nkrumahist-Tureist ideology. David was committed to the objective of pan-Africanism, the total liberation of unification of Africa under scientific socialism. His history is one of relentless uncompromising struggle for the People. David was undoubtedly a servant of the People. Known and respected as a leading organizer for the All-African People's Revolutionary Party (A-APRP), David stood firm in emphasizing the dire necessity for our scattered, suffering, struggling, disorganized masses to be organized. David, along with Kwame Ture, was one of the first members of the A-APRP. He was on the first Central Committee of the A-APRP, and served in that position until his transition.

As an A-APRP organizer David has been an inspiration to all. He has been on the front line of organizing and politically educating our disorganized masses. David participated in the founding of the Afrikan Anti-Zionist Front and the World-Wide Afrikan Anti-Zionist Front. David traveled to Africa, including Guinea, Ghana, Egypt, and Libya, as well as other places on a number of occasions, representing the A-APRP. David has a long working relationship with The EAST, December 12th Movement, the Nation of Islam, the Patrice Lumumba Coalition, and the New Afrikan

*People's Organization, amongst others. He was well-respected by
nationalist, pan-Africanist, and socialists worldwide.*

*David's consistent work is an example for us to emulate. Despite
his failing health, up until recently he participated fully in the
politics of the Party. His serious health problems did not deter
him from providing guidance and direction. David's daughter,
Donna, would assist him in his life's work to serve the People. She
would help to facilitate his continued work to help build the Party.
For example, she would ensure he had the necessary material
to prepare for the Party's political discussions. She would send
his political statements out that provided direction for the Party.
When people like Dave leave us, it is as if a page of history has
been removed.*

Baba Mzee Moyo[17]

Sunrise: August 11, 1943
Sunset: August 16, 2007

Mzee The Elder

It was another eventful day in the life of the People's pastor. First
order of business for the day was the weekly organizing meeting to
stop the genocide in the Darfur region of Sudan. The all-consuming
item on the agenda was the collection and allocation of money for
the shipment of supplies to the refugee camp in Gaga, Chad, Central
Africa. We succeeded in raising $16,200, the cost of the shipment
from Douala, Cameroon, to the refugee camp and had already paid
$5,000 for a shipment from South Kearny, New Jersey, to Douala,
Cameroon.

The money was given to Yayha Osman, a Darfurian, responsible for guaranteeing the shipment to the refugee camp. I planned to
join him when the shipment arrived in Chad. It was a great moment
when we consummated the business. In a couple of months, we had
succeeded in gathering seven hundred boxes, weighing eighteen
hundred pounds, in a forty-foot container. All told, we raised more
than $21,000.

Around the same time as our Darfur meeting, our day care centers—Alonzo Daughtry Memorial Day Care Centers I and II—were celebrating their thirty-sixty annual graduation. With the Darfur crisis, we addressed "the worst humanitarian crises in the world today," according to the United Nations (UN). With graduation, we are caring for the seeds of the future.

I learned that Mzee Moyo had made his transition while at the Harlem State Office Building for the Institute of the Black World's (IBW) Pan-African Unity Brunch, organized by its president, Dr. Ron Daniels. It was August 17th, Marcus Garvey's birthday.

I met Mzee around 1978, when we were organizing the Black United Front (BUF) in response to the police killing of a fifteen-year-old black youth named Randolph Evans. A yearlong boycott of downtown Brooklyn stores was implemented. The EAST, headed by Jitu Weusi, was among the major organizations that made up the BUF. Out of the EAST came the Uhuru SASA, an independent Afrocentric school, and what was formerly the African Street Carnival, now the International Arts Festival. Mzee was a key player in all of the EAST's operations.

Mzee was president of the Uhuru SASA Parent Council, director of EAST Caterers, and co-founder of Kente Productions Consultant Firm. He was chairperson of the Social Service Committee for Planning Board 3. He was a member of the Dance Africa Council of Elders and cofounder of the Kwanzaa Collectives. He served as chief of operations of the International African Arts Festival for over twenty years. Under his leadership, the festival reached the point where it was the largest of Global African Culture in the United States. Also, Mzee served as a homeless advocate for Colony South Brooklyn Houses. For over two decades, he assisted the homeless by coordinating Nat Turner Day Care Services for parents and organizing several food drives annually.

The viewing and funeral were concrete expressions of the pervasive love and appreciation the community had for Mzee. From the start of the viewing at 4:00 p.m., to the commencement of the ceremony at 6:00 p.m., and during the ceremony, there was a constant stream of admirers coming into our church, The House of the Lord. The church was packed—a two-deep, standing room around the walls of the sanctuary and balcony. It was the largest funeral at our church in recent memory.

While there were a few whites, the ceremony was all Africans. With the family, preceded by the drummers, we marched into the sanctuary. Veteran activist Adeyemi Bandele and I officiated with welcome, prayer, and scripture readings from St. John 14:1–3. "In my father's house there are many mansions…. I go to prepare a place for you…" The libation followed, conducted by Nana Nsia, Ana McKen, and Neil Clark. A close friend, Russell Benjamin, offered the prayer of comfort. Among those offering community expressions were Imam Obaba Oyo, Queen Mother Ma'asht Amm Amen, Jitu Weusi, and Sharonnie Perry. The eulogy was done by K. Mensah Wali. Music was supplied by Steve Cromity. The sons of Mzee—Baraka Moyo Smith and Zamani Moyo Smith—read the obituary and a poem.

The ceremony was celebrative and representative of several African cultures. Laughter and humor interspersed the solemnity and seriousness. There was a feeling of the unique African communal spirit. Though we were of different religions, political views, and ideologies, on this occasion, we were one African people. It is another testimony of the power and influence of Mzee, that he could bring so many different people in the African Diaspora into a Christian church, united as one African people.

The traditional repast was served in the Fellowship Hall, with enough food of wide variety to feed the hundreds, and to spare.

"The funeral seemed to be more of a celebration," said one of our neighbors.

"It was," I said, "The celebration of a life well-lived."

A special commendation needs to be paid to Mzee's daughter, Salima, and son, Baraka, and the rest of the family. Even though they were grieving, they organized their father's funeral with the highest professionalism and sensitivity. Other members of the family he left to mourn include stepfather, Vincent Byron; sister, Debris Smith; sons Ogdonna, Babu, and Yarul; and daughters Asha, Sala and Adenike; seven grandchildren, a great-grandson, and hundreds of extended family members and friends.

Preston Wilcox[18]

Sunrise: December 27, 1923, Youngtown, Ohio
Sunset: August 12, 2006, Harlem, New York

Eulogizing Preston Wilcox

Preston Wilcox was physically imposing and intellectually brilliant. He was intent on the pursuit of his purpose, and invincible in his determination to achieve his objective. He was innovative in his tactics and programming, insistent on being right and doing right. He was independent in his thinking and lifestyle, ingenious in his research. He was in the quest. He was insightful in his analysis of individual and institutional racism and classism. He was indefatigable in his fight against injustice and exploitation. He was incredibly effective in his enterprises.

He was involved in the struggles against police abuse and for community control of public schools, Black independent schools, black leadership at Schomburg, the African Burial Grounds, and the African Liberation and Black Power movements, to name a few of his many, many involvements.

All across New York, he could be seen carrying picket signs boycotting and demonstrating. Sometimes upfront, most of the time, somewhere in the line of march. He could lead, and he could follow. He wasn't afflicted by the ego inflating the "me first," or the "my way or no way." Nor was he provincial or a participant in the borough battles. He never argued for the hegemony of Harlem. He was too big for that. He was large enough to engulf people of African ancestry everywhere, knowing if we suffered anywhere, we suffered everywhere. We are inextricably bound together by blood, and no geographical lines could eradicate that fact. I am proud to say Preston was a frequent visitor at our church in Brooklyn. Even more, he participated in the myriad of programs in which our church has become famous. The last time I saw him was at our church for the monthly Saturday program of the Institute of the Black World, headed by Ron Daniels. Disease had ravished his body, leaving his once-straight frame bent, and his once-strong eloquent voice weak.

But his mind was still sharp, his eyes flashing with enthusiasm as we discussed many topics.

I don't know what his religion was, or if he was a member or affiliate of any religious institution or tradition. I do know he was profoundly spiritual—meaning, he was located in a universal context. He was connected to the Creator and the creation, from which flows the do-right values, integrity, truth, honesty, valor, compassion, and love, deep concern and tireless work for others.

Preston personified the academic activist. He was a scholar, but his scholastics were not confined to the ivory tower. He was always the professor—always teaching, instructing, guiding wherever he was, in the streets and in the suites, in the classrooms, bar rooms, pool rooms. The world was his university, and everybody was his student.

It was well-nigh forty summers ago, when I first met Preston. It was a tumultuous time in our struggle for freedom. Oppressed, colonized people across the world were on the move. Old demonic systems were being demolished. Here in the United States, the Civil Rights Movement was shaking the nation to its foundation. There were scattered urban revolts called "riots," and upheavals on campuses and schools across the country. And in June 1966, in Greenwood, Mississippi, and Kwame Ture a.k.a. Stokely Carmichael, screamed "Black Power!" and conscious, courageous people of African ancestry around the world resoundingly echoed back, "Black Power!" The struggle intensified, keeping coal on an already burning fire.

Churches were trying to find their roles and places amid the tumult. Black churches, which had a history of being the vanguard in the struggle for human rights and self-determination, had—to a significant degree—lost or forgotten their history and mission.

A group of churches formed the Metropolitan Urban Service Training (MUST) to teach and train ministers, and help them define their roles and missions. To achieve that objective, noted persons were invited to interact with us. We were very meticulous in our selection. We wanted persons of highest intellect with undaunted courage, sterling character, unquestioned commitment to our struggle, a consistent militancy—unbossed and unbought. Among the many who shared with us there were three, which I met for the first time and formed lifelong friendly, enjoyable, productive relationships:

Kwame Ture, Dr. John Henrik Clarke, and the person to whom we pay tribute today—Preston Wilcox. I will treasure these friendships until the bells toll for me.

The Ageless Freedom Fighter from Youngstown[19]

As I have said, Preston waged many struggles, and he initiated and implemented many programs. Four of them stand out in my mind:

1. **AFRAM— researching and cataloging our history and struggle.** We create, make history, then others claim it and record it. Preston pioneered AFRAM to correct that manipulation of history.

2. **The struggle around education.** He knew and taught that there is nothing so precious as the human mind, especially the minds of our children. Whoever controls the minds of our children, controls our future. Therefore, always the corrector, Preston fought gallantly for community control of public school, and struggled and sacrificed for black independence groups, including schools. Some argued for one or the other approach—public *or* independent schools—but Preston drew a circle and included both.

3. **"Blackenization" of the Schomburg Center for Research in Black Culture.** In the 1980s a black man appointed a white man as the archivist at this center. The black community was furious. Two tried and true brothers stepped forward to lead this struggle: Councilman Charles Barron, who, at the time, was the chairperson of the Harlem chapter of the National Black United Front; and the other brother, I am honored to eulogize today, Preston Wilcox. Every Saturday, for three and a half years, they demonstrated in front of the Schomburg Center. Finally, the director of Schomburg saw the light, and they agreed to replace the white man—but they wanted to replace him with the choice of Dr. John Hope Franklin. Councilman Charles Barron and Preston Wilcox said no. They wanted Dr. Howard Dodson,[20]

who, at that time, was director of the Institute of the Black World. That, dear friends, is how Dodson became director of the Schomburg Center.

Dr. Dodson is deeply indebted to Preston, as are countless others. Had it not been for Preston, where would they be? Wish to God that those who come to lofty positions would always remember how they got there. It wasn't by their intellect or their degrees or their physical attributes, but because of brothers and sisters, so often overlooked, forgotten and sometimes even disrespected, who turned up the heat in the streets.

4. **The African Burial Grounds.** Preston was very much involved in the early struggles to save the African Burial Grounds, unearthed during work on a new federal building in Lower Manhattan in the early 1990s. Had it not been for people like Charles Barron, Eloise Dix, Allie McLean, Alton Maddox, Sonny Carson, Noel Pointer, David Paterson, Gus Savage, Dr. John Henrik Clarke, and the person to whom we now bring our tributes, Preston Wilcox, there would have been African Burial Ground memorial—now taken over, managed, and directed by others as the names and contributions of those who fought for its preservation are blotted from the burial ground history.

Ah me, History thou art so unfair. Thou art but lies and distortions—a tale told by prejudiced scribes long removed from truth and facts. Yes, History, you may forget with all those who benefited from the sweat and blood of the forgotten, but we who are gathered here today, will never forget.

Every time we pass a schoolhouse, we will remember Preston. Every time we see children with book bags, on their way to classes, we will remember Preston. Every time we pick up a book, we will remember Preston. Every time we set pen to paper, we will remember Preston, the great scholar and educator. Every time we pass the Schomburg Center or enter its hallowed halls, we will remember Preston. Every time we see Dr. Howard Dodson, we will remember Preston. Every time we go down to the African Burial Grounds, we will remember Preston. Every time we find ourselves in a great cause, we will remember Preston.

And when we remember, we are really declaring to the world and to ourselves, Preston Wilcox is not dead. He lives in our memories and struggles for justice. He lives in the streets of Harlem and Brooklyn and throughout New York—indeed, the world. We shall heed the words of Marcus Garvey and look for Preston in the whirlwind. We shall look for him not buried beneath the ground. We shall look for him not on a wind-swept gravesite. But we shall look for him in the whirlwind of social change, and wherever people are struggling to lift the spirits of humankind, we shall see him then.

A Devout Malcolmite

Yes, Preston lives in our memory. But I believe he lives beyond the grave. I don't know about you, but I cannot believe that these magnificent bodies and minds we possess were meant only for a day. That the few brief years we sojourn in this valley of sorrow and tears constitute the totality of our existence. Perish the thought! I am convinced there is life beyond what we call death. Out there, up there, somewhere, there is life. Not life in these frail, tottering tabernacles of clay. But life in a new form, yet sustaining self-subconsciousness. All religions and sages have taught that life continues in some form, that nothing really ends. Everything is recycled or evolving.

The Bible says, "This corruption must put on incorruption. This mortal must put on immortality. Then shall be brought to pass the saying that is written, 'O death, where is thy sting. O grave, where is thy victory.'" A great Bible mystic said, "I saw a new Heaven and a new earth coming down from God…. There was no more sickness, sin, or death, for the former things have passed away."

There will be a family reunion and the circle will not be broken.

Yes, Preston lives in the great beyond. So long, old Struggler. You fought a good fight, you kept the faith, you finished your course, and there is a great reward awaiting you.

So long, old Struggler. Give my regards to our old friends—Malcolm, Kwame, Sonny, and Cenie. So long, old Struggler. If you see any of my clergy friends, give them my regards. Tell them I am still in the trenches. My head is bloody but unbowed. Tell them don't expect me soon, not that I am afraid to join them. I think I have more to do down here. But when the Lord calls me, I'll be somewhere listening for my name. And when God says put away your pen and paper, take off your marching shoes and lay your sword and shield down by the riverside and study war no more, I'll be ready!

The venerable Percy Sutton quoted a verse from Thanatopolis. I, too, have a favorite poem related to death. It comes from Robert Louis Stevenson:

> *Under the wide and starry sky*
> *Dig me a grave and let me lie.*
> *Glad I lived and gladly will I die.*
> *And I lay down with a will*
> *This be the grave that they made for me*
> *Here he lies where he longs to be.*
> *Home is the sailor*
> *Home from the sea*
> *And the hunter has come home from the hills.*

So long, old Struggler. So long. No more hot sand for you to tread. Your journey has ended now. So long, old Struggler. We're going to miss you. But one day, we will meet again. And in that day, there will be no more parting of the ways.

Vicki Ama Garvin[21]

Sunrise: December 18, 1915, Richmond, VA.
Sunset: June 11, 2007, New Yrok City

Memorial for a Warrior Woman

Vicki Ama Garvin requested that her memorial service be held at The House of the Lord Church. She had said that while she'd been a member of Abyssinian Baptist Church in Harlem since her childhood, when Adam Clayton Powell Jr. was pastor, and had marched with him when he boycotted stores on 125th Street in Harlem, but she wanted her memorial service at The House of the Lord Church because it preached and practice a theology of Black liberation.

My wife, Dr. Karen S. Daughtry, has her handwritten letter with all the details of the ceremony, the people she wanted on the program, and the venue. How easy it would be during these times of grief if deceased persons always left behind directions regarding their final wishes, including a will.

Dr. Karen Daughtry presided over the program and gave words of welcome. Adelaide Simms read Vicki's message for her memorial, and Elombe Brath served as master of the ceremonies. There was a video by Shabazz Productions, of Vicki's life from 1977, to age eighty-one, and a slide presentation of her life and travels. Judith Casselberry, Fred Ho, and Peggy Iman Washington did musical selections. There was a video message from Yuri Kochiyama, and remarks from several individuals, including Herman Ferguson, Brenda Stokely, and Viola Plummer. Her stepson and daughter—Lincoln and Miranda Bergman—gave special remarks. I gave the closing remarks and benediction.

It was a reunion of veteran strugglers sharing memories of a gallant warrior woman. There was a theme that some of the speakers touched upon: She was so little known, really known. Even the people with whom she struggled confessed that they really did not know her. In my remarks, I quoted W.E.B Du Bois, from a passage about the Episcopal priest Dr. Alexander Crummell, in his book, *The Souls of Black Folk*. In Discussing the life and times of Dr. Alexander Crummell, DuBois said that upon meeting him, "I instinctively bowed. The tragedy is we know so little of men."

I knew Vicki primarily from her membership in Sisters Against South African Apartheid (SASAA), *now* in ki-Swahili), an organization my wife started in 1986, which was later renamed Sisters Assisting South Africans (SASAA) after apartheid was abolished. She was quiet and unassuming. Never once did I hear her discuss her accomplishments and the important people she knew. She was always friendly and cooperative, but there was no question that she was sincere and dedicated.

Among my closing remarks, I said:

The ceremony has been so profoundly moving, I am reluctant to speak. Sometimes in moments of solemnity, silence is to be preferred to word noise, but I am compelled to make a few brief remarks.

I am glad and feel honored that she chose this church to have her memorial. I have always prayed and struggled that our church might be the religious place where the radicals, revolutionaries, nationalist, pan-Africanist, artists, athletes, grassroots would find a home, in addition, of course, to whosoever will, let them come. So among her many contributions, Vicki can claim an answer to my prayers.

Also, I am glad she came my way. I wish I had known her better. How many times have we said that about other people? Our challenge is to let her life inspire us to greater efforts to make a better world.

So Vicki, you said, "You never say goodbye to friends; you say goodbye enemies. You say, 'So long,' to friends." We will say bon voyage to you. We will always remember you.

Let us conclude with a portion of her obituary that you might comprehend the greatness of this warrior woman:

Victoria H. Garvin was born in Richmond, Virginia, on December 18, 1915, and grew up in Harlem.

In 1951, she was a founder of the National Negro Labor Council (NNLC), and became a national Vice President and Executive Secretary of its New York City chapter. With the NNLC, she worked with Coleman Young, later Mayor of Detroit, and organized cultural programs featuring Paul Robeson during his persecution. He remained a close friend until his death. In 1955, under pressure from the House Un-American Activities Committee and other repression, the NNLC disbanded.

In 1960, in the wake of McCarthyism, Vicki traveled to Africa. She lived first in Nigeria and then in Ghana, where she worked with Dr. W.E.B. Du Bois, Shirley Graham Du Bois, Alphaeus and Dorothy Hunton, and others, on the African Encyclopedia and anti-colonialist efforts. In Ghana, she lived with Maya Angelou and Alice Windom. When Malcolm X, whom Vicki had known in Harlem, visited Ghana, she introduced him to the ambassadors from China, Cuba, and Algeria, and using her French language skills, interpreted for his meeting with the Algerians.

In 1964, Vicki was invited to China by the Chinese ambassador in Ghana. She taught English for six years in Shanghai. She became friends with many of her young students and kept in touch with them. She also became close to then political exiles Robert F. and Mabel Williams. When Mao Tse-Tung issued a proclamation in support of the Afro-American movement in 1968, Vicki made a speech to a rally of millions. In China, she met and married Leibel Bergman and became a loving stepmother to his daughter, Miranda, and two sons, Christopher and Lincoln.

On their return to the United States, Vicki and Leibel first lived in Newark, where she was director of the TriCity Citizen's Union, a community organization for children and teenagers. In Manhattan, Vicki worked as area leader for Community Interaction at the Center for Community Health Systems of the Faculty of Medicine of Columbia University. Later they moved to Chicago. When the marriage ended, Vicki returned to her parent's home and cared for them until their deaths.

Vicki remained active in political and international circles, traveling back to China several times and making many trips to Africa and the Caribbean, often with her dear friend Adelaide Simms. She was an active supporter of many organizations, including SASAA/SASA, the Committee to Eliminate Media Offensive to African People (CEMOTAP), Black Workers for Justice, and the Center for Constitutional Rights. She spoke at events honoring Malcolm X, and at rallies in support of Mumia Abu Jamal and other political prisoners. Kwame Ture gave her the African name of "Ama." She was recognized as an "honored elder" for her many contributions and unwavering commitment to African liberation and internationalism, as well as her shining example of positive energy, dedication, and self-discipline.

In speeches before her serious health decline, Vicki urged younger generations onward. She said, "Of course there will be twists and turns, but victory in the race belongs to the long-distance runners, not sprinters.... Everywhere the just slogan is reverberating.... No justice, no peace!" She joined the ancestors on June 11, 2007, in New York City, at the age of 91.

Mae Mallory[22]

Sunrise: June 9, 1927
Sunset: 2007

Another Warrior Leaves the Battlefield

On July 8, 2007, Mae Mallory was funeralized at the historic House of the Lord Church. The 5:00–7:00 p.m. viewing was followed by the funeral, where I officiated and gave the eulogize. My scripture reading was from the Psalm 23, Old and New Testaments.

Mrs. Phyllis Pearson read James Weldon Johnson's "Go Down Death," which she improvised by inserting Brooklyn, New York, in place of "Yamacraw," and "Savannah, Georgia," and Mae Mallory for "Sister Caroline." Veteran activists Jitu Weusi, Paul Washington, and Councilman Charles Barron eloquently and movingly shared their experiences with Mae Mallory. All of them referenced her audacity, boldness, brilliances, and commitment to people of African ancestry. Family and friends were moved to tears, verbal responses, and hand clapping as Sister Peggy Washington sang "Precious Lord (Take My Hand and Lead Me Home)." To some of the people present, it conjured up memories of Mahalia Jackson singing during the funeral of Martin Luther King Jr., as that was his favorite song. Grandson Keefer Malloy read the condolences, and granddaughter Geraldine Brown read the obituary.

Mrs. Malloy was reposed in a bronzed casket, and arrayed in a white dress. She held a bouquet of flowers in her folded hands. "She looked so peaceful," mumbled visitors as they slowly passed the casket.

The casket was closed at the conclusion of the viewing, and reopened at the close of the eulogy. After another viewing, the family, followed by friends, were led to the fellowship hall for the traditional repast.

In attendance were veteran activist Herman Ferguson and his wife, Iyaluua, Elombe Brath, Joan Gibbs, and more.

The next day, family and friends gathered again at The House of the Lord Church for the journey to the cemetery. Prayers were said with the family, and the body, which had remained at the church overnight, was removed to the hearse. When cars were arranged, we started our journey. In the hot sun at the Frederick Douglass Cemetery, Mae Mallory was laid to rest. One observer commented, "It seems fitting that she should be buried in a cemetery named after one of the greatest of freedom fighters, Frederick Douglass."

My Eulogy for Mae Mallory

The following is my eulogy for Mae Mallory

What are the worse of woes that wait on age, what stamps the wrinkles deepest in the brow to view ones blotted from life's page and to be alone as I am now.

A week has passed, and we are here again. Last week, at this exact time, we gathered to wish bon voyage to another gallant warrior, Dave Brothers. Now, we come for Mae Mallory. They were strikingly similar in many ways. They were totally and completely committed to the freedom of all people, particular peoples of African ancestry. Dave outlived Mae by seven years. He died at 87.

The picture on the front of the program, with Mae Mallory seated in front of bookshelves packed with books, is an appropriate expression of one of Mae's love and struggles—education. She loved books and pencils and school. In that sense, she was a philosopher, a lover of knowledge and wisdom.

Earlier, Jitu Weusi said it well: "She was brilliant." She was an intellectual who brought sharp analysis and penetrating insights to our movement. She struggled to ensure quality education for all, but especially for people of African ancestry. She had a comprehensive understanding about the school system and independent schools. In those days—and to a small degree, today—there was a fierce battle between those who thought all our effort should go toward making the school system responsive to our needs. There were others, equally sincere, who believed that we should build our own schools and educate our own children. Mae Mallory believed in both. While we fight for quality education in the school system, we should work equally hard to create our own school system. Dissatisfied with the school system, she taught her own children at home. She was for integration of school, but believed there should be some separation. Her fight for integration, let us be clear, was not to be next to Euro-ethnics, but to be where the resources were. At the same time, she was fighting to equalize resources for all schools.

She believed in the importance of union, and so, held membership in 1199 and International Ladies Garment Workers Union (ILGWU). She was a nationalist, pan-Africanist, and concretized her belief by going to Africa to live in Tanzania for five years. She was serious about what she believed. She was no-nonsense, in-your-face, tough but compassionate. She exemplified the ideal of a well-balanced human being, a tough mind and a tender heart. She was ready and able to challenge any authority, Black or white.

It was this seriousness and sincerity that ripped away at her mighty heart. When people didn't measure up to her standards and expectations, she suffered severe let-down, disappointment, and frustration. A lesson we should learn—a hard lesson it is, too— is that there are no perfect persons on this side of history. We play our little part on the stage of life, and do the best we can. Sometimes we falter along the way. We make mistakes. Some decisions we make may not turn out to be the right decisions. But they had to be made. Jesse Jackson used to say, "I am a public servant, not a perfect servant."

It was around 1978, when I first met Mae Mallory. In 1976 a fifteen-year-old black youth was shot in the head by a white officer named Robert Torsney for no reason at all. The following year, almost to the day, a jury sentenced Torsney to two years of psychiatric treatment, weekly visits home, and two years of probation. His lawyers argued that Torsney had psychomotor epileptic seizures.

The community was furious. We-Jitu Weusi, Assemblyman Al Vann, Sam Pinn, and I, along with others, stepped forth and provided leadership. Out of that movement came the National Black United Front. Mae Mallory became a member of the organization. Not long after she joined our church.

I explained that there is a ten-week study period, a commitment of your life to the Lord Jesus Christ, and if you have not been baptized, you must be. Eagerly, she said yes, she still wanted to be a member. She was excited about the challenge, as I thought she would be.

We had many clashes. It is not an understatement to say she was a tough sister. But you like having those people around you—someone to tell you the truth, even when it hurts, or you are ambivalent about it—although they can make you feel uncomfortable.

There are three affirmations I've learned that help me during the time a love one has departed:

- *Purposeful. I believe the universe moves inexorable towards God's confirmation. We are here for a purpose. We may not always understand, and maybe most of the time we don't understand, but we affirm that God, the creator, is in charge.*
- *Goodness. I believe that goodness is inherent in the universe. That God is always at work trying to make good things happen. We sometimes get in the way, disrupting or delaying God's plan, but in the end, God will bend everything to make it work for the good.*
- *Eternity. I believe that life is eternal. Death does not end our existence. Death is but a moment of transition. We move on to a better life. This is the promise of scripture: "When this mortal shall have put on immortality, and this corruption shall have put on incorruption, then shall be brought to pass shall be written, O death where is thy sting; O grave where is thy victory."*
- *So I say to the family and to friends, I hope you can share my three affirmations. If you do, then you know that Mae Mallory is not dead. As the poem "Go Down Death" says, "She's only just gone home."*

Dr. Imari Abubakari Obadele[23]

Sunrise: May 2, 1930, Philadelphia, Pennsylvania
Sunset: January 18, 2010, Atlanta, Georgia

Free The Land!

One of the most dedicated, brilliant, creative, and courageous freedom fighters to emerge out of the struggles of the 1960s was Dr. Imari Abubakari Obadele. He succumbed to a massive stroke on January 18, 2010, in Atlanta. He was 79.

Dr. Obadele befriended Malcolm X and assisted him in his organizing efforts. Obadele had a prodigious intellect. He received a doctorate from Temple University. He was a prolific author, and his books and pamphlets included *The Foundations of the Black Nation* (House of Songhay, 1975), *War in America: The Malcolm X Doctrine* (Ugamma Distributors, 1977), and *Free the Land!* (House of Songhay, 1984).

Among Dr. Obadele's many achievements was his leadership in the founding of the Republic of New Afrika and National Coalition of Blacks for Reparations in America (N'COBRA).

The Republic of New Afrika (RNA) was a social movement organization that proposed three objectives. Firstly, RNA proposed the creation of an independent Black-majority country situated in the southeastern region of the United States. The vision for this country was first promulgated on March 31, 1968, at a Black Government Conference held in Detroit, Michigan. Proponents of this vision lay claim to five Southern states (Louisiana, Mississippi, Alabama, Georgia, and South Carolina) and the black-majority counties adjacent to this area in Arkansas, Tennessee, and Florida. A similar claim is made for all the Black-majority counties and cities throughout the United States. Secondly, the organization demanded several billion dollars in reparations from the US government for the damages inflicted on Black people by chattel enslavement, Jim Crow segregation, and persistent modern-day forms of racism. Thirdly, it demanded a referendum of all African Americans to decide on their citizenship, because it claimed Black people were not given the option to decide on their citizenship after Emancipation.

The idea of the Republic of New Afrika originated in a conference on Black government convened during the weekend of March 31, 1968, by the Malcolm X Society and the Group on Advanced Leadership (GOAL). A declaration of independence with a constitution and framework for a provisional government came out of the conference. It was signed by one hundred of the five hundred conference attendees. Robert F. Williams, living in China at the time, was chosen as the first president. Milton Henry (Brother Gaidi), an attorney, was named its first vice president. Dr. Betty Shabazz, widow of Malcolm X, served as second vice president.

N'COBRA started the primary program to obtain reparations for African descendants in the United States. It understands its work as part of the international movement for reparations. N'COBRA's International Affairs Commission (NIAC) arm works closely with Africans, African descendants, and supporters of reparations for Africans and African descendants throughout the world. Under its leadership, N'COBRA members were very active during the preparatory process for the World Conference Against Racism (WCAR) and the Non-Governmental Organization Forum and government conference held in Durban, South Africa, August 28–September 8, 2001. Members were also active in the African and African Descendants Caucus that was formed during the WCAR preparatory process, and which continues to work on reparations internationally. NIAC understands the connection between the status of Africans and African descendants in the United States and throughout the Diaspora. N'COBRA and NIAC acknowledge that the success of the movement for reparations for Africans anywhere advances the reparations movement for Africans and African descendants everywhere.

My first close association with Dr. Obadele started on January 25–26, 1980, when we gathered in the Robert Hotel in Chicago, Illinois, to put the final touches on organizing the National Black United Front (NBUF). Five of us—Florence Walker of Philadelphia, Pennsylvania; Skip Robinson of Tupelo, Mississippi; Ron Herndon of Portland, Oregon; Jitu Weusi of Brooklyn, New York; and Charles Koen of Cairo, Illinois—were on the organizing committee for the National Black United Front. I had been crisscrossing America, organizing and conferring with various leaders concerning an imperative for a National Black United Front, which would be mass-based, independent, nationalist, militant (or revolutionary), and pan-Africanist.

J. Edgar Hoover, head of the FBI at the time, along with law enforcement systems, had neutralized or decimated the Black Liberation Movement by the middle of the 1970s. We had invited twenty-one veteran leaders to endorse our organizing efforts. Attendees included Amiri Baraka, Dr. Maulana Karenga, Haki Madhubuti, and Oba T. Shaka. Other leaders included were Bob Brown, who represented the All African People's Revolutionary Party, which was headed by Kwame Ture (aka Stokely Carmichael), a representative from the Nation of Islam; Dr. Jacob H. Carruthers; and Dr. Conrad Worrill of Chicago's Center of Inner City Studies, who was to become chair of the National Black United Front, succeeding my resignation in 1986. Dr. Carruthers was chairman emeritus of the National Black United Fund

We started the meeting on Friday night, and for sixteen straight hours, we debated the various issues surrounding the National Black United Front. We concluded Saturday with a consensus on the necessity of a National Black United Front to further the liberation struggle. Later that Saturday evening, over 350 people crowded into the Reverend John Porter's Christ United Methodist Church to hear the various speakers expound on history, culture, and analyses on the existing conditions and the imperative for unity.

Dr. Obadele, who had just been released from prison, shocked the conferees when he entered the room. We had heard that he had been emancipated, but we had not been informed that he would show up at the meeting. He appeared as strong, energetic, and committed as ever. Some time was required before we could resume the business at hand. It was hard to refocus, seeing this brother whom we all regarded so highly. We took time to shake hands, to embrace, to exchange greetings, stories, and updates.

After that meeting, I continued to confer with Dr. Obadele on various issues and planning strategies. In some sense, Dr. Obadele personified the Black liberation struggle. Regrettably, after the 1960s, he became less known, even forgotten, than some of the other liberation fighters. Personally, I liked him very much. He was a giant in every sense of the word except for physical size. He was imposing but unassuming. He was without arrogance or ostentatious rhetoric. He was a great listener: eager to hear new ideas, tactics, analyses, etc. To me, he was always humble, friendly, and easygoing.

Forward Ever, Backward Never![24]

I had mentioned that Dr. Obadele had attended the National Black Forum on Unity in Chicago January 25–26, 1980. I came across an article in the *South Suburban Standard of Chicago* dated February 16–March 1, 1980, with a picture of some of the leaders who had attended. A couple of the paragraphs read:

> *Black leaders, activists, and scholars met in Chicago last Saturday to discuss, debate, and lay groundwork for a "National Forum for Black Unity," according to a spokesman at a press conference held at Robert's Motel.*

> *Twenty-one people were invited to represent the various degrees of ideological thoughts from the nationalists. These various factions saw the need to bury their ideological hatches as Blacks face greater oppression in the 1980s.*

Dr. Obadele was mentioned in *Front Page* newspaper in May 1981. The article records the founding of the National Black United Front, and lists some of the persons who attended. Here is a couple of paragraphs from the paper:

> *When the National Black United Front was founded in June 1980, one journalist wrote of the occasion, "The Black Revolution has begun in earnest, and on a scale much larger than anyone could begin to conceive." Indeed, the over 1,000 delegates from 35 states in America and four foreign countries who participated in the historic founding convention, represented the broadest and most dynamic consolidation of grassroots, radical, and democratic forces in the history of the Black Liberation Movement in America.*

> *Reverend Herbert Daughtry, elected Chairman of NBUF on the third day of the convention, characterized the phenomenal gathering as a "unique fusion of old blood with new," a combination he perceived as vital to the effectiveness of more*

intensive and sophisticated struggles for Black empowerment. And it was! Many veteran activists of the 60s era and prior— like Imari Obadele, Queen Mother Moore, Amiri Baraka, Mae Mallory, and Oba T'Shaka, to name a few—came to lend their experience and expertise to the fashioning of the new multidimensional organization.

The presence not only impacted upon newer, younger activists the continuity of *Black* people's struggle against oppression, but was indicative, too, of the urgency of these times. After all, many of those present at the convention, both the young and not-so-young, were, or had not been in the past, staunch antagonists. Separated by rigid ideological positions, egoism, and other human factors (and not so human ones, i.e. *COINTELPRO), they had remained isolated from each other in their efforts to foster* progress in the Black community.

J. Bruce Llewellyn

Sunrise: July 16, 1927, Harlem, New York
Sunset: April 7, 2010, New York, New York

Dorothy Height

Sunrise: March 24, 1912, Richmond, Virginia
Sunset: April 20, 2010, Washington, DC

When Giants Pass as a Duo

What is the worst of woes that wait on age?
What stamps the wrinkle deeper on the brow?
To view each loved one blotted from life's page,
And be alone on earth, as I am now.

—Lord Byron, *Childe Harold's Pilgrimage*

Within two weeks, three giants of the human spirit made their transition: J. Bruce Llewellyn, Benjamin Hooks, and Dorothy Height. It was my privilege to interact with all three persons at various levels.

J. Bruce Llewellyn

I interacted with J. Bruce Llewellyn at community meetings and social functions. Mr. Llewellyn was a successful businessman. His enterprises included banking, broadcasting, bottling, and groceries. He was also a founding member of 100 Black Men of America, Inc. He had a deep concern for the community, and he was very generous in his giving.

He was tough, aggressive, and hardworking in the pursuit of his objectives, as evidenced in a quote attributed to him when he was interviewed by the *Black Collegian* magazine. Mr. Llewellyn said, "There is no short road to success. It emanates from long, hard years of concentrated effort, from going the extra mile and doing what others will rarely do. Succeeding is tough. It's nerve-racking, gut-wrenching, and pain-inducing. However, there's an old saying, 'Hard work doesn't guarantee you anything, but without it you don't stand a chance.'"

Dorothy Height[25]

It is customary when events occur, or when giants of the human spirit pass away, to ask, "Where were you when the event occurred?" It was asked when Dr. Martin Luther King, Jr. was shot. I can vividly recall being on the telephone talking to a woman named Grace about publishing a book.

I know where I was when John F. Kennedy was shot. I was working in a dry-cleaning store when the owner, a kind, generous man named Mr. Cohen, came rushing to the back where I was, his eyes bulging and body shaking as he cried out, "President Kennedy has just been shot!"

When the World Trade Center was hit by a hijacked airplane, I was on my way from my church to East New York to campaign for Charles Barron. I smelled and saw clouds of smoke even before the radio announcer said, "The first World Trade Center has been hit by an airplane. It is falling down." Then he said, "The other trade center has been hit by an airplane. It is engulfed in fire, and it's falling down." I turned my car around and returned to our church to prepare for the fallout. I knew that crowds of people would be streaming into the church.

When I heard the news that Dr. Dorothy Height had died, I was in Augusta, Georgia, paying my monthly visit to our mother church and taking care of business regarding Legacy, our church's non-sectarian organization. It was around 4:00 p.m., and as I entered the house, I heard a CNN reporter announce the sad news. My mind conjured up the occasions I had been with Dr. Height. I cannot remember how far back, or specifically what we were doing, but I know we attended many meetings and conferences. I do remember the last, and most memorable, occasion was at the home of Alexis Herman, the former secretary of labor during the Clinton years, for a reception in honor of my daughter Leah Daughtry when she was named CEO of the National Democratic Convention in 2008.

Dr. Height was in a wheelchair but still vibrant. Her eyes were clear, and her mind was lucid. I remember how people gathered around her, kneeled, bowed their heads, and praised her for her contributions. The scene reminded me of several other experiences with icons of the movement.

One of those experiences took place at the sixth Pan-African Congress in Tanzania, with Ras Makonnen.[26] We were gathered around him on a warm summer evening, sitting and standing on the green grass, hanging onto every word that fell from his lips as he recounted his years of struggle.

And there was Rosa Parks who visited our church in Brooklyn. She sat in my office, unassuming and petite, and we were mesmerized as we gazed at her. She was soft-spoken and said a few words. It wasn't necessary for her to speak. We were satisfied just being in her presence. As she walked slowly through the fellowship hall on her way up to our pulpit, people bowed. Some tried to reach out and touch her.

There was a similar embracing of Ella Jo Baker[27] at the church, but only a few people knew who she was. Only those who were involved in the civil rights, union, and student movements were familiar with her. Mrs. Baker had been a feisty fighter and organizer. She had played a major role in civil rights and union organizing, and she was known for being fiery and vocal.

Hail to a Queen

Whenever I met or interacted with Dr. Dorothy Height, I felt as W.E.B. Du Bois did when he met the imminent Episcopalian theologian Alexander Crummell. "I instinctively bowed."

Dr. Height's very presence always triggered a panoramic view of history in my mind: The Urban League, the NAACP, the Brotherhood of Sleeping Car Porters, the many photos of her with presidents, heroes and heroines, Freedom Strugglers, Dr. Martin Luther King, Jr., Whitney Young, Roy Wilkins, A. Philip Randolph, Jesse Jackson, James Farmer of the Congress of Racial Equality, unnumbered artists, politicos, opinion-makers, and movers and shakers of every description.

When we were left alone, Dorothy Height always asked about my family. However difficult her days were and painful her body, she was always concerned about others. My daughter, Leah Daughtry, remembered that Dr. Height was a lone woman among the six leaders of the Civil Rights Movement. At the 1963 March in Washington DC, she gave up her speaking slot so that a young, little-known minister from Georgia could have more time. His "I Have a Dream" speech is now legendary. She was a courageous and vigorous fighter for justice. She was self-effacing and always prepared to give others the spotlight if it meant achieving the objective.

She was so proud of Leah. In Leah she saw a representation of the fruit of her struggles. Dr. Height's influence extended to four generations: her generation, my generation, my children's generation, and that of my children's children. There have been few, relatively speaking, in the long history of the human family, who can boast of such a long record of achievements and impact.

Excerpts from her obituary help tell the story:

Dorothy Irene Height, the celebrated civil rights leader and Chair Emerita of the National Council of Negro Women, transitioned to eternal life on April 20, 2010, in Washington, DC. Dr. Height dedicated her life to service and leadership, working tirelessly to the very end. A recipient of the Congressional Gold Medal, awarded in 2004, and the Presidential Medal of Freedom, among hundreds of other honors, Dr. Height has worked on every major advancement in civil rights and justice for women and people of color dating back to the 1930s. She gave counsel to every American president from Dwight D. Eisenhower to Barack Obama.

Born on March 24, 1912, Dr. Height awakened early to the social injustice of segregation and became active with organizations as a teenager. As a young social worker in her 20s, she helped New York City resolve the Harlem Riot of 1935, and helped organize protests against lynching. She soon went on to work for the desegregation of the armed forces and for access for all people to public accommodations.

As the only woman leader among the civil rights leadership known as the "Big Six" Leadership (which included Martin Luther King Jr., Roy Wilkins, Whitney Young, A. Philip Randolph, John Lewis, and James Farmer), Dr. Height played a critical role in helping her colleagues put aside their factional differences and forge a united front. At her urging during the March on Washington in 1963, Dr. King was given no time limit, compared to the other leaders, and was scheduled to be the last speaker that day to deliver what would become known as the "I Have a Dream" speech. As she wrote in her memoir, Open Wide the Freedom Gates, "I do not think there was anyone who really would have wanted to follow him! It was a riveting sermon that struck the conscience of America…. A moment of grace, of transcendence, touched the thousands who were there and the millions more who watched from afar on television."

In a soon-to-be published book, Living with Purpose, Dr. Height left the following advice to meet today's challenges: "To move forward, we have to look at the world as it is becoming rather than how it has been. We have to see how we have to stretch ourselves to become related to this ever-changing scenery. We have to gain recognition not only that no one stands alone, but on a positive side, that we also need each other…. In the long run, it is how we relate to each other and how well we work together that will make the deciding difference.

A Homegoing[28]

All over the sanctuary, people were clustered into groups, exchanging pleasantries. Black funerals are special. They are a unique blend of sorrow, joy, festivity, fashion, and gloom. It is a gathering of the greats, the near-greats, and the wannabe greats, mixing and mingling, and sharing pain, joys, achievements, and failures. Everyone is forced to be together, and they are exceedingly cordial and friendly. Everyone is forced to recognize the frailty and ephemeral of each and all.

During all of the chattering, there were several preludes, starting with the Carillon by Dr. Edward M. Nassor, Carillonneur of the Washington National Cathedral, then the organ by Jeremy Filsell, an artist in residence at the Washington National Cathedral. The final prelude was a choral performance by the Howard University Choir, conducted by Dr. J. Weldon Norris. At 9:30 a.m., the choir, robed in blue with white seams around the shoulders and hem, started singing a medley of spirituals, including "Lord, I Don' Done."

Without a cue, the mass choir became still and quiet. At 9:58 a.m., walking slowly to their seats were US President Barack Obama and Vice President Joe Biden, with their wives Michelle Obama and Jill Tracey Biden.

There seemed to be several minutes of absolute silence, and then the "Resurrection Anthem" was sung. Down the long nave, three young people carried candles on a long pole. They were followed by a long procession of colorfully robed clergy and the family of Dr. Height. Eight young, uniformed men and women carried on their shoulders the mahogany coffin of the venerable lady whom we were to bid adieu.

"'I am the resurrection and the life,' said the Lord," intoned Dr. H. Beecher Hicks, Jr.

The welcome was extended by the Very Rev. Samuel T. Lloyd III, the Dean of Washington National Cathedral. He opened with, "Doctor Dorothy Height lived a life filled with courage and grandeur. We now give her back to God." Prayers were offered by the Right Rev. John Bryson Chane and Dr. Hicks.

The first reflection was expressed by Dr. Dorothy Height's nephew, Dr. Bernard C. Randolph, Sr. He spoke for only several minutes.

His eighty-year-old body needed assistance as he walked from his seat to the podium, but his voice was clear as he said, "My aunt, Dr. Height, was a mentor to all of us."

Bebe Winans of gospel music's famous Winans family, sang a couple songs, including the old spiritual, "Climbing Jacob's Ladder," and "Stand," a contemporary gospel song made famous by Donnie McClurkin. I was puzzled by the position in the service of the two songs, as they didn't seem to fit together. Leah told me later that Dr. Height requested "Climbing Jacob's Ladder," and Bebe wanted to sing "Stand" because Dr. Height had enjoyed it when he'd sung it for her on a cruise. And he did sing. The staid and sad demeanor of the audience was pierced. Amens and hallelujahs could be heard mumbling across the congregation. Hands went up, and the people stood on their feet. Some wept as Bebe Winans's amenable voice rang out:

> *Tell me, what do you do*
> *When you've done all you can do*
> *And if seems like it's never enough?*
> *Tell me what do you say*
> *When your friends turn away*
> *And you're all alone, so alone?*
> *Tell me, what do you give*
> *When you've given your all and*
> *Seems like you can't make it through?*
> *Well, you just stand*
> *When there's nothing left to do*
> *You just stand*
> *Watch the Lord see you through*
> *Yes, after you've done all you can*
> *You just stand... Stand!*

Camille O. Cosby gave a five-minute reflection, saying, "Dr. Height gave her time and energy to those who were in need, no matter how she felt."

The twenty-third Psalm was sung in a melodious rendition by Al Johnson, and a second reading was done by Dr. Barbara L. Shaw, the interim chair of the National Council of Negro Women.

Then President Obama gave his tribute. He spoke for thirteen minutes. "We have come to celebrate the life of Doctor Dorothy Height, and to mourn her passing. Her life lifted the lives of others.… She came by the White House not one time, two or three times, but twenty-one times." He went on to describe how she fought for justice, civil rights, and women's issues. She insisted upon taking her place among the male civil rights leaders. She deserved a place in the pantheon of other heroes and heroines."

The president singled out her spirit of humility. He said, "Doctor Height never cared about who got the credit."

After his speech, the president slowly returned to his seat.

Another musical tribute was performed by Denyce Graves. The Right Rev. Vashti McKenzie, D.D., of the eighteenth Episcopal District of the African Methodist Episcopal Church, and that denomination's first female prelate, proclaimed a gospel lesson. The homily was delivered by Dean Lloyd. He said that Dr. Height was provocative, unstoppable, and forceful; she was tireless and dedicated to justice. Mr. Lloyd concluded with quotes from James Weldon Johnson's "Go Down, Death." Afterward, Dr. Hicks led the congregation in the Lord's Prayer.

To Perpetuate Dr. Heights Memory[29]

My wife, Dr. Karen Smith Daughtry, and I were celebrating our forty-eight wedding anniversary on our favorite Caribbean island. It was not an easy decision to leave in order to attend the funeral of Dr. Dorothy Height. It meant I would have to leave in the middle of our anniversary on April 28th to make the funeral on Thursday, April 29, 2010, at the National Cathedral in Washington, DC. In addition, there were the challenges of time, travel, and cost. I would have to depart on a different flight than we were originally scheduled to take.

The difficulty for us came with the change in the date of the funeral. We were informed that it was originally scheduled for Saturday, May 1, 2010. Our anniversary vacation ended on April 30, and we would easily have been able to make the funeral. We later learned that President Barack Obama wanted to do the eulogy, and he only had an open time slot of 10:00 a.m. on Thursday on his calendar.

I arranged a 2:50 p.m. flight off of the Caribbean island. I arrived in Newark at 10:00 p.m. and took a 3:00 a.m. Amtrak train to Washington, DC, arriving at 6:55 a.m. I went straight to the cathedral. Guests were asked to arrive at 8:00 a.m. for the scheduled 10:00 a.m. funeral service of Dr. Dorothy Height.

And for what was all of this sacrifice, hardship, and disruption of our wedding anniversary, and the denial of my wife in our time in the sun? (My wife decided to stay.) After all, Dr. Height was dead. Nothing I could do would bring her back. But my presence might, in some small way, help perpetuate her memory and contribute to her immortality.

After days of agonizing and constantly praying over the decision of leaving, I decided to go to the funeral for the following reasons:

- Dr. Height was one of the most amicable persons I have ever met. I had the highest admiration for her. I thought I owed it to her to show the world how much she was loved.
- I wanted to do all that I could to immortalize her and perpetuate her memory.
- It was a rare historic moment. I have always had the desire to be present at great moments of history. It helps to make a decision by asking, "Will I be able to do this again?" or "Will this moment happen again?" In the case of Dr. Height's funeral, the answer was no. No, this will never happen again, but I will have the money, the time, and many more anniversaries, if God spares our lives.
- As one who writes, I feel compelled to leave a record on the pages of history. Therefore, I feel driven to be at historic events.
- By reconnecting with old friends or renewing old friendships, there is the potential for the sharing of ideas and information, which can have far-reaching consequences.
- I possess parental pride. My daughter, Leah, was asked to be the national coordinator of the funeral arrangements. To see and spend time with her, to observe her as she orchestrated and coordinated the event, and to see the end result of her labor,

which has always been superlative, was worth whatever I had to do to get to the funeral.

It was 7:35 a.m. when the Amtrak train pulled into Washington, DC's Union Station. Rushing out of the station, I met Mark Thompson, who was waiting inside a car. It was decided that it would be best if he parked near a schoolyard several blocks away from the cathedral so that we could catch a cab. During the ride, Mark requested a ticket for a friend, which I was able to secure.

After parking near the schoolyard, we started our trek up the long, hilly blocks. Thank God a cab came and rescued us. We were dropped off a little distance away from the cathedral, which reminded me of a medieval castle. It sat imposingly, surrounded by trees and manicured lawns. Nothing had changed since I was last there for the Inaugural Prayer in January 2009. We were met at the entrance by Leah's smiling assistant, Lisa, who ushered us into the great cathedral. It was now about 8:30 a.m.

One of the Big Six[30]

The final reflection was expressed by the Honorable Alexis M. Herman, the twenty-third secretary of labor of the United States. She only spoke for four minutes. At times, her voice faltered, and it appeared that she would not get through the remarks. Mrs. Herman had taken care of Dr. Height for many years, and she was steadfast and loyal to the end. My daughter, Leah Daughtry, had been Alexis Herman's protégé for many years, and Mrs. Herman asked her to coordinate the funeral arrangements.

In the few minutes she spoke, Mrs. Herman captured the essence of Dr. Height and the love that we all had for her. She said, "Dr. Height was a woman who loved flowers, hats, the Washington Redskins, the New York Yankees, and good parties. She would be the last to leave a party." Mrs. Herman mentioned that there were three curtain calls for Dr. Height, when it appeared she would be leaving.

"Dr. Height was really preparing us for her transition," she said. "Mrs. Height always said, 'Keep fighting and never take yourself out of the game.'"

Mrs. Herman went on to say that Dr. Height's favorite scripture was Psalm 139. She invited Dr. Height's longtime friend, Dr. Maya Angelou, to read the psalm. Dr. Angelou came to the front of the church in a wheelchair. A mike was brought before her, and in a strong emotional voice, she read the Scripture.

We all stood and sang the National Black Anthem, "Lift Every Voice and Sing." Bishop Chane gave the dismissal, "Let us go forth in the name of Christ. Hallelujah! Hallelujah!"

We all responded, "Thanks be to God. Hallelujah! Hallelujah!" and sang "This Little Light of Mine," as the recession proceeded up the nave, and the body of Dr. Height was taken to the burial ground.

Leah looked at her watch and it was 11:30 a.m. She said, "We ended on time." She was pleased with herself and all those who had assisted in coordinating the funeral arrangements. Even though the profound and unforgettable ceremony was over, people refused to leave the sanctuary.

As we walked out of the church into the sunlight, we met Congressman Walter E. Fauntroy and other ministers. I thought back to the trip Congressman Fauntroy and I had made in the waning days of the Iraqi War. We had gone to Iraq in a desperate attempt to prevent the war, and Congressman Fauntroy had remained in a meeting to meet with Tariq Aziz, the former deputy prime minister of Iraq. Congressman Fauntroy was able to obtain an agreement from the Iraqi government. He was so excited. He called me when he returned from Iraq. He was at New York's JFK Airport, on his way to Washington, DC. He exclaimed, "We have made history! I have an agreement from the Iraqi government. I'm on my way to meet with Secretary Colin Powell."

Mr. Fauntroy said, "I attended Benjamin Hooks's funeral, and it lasted for five hours. This funeral only lasted an hour and a half—" Before he finished his remark, I blurted out with a fatherly pride, "It's because my daughter coordinated the funeral arrangements for Dr. Height." We all laughed, and Congressman Fauntroy said, "I know, I know. She's a genius."

I decided to return home instead of going to the reception. I had been on the move for almost twenty-four hours. While I take pride in my perpetual energy, I was beginning to feel a bit weary. After being dropped off at the station, I paused for lunch at B. Smith's restaurant at Union Station. They make delicious vegetarian barbecue ribs. After twenty-seven years as a vegan, I still like the taste of barbecue ribs. There was a time when I was known to be the connoisseur of barbecue ribs. Occasionally, I find a restaurant that could give me the taste without the flesh.

As I climbed onto the train, I rehearsed the past twenty-four hours. I felt proud of my daughter. I don't know if anyone, besides mothers and fathers, can truly appreciate the glorious feelings parents have when watching their children succeed magnificently. To succeed in anything is wonderful, but magnificently succeeding in a monumental enterprise or work is more than words can describe. To be with my daughter—sitting next to her, occasionally walking with or standing around her (always giving her space); praising her to anybody, but especially to the high and mighty as often as I can; hearing the constant praises for her competence and cordiality; walking away from the event and getting into her chauffeur-driven car that speeds across the city to my destination; watching and listening as she takes care of business on her Blackberry phone, and having interesting conversations with her on a range of topics—it doesn't get any much better than that.

Lenzy Kwaku Ofori Payton[31]

Among the well-known personalities who made their transition in 2010—Benjamin Hooks, Bruce Llewellyn, and Dorothy Height—was a lesser-known personality who joined the ancestors: Lenzy Kwaku Ofori Payton. Ofori's impact in the black community was equal to, or even surpassed, the aforementioned.

The media—Black and White—took little notice of his passing, but those of us who knew him will remember him and sorely miss him inside "the hood." The service was held at the Woodward Funeral Home, and there was standing room only, with crowds in the vestibule and on the sidewalk.

It was an overwhelmingly African, Pan-Africanist, and revolutionary gathering. The attire was predominately African. I was asked to do the invocation. I thanked God for sending Ofori along our way, and for his contributions to the Freedom Struggles. Before I prayed, I talked about my relationship with him.

A word characterized his life: *ubiquitous*. He seemed to have been everywhere.

Wherever there was a crisis or a gathering of importance, he was there. Donned in his African apparel, Ofori attended innumerable marches, rallies, demonstrations, and boycotts. Frequently, he was at my church and could be counted on to be present at all of the important meetings or events. He was often at my church when Sonny Carson and I were the only ones present. Sometimes, Atiim Ferguson came as well. After the passing of Sonny Carson, Ofori was often at the church with Atiim. The three, and sometimes four, of us would sit and rehearse the doings of yesteryear, analyze the present, and make plans for the future.

Two more words describe Ofori. *Loyalty* characterized him. He was as loyal as they come. When I first met him many years ago, he was with Sonny Carson. He remained by Sonny's side until his death.

Ofori never gave the impression that he was jockeying for the top spot or to get ahead. He was content to stay in the background. He had a genuine humility that radiates from those who are secure and confident in themselves. He could lead when he had to and follow when it was necessary. He had a quiet, friendly, and serene aura about him. He spoke softly with a winsome smile.

The final word that described him was *commitment*. He was totally committed. All who knew him never had any doubts about his commitment to our struggle for freedom.

The last time I saw him was at my church. Ofori, Atiim, and I had met to discuss securing construction contracts. He passionately expressed his determination to achieve significant contracts for the community.

Ofori is now gone, but he will never be forgotten. We will remember his life and times as recorded in his obituary:

The journey of Ofori's life led him to participate in many important struggles to improve the lives and circumstances of others. His involvements were many. He worked with troubled youth and on housing, men's health, feeding and housing the homeless, job development, summer employment programs, festivals, political campaigns, boycotts, demonstrations, and direct action.

Ofori's life was a testimony to the adage "Actions speak louder than words." He was a delegate at the National Black Political Convention held in Gary, Indiana, in 1972. He was part of the Committee to Honor Black Heroes trip to Ghana with Sonny Carson, and the Emancipation Day program returning a runaway slave back through the "Door of No Return" at the slave castles in Ghana in 1998. He was part of the funeral ceremony of the Asantehene, King of kings of Ashanti, Kumasi, Ghana, in 1999. To be a witness to, and participant in, these powerful historic moments were among the most unforgettable memories of Ofori's lifetime.

Ofori was always busy. His keen mind never slept, but in his commitment to the community and culture, there was always time for his family. He and his wife, Santina, had a loving bond that others dream of. He was kind, loving, respectful, and always maintained an easy sense of humor. Likewise, as a father, a role he took seriously, he prepared his sons and daughters to be ready for academia and intellectual pursuit. There was not a brighter smile than when he spoke of his children, no matter what the pursuit. He delighted as each one matured and began their adult journey in life. Ofori held a deep and abiding love for his family, fully knowing that love never dies, but lives forever.

Professionally, Ofori served as Executive Director of Central Brooklyn Housing Council, working for better housing and economic development opportunities for minority contractors.

Geronimo Pratt[32]

Sunrise: September 13, 1947, Morgan City, Louisiana
Sunset: June 3, 2011, Tanzania

Uhuru Sasa (Freedom Now)

The last time I saw Geronimo Pratt was at Sekyiwa Kai Shakur's wedding in 2003. The lovely, shiny day in Georgia came close to equaling the beautiful wedding at the scenic home of Afeni Shakur, purchased for her by her son, Tupac Shakur. The spacious dwelling sitting on the expansive terrain of manicured grass, tall trees, and rolling hills, added to the majestic beauty of the affair.

As I prepared to officiate Sekyiwa's wedding, I thought about the conversation I had with Tupac before his death. We were sitting in a jail cell at Rikers Island in New York City. He was waiting to be transferred upstate to the Clinton Correctional Facility. He related to me how he was going to marry Jada Pinkett (who is currently the wife of actor Will Smith). Tupac had had a crush on Jada that went back to their high school days in Baltimore, where they studied performing arts. He was very detailed in how he wanted the wedding to be performed. I did not get a chance to officiate the wedding for him, but I performed the wedding for his sister.

Geronimo Pratt was Tupac's godfather. He was very jovial, and we had a great time laughing and rehearsing old memories at the wedding. He would soon return to Tanzania. We decided that we would take a picture together. I always liked him. He was one of the sincerest, committed, and fearless brothers not only in the Black Panther Party, but in the movement of that day.

Geronimo was sixty-three years old when he died. The cause of his death was a heart attack. He played quarterback on his high school football team. He served two years in combat tours in Vietnam and earned the rank of sergeant. To his credit, he earned a Silver Star, two Bronze Stars, and two Purple Hearts. After military service, he moved to Los Angeles, California, and studied political science at the University of California, Los Angeles (UCLA).

Geronimo, the Black Panthers, and COINTELPRO

Geronimo was recruited by Bunchy Carter and John Huggins into The Black Panther Party. He rose to become the Minister of Defense of the local chapter. In 1971, his wife Saundra was killed. She was eight months pregnant. The murder was blamed on Party discord between the supporters of Huey Newton and Eldridge Cleaver. Geronimo and his wife were members of the Cleaver wing of the Party. In 1972, he was falsely accused, tried, and convicted of the kidnap and murder of Caroline Olsen in 1972.

Geronimo spent twenty-seven years in prison, eight of which were spent in solitary confinement. In 1997, he was freed when his conviction was overturned on the grounds that the prosecution had concealed evidence that might have exonerated the defendant. The government had not included that Julius Butler, the eyewitness against Geronimo, was an informant for both the FBI and the LAPD. An appeals court ruled that this fact was favorable to the defendant, and it was hidden by a law enforcement agency. It was germane to the jurors' decision to convict.

Geronimo was defended by the world-renowned attorney Johnnie L. Cochran, Jr. He always maintained his innocence. Eventually, Geronimo received $4.5 million as a settlement for false imprisonment. The City of Los Angeles paid $2.75 million of the settlement, while the federal government paid $1.75 million.

Geronimo was convicted during a time in US history when the law enforcement, particularly the FBI, had developed calculated, coordinated, and concentrated strategies to disrupt and destroy Black movements and all protests. The FBI program was called COINTELPRO, an acronym for a series of FBI counterintelligence programs. Under the leadership of J. Edgar Hoover, they would employ any means—including murder, deception, forgery, and more—to achieve their objectives.

I had the occasion to co-chair the hearings in Washington, DC, on FBI activities in the 1960s and 1970s. Many organizations and individuals targeted by the FBI testified. They included Kwame Ture[33] of the All-African People's Revolutionary Party; Minister Louis Farrakhan of the Nation of Islam; Dr. Maulana Karenga of the formerly US Organization, and now the National Association of Kawaida

Organizations; the National Black United Front, which I chaired at the time; Amiri Baraka of League for Revolutionary Struggle; and the Black Panther Party. The audience was stunned as each group presented its testimony of how the FBI had infiltrated and disrupted their organizations, and even killed some of its members. It became clear that the conflict between the US organization and the Panthers had been staged by the FBI. Dr. Martin Luther King, Jr. was one of the FBI's prime targets. It was their intention to drive him mad or cause him to have a nervous breakdown. Hoover hated Dr. King with a passion.

In 1966, the Black Panther Party came into existence, or became known in Oakland, California. It challenged people of African ancestry to become more aggressively involved. It viewed the US government as racist and imperialist. The Party grew rapidly in the ghettos and colleges.

Because of its influence, the Black Panther Party became the prime target of law enforcement. According to internal memos of the LAPD and the FBI, the law enforcement had set up an operation designed to challenge the legitimacy of the authority exercised by Geronimo in the Los Angeles Panthers. There was another memo that said the FBI was working on measures to neutralize Geronimo as an "effective Black Panther functionary."

It is incredible to contemplate the number of innocent men and women who have been imprisoned, and even killed, by those who are paid to uphold the law. When the law enforcers become the lawbreakers, the foundation of a society is threatened.

Dr. Ronald "Ron" G. Walters[34]

Sunrise: July 20, 1938, Wichita, Kansas
Sunset: September 10, 2010, Bethesda, Maryland

Scholar Activist

Dr. Ronald "Ron" G. Walters was quiet, unassuming, soft-spoken, scholarly, friendly, charitable, courageous, tough, and committed. He was all of the aforementioned characteristics and more. He was an activist, strategist, organizer, author,[35] and a radio and television commentator.

His father was a musician, and his mother was a civil rights investigator for the state. His undergraduate years were spent at Fisk University. It is not as well-known as many aspects of his life, but Dr. Walter's tenor voice blended well with the famous Fisk Jubilee Singers. He graduated in 1963—the year Martin Luther King, Jr. gave his "I Have a Dream" speech at the March on Washington.

Dr. Walters began his illustrious academic career at Syracuse University, and he headed the Department of African and Afro-American Studies at Brandeis University in Boston, Massachusetts. He was a professor and chair of the Department of Political Science at Howard University. From this vantage point, Dr. Walters influenced many budding scholars and activists. He played a major part in helping to organize the Congressional Black Caucus.

In 1996, Dr. Walters accepted an appointment at the University of Maryland, where he directed the African American Leadership Institute, and he was the Distinguished Scholar at the James MacGregor Burns Academy of Leadership. It is reported that he had agreed to return to Howard University as a Senior Research Fellow and Lecturer.

Herb Boyd, the eminent author and columnist, wrote:

For more than a generation, Walters was among the leading Black thinkers in the nation, operating in the precincts of national politics with the same commanding authority he had in the classroom. While Dr. Walters' scholastic achievements and prodigious intellect were well-known, his activism in the Civil Rights and Black Liberation Movements had often gone unnoticed. He led one of the first lunch counter sit-ins as a teenager in his hometown of Wichita, Kansas. Later, Dr. Walters became a leader of the Youth Council of the National Association for the Advancement of Colored People (NAACP). With his cousin, Carolyn Parks, Dr. Walters organized a sit-in protest at the Dockum Drugstore in Wichita. Every day, Black youths sat in silence at the lunch counter and endured harassment from white customers. This happened two years before the Greensboro sit-in. Both sit-ins were pivotal points of the Civil Rights Movement. It has always been fascinating to me and provided meat for study that an act can be done for years and

go unnoticed, seemingly accomplishing little or nothing, but the
same act, done at another time, can change the flow of history.

When the Civil Rights Movement slowed down or took more
assertive cultural and political expressions, such as Black Power
and Black liberation, Dr. Walters, unlike many of his peers,
joined the militancy. He brought his vast intellect and experience
to the Black Freedom Movement, which was predominantly led
by grassroots, radical, and revolutionary nationalists/Pan-
Africanists.

In the *Daily Challenge,* on September 15, 2010, George E. Curry
recorded Dr. Walters's reluctance to accept honorariums for speaking
engagements, and that he led a crusade to force Dr. Walters to start
charging for speaking engagements. Mr. Curry wrote that both of
them were on a panel at Columbia University, and in passing, Mr.
Curry learned that Dr. Walters had agreed to serve on the panel for
only expenses. He said to Dr. Walters, "I'm getting paid, and they
are taking care of my expenses. Others on this panel are getting
paid, too. You must stop letting people exploit you like this. If the
university can pay thousands of dollars to rappers, they can afford to
pay for your exceptional intellect." But Dr. Walters never put a price
tag on his service and speaking engagements for the community. He
was eager to come to any conference or meeting at his own expense,
especially if it were demonstrated that the sponsoring group didn't
have the funds.

A Political Savant[36]

In the early 1980s, Dr. Ronald Walters attended the founding
convention of the National Black Independent Party in Philadelphia,
Pennsylvania. Contemporaneously, we were organizing the founding
convention of the National Black United Front (NBUF) in Brooklyn,
New York.

The Sermon, a 1980 film by Robert Knight of Pratt Institute,
captured aspects of the Freedom Struggle, focusing primarily on the
Black United Front. Dr. Walters concluded the film by saying, "We

must continue organizing at the base. If our liberation struggle is to be won, it must involve the masses."

All along the Freedom Trail, Dr. Walters and I interacted at various times in different ways. We worked closely together during Jesse Jackson's campaign for the US Presidency in 1984. During those times, I had a chance to witness Dr. Walters' strategic perspicacity, keen intellect, organizing skills, and his calm and thoughtful demeanor.

I shall never forget the infamous plane ride from Washington, DC, to Dallas, Texas, in 1984. After Jesse won the Democratic Presidential Primary elections in Washington, DC, we headed in a private jet to Dallas for the presidential candidates' debate. At the rear compartment of the plane were the news reporters, and at the front were the staff, advisers, confidantes, and Secret Service. Dr. Walters sat in the front row, to the right of the plane, and I was seated near him. .Behind us sat former Congressman, the Rev. Walter E. Fauntroy, in the middle was Jesse Jackson, and next to him was Dr. Walters. The plane went through a storm. It was as though we were riding a bronco bull on a rollercoaster ride. The plane was creaking—seemingly about to come apart at any moment. People were crying, throwing up, praying, singing—anything that would get their minds off of the horrifying ordeal. When I looked back, the calmest person on the plane was Dr. Walters. His usual brooding face had not changed. He continued to offer Jesse advice and analyses in a reassuring voice.

When we finally landed, Jesse kissed the ground. The smell of fumes was everywhere. The Secret Service grounded the plane. On our way to the debate, Dr. Walters continued to advise Jesse. By all accounts, Jesse Jackson did exceptionally well in the debate. It deepened respect for him, particularly when it was learned of the heart-stopping incident we had just experienced on the plane. A few months later, that same plane crashed, killing all sixty passengers, including the crew that we had come to know so well.

Another experience I had with Dr. Walters was when Jesse had assigned us to put together the constitution and by-laws of the Rainbow Coalition. At times, the meetings were raucous and fiery.

The steady decorum and wisdom of Dr. Walters always brought the meeting back to seriousness and order.

We worked together on the Democratic Party Platform Committee, representing Jesse Jackson and the Rainbow Coalition's positions. I remembered there was an issue regarding a Palestinian-Israeli conflict. I thought that the participants were so blatantly overwhelmingly supportive of Israel, as to deny any semblance of justice for the Palestinians, that I decided to walk out of the meeting. As I headed down the hall, Dr. Walters came running up to me, and said, "I know how you feel, and I'm on your side, but this is not the issue for you to walk out on. There are many other issues that we need to stay and fight for." Immediately, I saw the wisdom of Dr. Walters's argument. Following him, I returned to the meeting.

On some of Jesse's trips abroad, Ron Walters and I traveled together, and it was always a delight and an educational experience being with him. He had a colossal storehouse of knowledge and a way of imparting it that never made you feel intimidated, small or stupid.

Those of us who knew Dr. Walters miss him very much. Somehow future conferences, meetings, and seminars will not be quite the same without him. Whenever we meet at a serious debate or discussion, we will instinctively look for him—and listen for his quiet voice. While Dr. Walters is gone from us in the flesh, thank God for the hope that we will see him again in the eternal presence of God.

Patrick Gary "Nation Allah" Graham[37]

Sunset: January 11, 2011,

Henry "Shasha" Brown

Sunrise: Unknown
Sunset: January 21, 2011,

On Tuesday, January 11, 2011, Patrick Gary Graham, also known as "Nation Allah," a member of the Nation of Gods and Earths, made his transition. He was funeralized at The House of the Lord Church. On Friday, January 21, 2011, Henry "Shasha" Brown made his transition. He was also funeralized at The House of the Lord Church.

Mr. Brown was a proud and committed brother and an acknowledged member of the Black Liberation Army, which was said to have been the armed wing of the Black Liberation Movement of the late 1960s and 1970s. He was a frequent visitor of our church. I felt so strongly about him that I made a special call from the hospital.

The passing of these men conjured up in my mind the killing of Twymon Myers, who was also said to be a member of the Black Liberation Army. I eulogized Mr. Myers in a sermon titled, "Who Will Weep for Twymon Myers?" It was delivered at The House of the Lord Church in 1973. I think that message is still insightful, challenging, and relevant for today's youth.

Who Will Weep for Twymon Myers?

On November 14, 1973, Twymon Myers was killed in a gun battle with policemen. It was alleged that he had killed policemen, robbed banks, and that he was a member of the Black Liberation Army. No, I don't know Twymon Myers. I don't know if he killed anybody or robbed anything, and I don't know if he was a member of the Black Liberation Army. I don't even know if there was such a thing as "The Black Liberation Army." Even if he were guilty of all of the accusations lodged against him, it would not alter what I am going to say this morning.

Policemen in the exploited communities, primarily the Black and Puerto Rican communities, are guilty of two sins. Forgive me for the generalization. I know that there are good cops.[38] Many have put their lives on the line by protecting others. I say, God bless them. But the number of good cops has been so small as to make their influence insignificant.

The first sin is the Sin of Omission. Most of the policemen have been neglectful. They have not earned their pay in the exploited communities. They have done little or nothing against the ghetto crimes, rapes, muggings, purse snatchings, dope dealings, burglaries, etc. How is it that any child can point out the dope dealers, and the policeman can't find them?

There is a proverb in the exploited community that the hardest person to find when you need one is a policeman. For instance, if you call the police department and say somebody has been shot and is bleeding profusely, you might get a response in several hours—that is, if you're lucky. If you call and say a bank was robbed, the policemen will be there before you put the phone back in place.

Several weeks ago, a man was hit by a car outside the church. His head was busted open, and blood was all over the place. His mother was near hysteria. A number of calls were made to the hospitals and police departments. One police car came and parked. The policewoman made more calls, and the car remained parked. The police officer never got out of her car.

Another police officer came by. I stopped him and pointed to the bleeding man on the ground. He said, "Sorry, I can't do anything." I said, "You've got to do something. Make more phone calls. Give the guy first aid or put him in the car and take him to the hospital." He looked at me and said, "I'm sorry," and he sped away.

In addition to the Sin of Omission is the Sin of Commission. The recent publicity of police crimes makes it unnecessary for me to comment about them. Who brought all of the dope out of the police station? The answer is the policemen. No wonder the policemen have difficulty finding dope dealers. They're dealing with the stuff themselves.

There is a peculiar sin of which the police department is guilty, and it is racism. We need a lot more than a handful of Black and Puerto Rican policemen. A few Black and Puerto Rican policemen will not solve the problem. In fact, it might exacerbate it. It is well-documented that if a few members of an oppressed class are placed in positions of authority, they will exceed the oppressors in cruelty.

In his book, *Crisis in Black and White,* Charles E. Silberman quoted a study by Stanley Elkins documenting that the Jews in the concentration camps were as brutal as, and in some cases, more so than their Nazi slave masters. Some of the Jews tried to imitate the Nazis in their walk and talk, and they even tried to wear clothes as the Germans did in the camps. The same thing happened in slavery. Having been reduced to absolute dependency, the blacks who were placed in charge of other Blacks showed their white slave masters that they could be as vicious as they were.

I don't know if it still exists, but it is a fact that a few years ago, Black police officers were feared just as much, and in some instances, more than the white officers. A remedy to the fear is a community drive to get more Black and Puerto Rican officers hired, and let them know that they are answerable to the community. When a few Black officers are placed in a precinct with hundreds of white officers, they feel threatened. To prove themselves, and for other psychological reasons, the Black officers attempt to out-do the white officers.

I think the Guardian Society, an African American police officers organization, community consciousness, and Black awareness have eliminated most Black policemen's cruelty to Blacks. To the exploited community, the policemen have been symbols of racism in the wider society.

I grew up in Bedford-Stuyvesant and Jersey City. It was part of my childhood experience to be beaten up in a police precinct. One didn't have to do anything but to just be there and be Black! Author James Baldwin related an incident that happened to him when he was just a lad of thirteen years, in which he was walking across the street when the police stopped him for no reason, beat him, and made fun of his male anatomy.

I can list prominent people who received inhumane treatment by the police. I think every Black person has known at least one friend who was brutally beaten up or killed by policemen. Almost every Black person can say that he, or a member of his family, has been racially insulted by policemen.

My generation and the one before me didn't organize to retaliate. I don't know if it had to do with wisdom or cowardice. We took out our hostility on each other. When the cops beat us, we went home and beat our wives or shot or cut the poor fellow down at the bar. In our day, we knew that it would not always be like this. So it doesn't surprise me, and it ought not to surprise anyone else, that there is talk about Black organizations who are committed to killing policemen. Let us not be too harsh in our judgment of the policemen.

They are the reflections of the prejudices of the larger society. The policemen are the keepers of the system. They are here to do the dirty work.

The Rev. Fred Shuttlesworth[39]

Sunrise: March 18, 1922, Mount Meigs, Alabama
Sunset: October 5, 2011, Birmingham, Alabama

A Pastor's Pastor

Wednesday, October 5, 2011, the Rev. Fred Shuttlesworth made his transition at eighty-nine years old. In my opinion, Rev. Shuttlesworth never received the honor and recognition he deserved. Although the Birmingham-Shuttlesworth International Airport was named after him, and other honors were conferred upon him, they were nothing compared to what he deserved. Perhaps there are no honors that would truly do him justice. Maybe in the future, truth will get a hearing, and the world will come to appreciate who he was and what he contributed.

This is my tribute.

A Legend of the Civil Rights Movement

A while back, at the weekly Thursday meeting of the National Religious Leaders of African Ancestry (NRLAA), the Rev. C. Herbert Oliver, former president of The Ocean Hill Brownsville School Board, reported that Rev. Fred Shuttlesworth was very ill and was being harassed by the IRS for back taxes. A lien had been placed against his assets, along with those of his wife—even those assets she acquired prior to her marriage to him.

It was a deeply disturbing moment for the attendees of the meeting. There was a silence that seemed to last an hour while each of us remained lost in our own thoughts regarding the life and times of Rev. Shuttlesworth. He had become a legend to all of us. I would call him an icon, but he hated the term.

I thought about the last time Rev. Shuttlesworth was in New York. Rev. Oliver, a longtime friend of Rev. Shuttlesworth, had invited him to NRLAA's press conference at City Hall, and our subsequent meeting at The House of the Lord Church regarding the crisis in Darfur. Rev. Oliver, who had previously pastored a church in Birmingham and was a part of the Civil Rights Movement, particularly in Birmingham, had assisted Rev. Shuttlesworth in forming the Alabama Christian Movement for Human Rights (ACMHR). At the press conference and in the meeting, Rev. Shuttlesworth spoke poignantly and eloquently about his experiences growing up in the South and being a leader of the Civil Rights Movement. He was impressed with what we were doing in NRLAA, and sought membership. He eagerly received a unanimous vote of acceptance.

The esteem in which those who knew Rev. Shuttlesworth, or about his contributions, was manifested in how then President-Elect Barack Obama related to him. Although in a wheelchair, Rev. Shuttlesworth participated in a march across the Edmund Pettus Bridge in Selma, Alabama, commemorating Bloody Sunday, a pivotal event in the lead up passage of the Voting Rights Act of 1965. Mr. Obama, seeing the reverend in the wheelchair, came over and pushed him across the bridge. Later, he wrote the following letter that the Reverend's wife gave to Rev. Oliver to share with us.

July 24, 2008

Dear Rev. Shuttlesworth,

I heard that Birmingham International Airport will be renamed in your honor, and I just wanted to send this small note of congratulations. You have led a remarkable life fighting for civil rights, and this is a fitting recognition of your service to the people of Birmingham, and our country as a whole.

Leaders like you built the Civil Rights Movement and made it into a transformative force in American history. For decades, you have kept the fight for opportunity and equal justice alive and nurtured the next generation of leaders. You are a giant on whose shoulders I and my generation now stand.

Congratulations again on this great honor. As a beneficiary of your lifetime of sacrifice, I intend to repay the debt I owe your generation by fighting for a better future for the children growing up today. I wish you continued health and blessings.

Sincerely,

Barack Obama

President Obama also made a statement upon learning of Reverend Shuttlesworth's death.

Statement by President Obama on the Passing of Civil Rights Leader Fred Shuttlesworth, October 5, 2011

Michelle and I were saddened to hear about the passing of Rev. Fred Shuttlesworth today. As one of the founders of the Southern Christian Leadership Conference, Rev. Shuttlesworth dedicated his life to advancing the cause of justice for all Americans. He was a testament to the strength of the human spirit. And today we stand on his shoulders, and the shoulders of all those who marched and sat and lifted their voices to help perfect our union.

I will never forget having the opportunity several years ago to push Rev. Shuttlesworth in his wheelchair across the Edmund Pettus Bridge—a symbol of the sacrifices that he and so many others made in the name of equality. America owes Reverend Shuttlesworth a debt of gratitude, and our thoughts and prayers are with his wife, Sephira, and their family, friends, and loved ones.

A Season of Transitions

During the time of Rev. Fred Shuttlesworth's death, eight other people I knew made their transitions. It was unprecedented. Never in all of my decades of ministry have so many people whom I have known or struggled with died so close to each other:

- Dr. Jay Sanford, the husband of Dr. Adelaide Sanford, died Sunday, October 9, 2011
- Dr. Derrick Bell, a civil rights activist and the author of *Faces at the Bottom of the Well*, died October 5, 2011
- Vanessa Cooper, the wife of radio legend Imhotep Gary Byrd, died October 13, 2011
- Charles Peay, a close friend
- Frances Wallace, the mother of ACORN leader Bertha Lewis, died October 10, 2011
- Bishop Landon E. Penn, pastor of Universal Temple Churches of God
- Benjamin M. Priestley, died October 10, 2011; and

Charles Peay

Around 1965, I conducted a revival in Montclair, New Jersey. At the conclusion of the service, a young lady named Virginia "Gin" came up to me and asked if I could visit her sister Maxine in a hospital in Brooklyn. I immediately responded in the affirmative, and upon my return to Brooklyn, I went to the hospital. I met Maxine; her husband, Charles Peay; her sister, Eloise McConnell; and other members of the family. As I continued to visit Maxine in the hospital, it was decided that we would do Bible studies at Mrs. McConnell's home. When Maxine came home from the hospital, we decided to shift the Bible studies to Mr. Peay's home.

The Bible studies continued at the home of Roger Turner and his wife, Tee. From the Bible studies, Roger became a minister and a pastor. Eloise McConnell joined our church and influenced members of her family to do the same. They became one of strongest families in our church. We prayed together for many nights as Maxine grew progressively worse. I always admired Charles' strength, loyalty, patience, and kindness. During the lengthy period of Maxine's illness, he remained devoted and steadfast. I can see him now with deep affection and pain on his face during those nights that Maxine would audibly express her suffering. We continued to hold Bible studies until Maxine's death. I was invited to preach at her funeral in Jenkinsville, South Carolina.

It was through Mr. Peay's concern and generosity, my wife and I were able to purchase our first home. Mr. Peay and I continued our friendship for years thereafter.

Bishop Landon E. Penn

I first met Bishop Landon E. Penn, the presiding prelate of the Universal Temple Churches of God, around 1969. He had just started his first church. He once came to preach for us at our church at 1393 Pacific Street, and delivered a powerful sermon. I remember thinking at that time, "Never a man spake like this man."

Across the years, our friendship deepened. Bishop Penn had a great love of the Church and concern for the community. He was able to bridge the dichotomy of church and community. He was prophetic and programmatic.

A portion of his obituary read:

> *As Pastor for 42 years at Universal Temple Church of God, Bishop Landon Penn has and will continue to be known worldwide as a profound and great thought-provoking preacher. He has demonstrated the art of successfully combining economics, human welfare, and community activity with practical religion. This great man of God advocated for people to have more abundant lives, spiritually, morally, and economically. His achievements in the community were evident by the numerous proclamations, citations, service awards, congressional recognitions from churches, and political and community leaders. In October 2002, the New York City Department of Housing Preservations and Development dedicated two- and three-family houses located at 501–513 Thomas S. Boyland Avenue in Bishop Landon Penn's honor. The housing complex is named The Bishop Landon E. Penn Homes.*

Benjamin Priestly

Benjamin Priestly served as an editor for the *Frontline Newspaper*, the official organ of the National Black United Front (NBUF), during the years when I was the chairman. He was a hard-hitting, honest, and skillful writer. Even more, he was one of the most dedicated members of NBUF. I will always remember his kindness and thoughtfulness toward me whenever I visited Portland, Oregon, where Ron Herndon was chair of NBUF's local chapter.

A stanza from Childe Harold's poem "Pilgrimage" expresses what I feel upon the passing of these people who have impacted my life:

What is the worst of woes that wait on age?
What stamps the wrinkle deeper on the brow?
To view each loved one blotted from life's page
and be alone on Earth
as I am now.

Oswald "Ozzie" Thompson

Sunrise: December 5, 1926, Bronx, New York
Sunset: :Unknown

From police officer to activist

Still reeling from the news that Deacon Betty Brazell had passed, I received word that Ozzie Thompson had died. It was as if I had been hit with left and right punches. By the time I'd caught my breath from one death, I'd been hit by another.

Ozzie was born in the Bronx December 5, 1926. Ozzie had many admirable qualities. He was committed. His commitment to the cause of African ancestry was second to none. This commitment motivated his other qualities. He was always there for everybody. As Congressman Charles Rangel said at a tribute at his funeral, "He was always there." I cannot count the times that on marches, rallies, demonstrations, and boycotts that I would look around and Ozzie would be standing next to me. All he would say is, "I'm here." He was the official security for all of us who were trying to effectuate change. You didn't have to send for him or ask for him, he would just show up. He answered the call springing deep from within him for a brother or sister in need of help.

He was courageous. Although he was a retired police officer with twenty-seven years on the job, he was relentless in exposing and fighting police brutality. It is one thing to fight enemies from a distance—and that's commendable. But it is another thing, a more courageous thing, to fight the enemy working in the same system— enemies that you work and eat with daily. He was what a cop ought to be: tough on crime, and equally tough on police abuse of power. Moreover, his concern went far beyond police-community relations. It was said of him, "When you want something done, you call Ozzie."

He was always friendly. He was "Mr. Cordiality." Oftentimes, those who fight evil become like what they fight, or they lose their sense of humor, gentleness, and friendliness, becoming raw, callous, and mean. Even the people they claimed to be fighting for became frightened of them or kept their distance from them. Ozzie, however, maintained his cordiality and humor and compassion until the end.

We will miss him very much. It will be a long time before I will be able to march, demonstrate, boycott, or attend any serious functions—particularly controversial or dangerous functions—and not be looking for him.

Always, I thank God for the hope that we will see our friends and loved ones again. It is God's plan.

Rosa Parks[40]

Sunrise: February 4, 1913, Tuskegee, Alabama
Sunset: October 24, 2005, Detroit, Michigan

A Rosa Parks Moment

The Rosa Parks Memorial Service, at The House of the Lord Church, was phenomenal. We were blessed with lessons in strength, understanding, and the true power of African Americans. After the opening prayer and welcome, the litany of thanksgiving from Rosa Parks's memorial service in Washington, DC, was read in unison: "For the life of this woman of honor, Rosa Parks, we say thank you."

Indeed, we are very thankful. Not only for what Rosa Parks did for her people, but what many other Black women have done as well.

Councilman Charles Barron reminded some and informed many that African-American women were the ones who truly started the Civil Rights Movement, along with the Montgomery Bus Boycott. Barron spoke of such women as Jo Ann Robinson, who was a prominent figure in the Montgomery Bus Boycott, and the president of the Women's Political Council. He then went back several more years and spoke of the courage of Harriet Tubman, who risked her life and traveled back to the South nineteen times after she had freed herself, to free others who were slaves. He spoke of the selfless decisions that these women made on behalf of themselves and all of the other people they saw suffering at the hands of injustice. It was because of Harriet that women like Rosa Parks continued to be created.

Barron ended his speech with a challenge for the audience to "Have a Rosa Parks moment." This was something that made sense to me, and seemed like something our generation has forgotten.

The spirit of wisdom definitely filled the room. The point of timing came up several times.

It is believed that had it not been time for Rosa Parks to take a stand by remaining in her bus seat, after her arrest, she may have been kept in prison and forgotten about, or even killed, as some others had been before her. But since it was the time for injustices to be brought to the light and stopped, she made history. The Montgomery Bus Boycott catapulted Parks into a position of leadership that she had been displayed even before this one incident.

Years before, Parks and her husband, Raymond Parks, were both members of the Montgomery, Alabama, branch of the NAACP. Rosa Parks served as the branch secretary and youth advisor. Her actions as an activist even helped to place a young Martin Luther King into the position to lead the bus boycott, although the spotlight only led the nation to see King's strong leadership skills.

Charles Barron gave us another example about timing. In the early 1960s, Harlem pastor, activist and congressman Adam Clayton Powell Jr., cried out for "Black Power!" at a rally. Although his message was well-received, his idea of Black Power went undetected, which may have meant that Powell was before his time, and the Black community was not ready to step up in the capacity that he had in mind and protest for Black Power. However, years later, in 1966, when Stokely Carmichael, also known as Kwame Ture, declared these same words, "Black Power," at a rally, the phrase caught on and a new revolution was born.

Barron also went on to remind us of the power of the African-American people. He noted that the Black population in the city of New York is larger than the populations of major cities like Dallas, Texas, and San Diego, California, yet we do not hold the power when it comes to such things as education, politics, and employment.

Also on the program were winners of the 2005 McDonald's Gospel Fest winners Tamika Smith and Linwood Smith Jr., and spoken-word artist Tylibah Washington. The Anointed Voices performed a rendition of "Lord I Am Available."

When I spoke, I seized on Councilman Barron's idea of "a Rosa Parks moment" and the Anointed Voices' "Lord, I'm available unto you." I sought to challenge the audience to make themselves available to God so that they could have a Rosa Parks moment. Whoever they were, no matter how unlikely they may feel being used to do mighty things, history reveals some of God's choicest servants have come from the most unlikely places and people. Also, I emphasized timing. The Bible says, "Be not weary in well-doing, for in due season, we shall reap, if we faint not."

Again, I quoted Victor Hugo, "Nothing is so powerful as an idea whose time has come." Also, to inspire, educate, and challenge, I touched on some of the great deceased leaders who had visited our church: Evangelist John Lawrence, Joshua Nkomo, Kwame Ture, Ella Baker, Ozzie Davis, Judge Bruce Wright, Dr. Betty Shabazz, and of course Rosa Parks. Surely, I reminded the audience that their spirit is still with us and abides in this church.

In closing, Dr. Karen Daughtry reiterated how the power of possessing an idea whose time has come can propel an ordinary person into an extraordinary position of leadership. The evening ended with the understanding that in 2005, it is not too late for us to have Rosa Parks Moments, and when we all begin to feel comfortable with having these sorts of moments, history will begin to be made again.

Resolution 1240: Rosa Parks Memorial Day

On Friday, November 18, 2005, the New York City Council, which includes Domenic Recchia, Charles Barron, Yvette D. Clarke, Eric Goila, and Simcha Felder, held a meeting at City Hall to introduce Resolution 1240, declaring December 1st Rosa Parks Day. Fifty years ago, on December 1, 1955, Rosa Parks refused to move from her bus seat. Resolution 1240 has detailed requests as to how December 1st should be treated by business owners as well as the school system. The resolution suggests that all business owners close on this day, or allow employees the day off if they wish. It also calls for all schools to use this day to teach students regarding the life and times of Rosa Parks, and the contributions she made toward the betterment of people of African ancestry in particular, and the human family in general.

Currently, Oakland, California; Baltimore, Maryland; and Cleveland, Ohio, have already designated December 1st as Rosa Parks Day. It is hoped that everybody will support the resolution, but it is fairly certain that the resolution will pass. Councilmember Yvette D. Clarke, a primary sponsor of this resolution, supported the bill, saying, "Rosa Parks stands apart from any icon." Clarke continued on to say that the hearing announcing Resolution 1240 should not be taken lightly.

City Council Chair Domenic Recchia also urged the support of the resolution to make December 1st Rosa Parks Memorial Day. The New York City Council is pushing for more cities in the South such as Montgomery, Alabama, to recognize and celebrate Rosa Parks Memorial Day. One council member noted the irony of Red Cross trying to kick Hurricane Katrina evacuees out of all hotels on this same date.

After all of the Council members had offered their remarks, the community members were granted the opportunity to express their sentiment toward Resolution 1240. The first speaker was Controller William Thompson, the first Black person to hold that position. Thompson said that had it not been for Parks, Black people today would not be sitting in positions of power. He spoke of the power of the boycott in 1956, explaining that more than thirty thousand pieces of literature urging a boycott were distributed, which helped to make the boycott more successful.

Next up to speak was Borough President Marty Markowitz, who said Parks helped to inspire white people to look inward to see that racism existed and it was detrimental to all people. I then spoke and reflected on the time that Rosa Parks visited The House of the Lord Church. I said how proud I was of the effectiveness of a couple of the

Council members that I have known since they were young. Councilmember Yvette D. Clarke was a Randolph Evans Scholarship recipient, and Charles Barron is a longtime member in The House of the Lord Church, and formerly my chief of staff. I said that once the resolution is adopted, it will inspire everyone, however humble their station in life, to perceive themselves as potential history makers.

Clarence Thomas, a third-generation longshoreman and former Black Panther, traveled hundreds of miles from Oakland, California, to demonstrate the importance of Rosa Parks Memorial Day. He added that in Oakland, on December 1st, flags will fly half-mast. He ended his words of admiration for Rosa Parks by saying that a revolutionary does not have to have a gun.

Nana Soul of Artists and Activists United for Peace made a statement and closed with "Black Power," a slogan which was later criticized by one of the council members. The point that the councilmember made was that he did not believe that Rosa Parks only stood for Black power and justice, but for the justice of all people.

As I was heading out, his comment forced me to stay and approach the microphone to respond to the council member's comment. When Stokely Carmichael, aka. Kwame Ture, first gave expression to the idea of "Black Power" during the march from Selma to Montgomery, Alabama, it was never intended to be anti-white or anti-anybody. Nor was it put forward as a call for violence. It was pro-people of African ancestry. It was a challenge to black people to look within themselves and to appreciate themselves, their families, and the history of their people. And out of their individual genius, which flows in their genes from the greatness of their ancestors, to create institutions of education, economics, and politics—in a word, create viable communities.

I emphasized that Black Power was a call for group solidarity as the means toward empowerment, which would lead to the creation of the aforementioned institutions. Group solidarity is the American way toward group advancement. I rehearsed the history of President Linden Johnson's becoming president of the United States after the death of President Kennedy. I referred to a statement made by President Johnson. He said when he became president, he felt as though he were Irish by osmosis. What he meant was that when Kennedy became president, he saturated the White House with Irish. Significantly, the country did not react with anger or resentment or indignation. In fact, it was considered amusing. Everybody knew President Kennedy had come to power because of Irish solidarity—in other words, Irish power.

It was then cleared up that the council member was not trying to dismiss the ideal of Black Power, but wanted to point out that this day should be viewed as a token of appreciation for Rosa Parks and all that she gave to this nation.

Radical Rosa

In favor of all who supported designating December 1st as Rosa Parks Commemoration Day, the City Council passed Resolution 1240 on November 30, 2005. I would like to now give a better understanding of what is included in Resolution 1240.

On November 18, 2005, a committee of the New York City Council focused on Cultural Affairs Libraries and International Intergroup Relations, held an initial hearing to discuss this resolution, which would be in commemoration of Rosa Parks as a Civil Rights icon. The full context of Resolution 1240 includes historical facts such as her date of birth, February 4, 1913, along with the date of her passing, October 24, 2005. It also speaks of Parks' life growing up in Montgomery, Alabama. Born to James and Leona McCauley, Parks spent a majority of her educational years at underrated all-Black schools. Forced to abide by Jim Crow rules in the South, Parks was unable to eat at all white diners, and had to drink from a separate water fountain. At an early age, Parks grew to understand the limitations that were put on Black people but refused to believe that she deserved the second-class treatment that her and her people were receiving.

Resolution 1240 also detailed a description of the day a half-century ago that Rosa Parks felt enough was enough. It explains how on city buses, there were "Black seats," but that section did not contain a specific number of seats and would fluctuate depending on how many whites rode the bus that day. On December 1, 1955, the bus driver insisted that four Blacks move out of their seats so that the white section could be expanded. Rosa Parks decided not to move out of her seat and was arrested. She was then convicted of disorderly conduct and fined fourteen dollars. Resolution 1240 also cites Rosa Parks's literary works, including a children's book published in 1993, and called *Rosa Parks: My Story*, along with her autobiography *Quiet Strength*, published in 1995.

The Resolution concludes that because of all of Parks's heroic acts, including the one that ignited the bus boycott, she was named "Mother of Civil Rights."

On December 1st, I participated in the rally on Wall Street that was organized by members of the anti-war movement, along with Rosa Parks Day supporters.

In conjunction with this rally, a march will be held in New Orleans on December 10, 2005, in support of the Hurricane Katrina evacuees, who were dispersed across the nation, and are now facing eviction from their temporary housing at various hotels and motels.

At the Rosa Parks rally, organizers highlighted Rosa Parks's struggles for human rights. They called for the immediate withdrawal of American troops from Iraq and an end to the war. I recalled my association with Rosa Parks and other leaders. Also, I reminded everybody of my early opposition to the war, and that two weeks before the war started, I led the last multifaith, multiracial delegation to Iraq in the quest for peace. I concluded that surely, if Rosa Parks were here, she would be opposed to the war, as she and Dr. King and others were opposed to the Vietnam War.

Endnotes

1   "Go Down Death," from *God's Trombones* by James Weldon Johnson. Copyright © 1927 The Viking Press, Inc., renewed 1955, by Grace Nail Johnson. Used by permission of Viking Penguin, a division of Penguin Books USA Inc.

2   This is a version of articles that originally appeared in the February 9, 2005 edition of *The Daily Challenge*, published in Brooklyn, New York. Mr. Thomas Watkins, publisher.

3   Horace Julian Bond, a founding member of the Student Nonviolent

Coordinating Council (SNCC) and the Southern Poverty Law Center, died August 15, 2015.

4   Marion Barry, an NAACP leader who became the first black mayor of Washington, DC, died November 23, 2014. Unfortunately, today he is more widely known for the sting on that videotape of him using illicit drugs while mayor.

5   A characteristic of great minds is the ability to focus yet meander without losing the focus. I saw it on the campaign trail with Jesse Jackson when he ran for president of the United States in 1984. I had been asked to campaign in Manchester, New Hampshire. On this particular Sunday, the campaign staff and supporters had gathered in the office of this synagogue, and a heated debate charged the office about an apology for something Jesse had said. Sometime earlier, Jesse had called New York, "hymie town," another way of saying "Jew town." When it became public, Jesse first denied it, then subsequently, confessed he had said it.

It really shouldn't have caused the furor it did. Other people had said the same thing. It spoke to the Jewish influence in New York. What's wrong with that? I wish there was a town somewhere in America where black people were so dominant that I could call it "Joe's town." The question for me, which raises ethical concerns—and would be true for any people—is not what you have, but how you get it, and what are you doing with it? However, there were those who didn't like, nor trust, Jesse, and this was their opportunity to vent their wrath In any event, the argument raged on. One side argued, "Don't do it Jesse!" The other side argued, "You gotta do it," with equal passion. Jesse was seated at a desk. He was focused on his writing. Occasionally, he would look up and listen with a distant look in his eyes. Sometimes he would make a comment. You knew he was listening, but you knew his mind was somewhere else also. All the time, he was focused on his writing. Finally, when he had heard enough, he looked up and said, "I'm going to do it. My instinct tells me it is the right thing to do." All arguments ceased. I went over, put my hand on his shoulder and said, "OK, let's do it."

He went forth to a packed synagogue. When he was finished, he received a standing ovation. The rabbi and his family came to Jesse for pictures and autographs. We left the synagogue on cloud nine. We were sure we had put the "hymie town" thing behind us. How wrong we were. Early the next morning, the first question the news people asked was, "Are you going to resign?" The bloodhounds never let up.

Even today, they are those who still think he did wrong and should apologize again.

6   At the conclusion of the historic march from Selma to Montgomery, Alabama, in 1966, Kwame Ture, aka Stokely Carmichael of SNCC, stood on the state capitol steps and screamed, "Black Power!" to the thousands assembled, and it would change things forever. Blacks everywhere began thrusting their fists in the air and screaming "Black Power!" However, it created serious division among people of African ancestry regarding the timing, effectiveness, and strategy of organizing around the words *black power*. It was in that climate that James Forman made his move for reparations and the African Liberation Movement.

7   A version of this section originally appeared in the February 16, 2005 edition of *The Daily Challenge*, published in Brooklyn, New York. Mr. Thomas Watkins, publisher.

8   Attorney Roger Wareham, Esq., of the December 12th Movement, Councilmembers Perkins and Barron, and I spoke at the press conference. All of us emphasized the demand for reparation. The councilmembers both discussed their particular bills:

The Queen Mother Moore Reparation Bill, introduced by Councilman Charles Barron to establish a commission to investigate slavery and its business connections in New York City, and

The Corporate Compliance Bill introduced by Councilman Bill Perkins to establish law requiring corporations doing business with city governments to produce all records pertaining to their historical relationship to the transatlantic slave trade and slavery.

9   A version of this article originally appeared in the June 17–19, 2005, weekend edition of *The Daily Challenge*, published in Brooklyn, New York. Mr. Thomas Watkins, publisher.

10   I have an interesting story related to the church, which always inspires my faith to trust God, even when things seem to be going against what I perceived to be my best interest. We were in the process of buying the church. We agreed upon a price.

When we went to close the deal, the owners had changed their mind. I was angry and despondent. It seemed that it was the perfect church for us. It even had a basketball court in the gym. Everybody knows my love for the sport. After a period, the church burned to the ground. I was told there was an electrical defect. There is a parking lot where the church once stood. After time had elapsed, we were directed to the church on Atlantic Avenue where we have remained to the present. The church on Atlantic Avenue is much larger, it cost considerably less, and the location was perfectly suited for our ministry. The church is easily accessible to all modes of transportation and the centers of power, i.e., the Board of Education, an Economic Center Piece, Borough Hall, City Hall and Wall Street. And as everybody knows, we have walked to those places many times, raising the issues of justice. In fact, we made a tradition of walking across the Brooklyn Bridge. So now, when it seems things are going against me, I think of the church that is no longer in existence, and remember that God had something better in mind for me.

11   This is a version of articles that originally appeared in the Feb. 15, 2006, Feb. 17–19, 2006, weekend edition, and Feb. 22, 2006 editions of *The Daily Challenge*, published in Brooklyn, New York. Mr. Thomas Watkins, publisher.

12   Dr. Benjamin Mays, a Baptist minister, was the first dean of the School of Religion at Howard University in Washington, DC, and the sixth president of Morehouse College in Atlanta, Georgia. He died in 1984, at one hundred years old.

13   Federal Bureau of Investigation.

14   Counterintelligence Program, a covert FBI operation conducted between 1956 and 1971, to discredit and neutralize civil rights and other organizations using illegal tactics, including deception, infiltration, and domestic spying on US citizens.

15   I want to thank Imhotep Gary Byrd for expanding upon my superstar characterization to include our people as a whole, and not just scattered individuals.

16   This is a re-edited version of the article "A Weekend of Tears and Challenges: Remembering Dave Brothers and Others" that originally appeared in the July 6-8, 2007, Weekend Edition of *The Daily Challenge* newspaper, published in Brooklyn, New York, Mr. Thomas Watkins, publisher.

17   This is a version of an article that originally appeared in the August 29, 2007 edition of *The Daily Challenge*, published in Brooklyn, New York. Mr. Thomas Watkins, publisher.

18   This is a version of an article that originally appeared in the August 30, 2006 edition of *The Daily Challenge*, published in Brooklyn, New York. Mr. Thomas Watkins, publisher.

19   A version of this section originally appeared in the September 1–4, 2006 edition of *The Daily Challenge*, published in Brooklyn, New York. Mr. Thomas Watkins, publisher.

20   Dr. Howard Dodson served as director of the Schomburg Center for Research in Black Culture from 1984 to 2010.

21   This is a version of an article that originally appeared in the October 31, 2007 edition of *The Daily Challenge*, published in Brooklyn, New York. Mr. Thomas Watkins, publisher.

22   This is a version of articles that originally appeared in the July 13–15, 2007 weekend edition of *The Daily Challenge* newspaper, published in Brooklyn, New York. Mr. Thomas Watkins, publisher.

23   This is a version of articles that originally appeared in the February 5–7, 2010

      Weekend edition of *The Daily Challenge*, published in Brooklyn, New York, Mr. Thomas Watkins, publisher.

24   This is a version of articles that originally appeared in the February 17, 2010 edition of *The Daily Challenge*, published in Brooklyn, New York, Mr. Thomas Watkins, publisher.

25   This is a version of an article that originally appeared in the May 14, 2010 edition of *The Daily Challenge*, published in Brooklyn, New York. Mr. Thomas Watkins, publisher.

26   T. Ras Makonnen (October 7, 1909–December 18, 1983) was a Guyana-born Pan-Africanist.

27   Ella Jo Baker was an organizer of the US Civil Rights Movement, known best as a key advisor and strategist for the Student Nonviolent Coordinating Council (SNCC).

28   This is a version of an article that originally appeared in the June 4–6, 2010 weekend edition of *The Daily Challenge*, published in Brooklyn, New York. Mr. Thomas Watkins, publisher.

29   This is a version of an article that originally appeared in the May 28–31, 2010, holiday weekend edition of *The Daily Challenge*, published in Brooklyn, New York. Mr. Thomas Watkins, publisher.

30   This is a version of an article that originally appeared in the June 9, 2010 edition of *The Daily Challenge*, published in Brooklyn, New York. Mr. Thomas Watkins, publisher.

31   This is a version of an article that originally appeared in the May 24, 2010 edition of *The Daily Challenge*, published in Brooklyn, New

York. Mr. Thomas Watkins, publisher.

32   This is a version of an article that originally appeared in the July 1–4, 2011 holiday

edition of *The Daily Challenge*, published in Brooklyn, New York. Mr. Thomas Watkins, publisher.

33   Kwame Ture, formerly known as Stokely Carmichael, was a leader in the Student Nonviolent Coordinating Committee (SNCC), an honorary prime minister of the Black Panther Party, and later, head of the All-African People's Revolutionary Party.

34   This is a version of an article that originally appeared in the October 6, 2010 edition of *The Daily Challenge*, published in Brooklyn, New York. Mr. Thomas Watkins, publisher.

35   One of his books was *White Nationalism, Black Interests: Conservative Public Policy and the Black Community,* African American Life Series, Wayne State University Press, August 2003.

36   This is a version of an article that originally appeared in the October 8–11, 2010 edition of *The Daily Challenge*, published in Brooklyn, New York. Mr. Thomas Watkins, publisher.

37   This is a version of an article that originally appeared in the February 9, 2011 edition of *The Daily Challenge*, published in Brooklyn, New York. Mr. Thomas Watkins, publisher.

38   This sermon was delivered in 1973, the year that the Knapp Commission Report on police corruption was released, and police corruption was at the fore of public discourse. The Knapp Commission, created by then New York City Mayor John Lindsay, conducted three years of investigation and public hearings on the subject largely in response to revelations of widespread police corruption by whistleblower Patrolman Frank Serpico.

39   This is a version of articles that originally appeared in the October 12, 2011, and December 19–21, 2008 editions of *The Daily Challenge*, published in Brooklyn, New York. Mr. Thomas Watkins, publisher.

40   A version of this article originally appeared in the November 16, December 1–4, 2005 editions of *The Daily Challenge*, published in Brooklyn, New York. Mr. Thomas Watkins, publisher.

3

Educators

Dr. William Manning Marable[1]

Sunrise: May 13, 1950, Dayton, Ohio
Sunset: April 1, 2011, New York, New York

An Exceptional Intellectual

On April 6, 2011, the *Afro Times* newspaper carried the headline, "Police Shootings of Blacks in Miami Draws Outrage." The opening paragraph read, "The recent fatal shootings of seven African-American suspects by Miami police officers is stirring outrage in many inner-city neighborhoods, prompting the city commission to hold a hearing on Thursday to allow family members and activists to air their grievances." The article was written by Curt Anderson.

Back in 1980, Miami was in fire and smoke from a riot sparked by—guess what—the police's violence towards people of African ancestry. As the head of the National Black United Front (NBUF), I was invited by the community to come to Miami. When I returned home, I wrote an article entitled "Miami: One More Warning," for the *Big Red News*.

In the article, I wrote:

> *Miami has been accurately described as war-torn. After spending several days there, the question uppermost in my mind, indeed in*

everyone's mind, is "Why did it happen? Is this a return to the sixties?"

Why did it happen? The one word which comes closest to answering the question is racism. Racism manifests itself in the oppression of one people and the elevation of other people. This takes the shape of joblessness, miseducation, dilapidated housing, inadequate medical services, police brutality and murder, white terrorism, and the emasculation of black leadership.

It reaches a point where one act ignites the fuse. In Miami, it was the fatal beating of a Black man named McDuffie by four white police officers, and their subsequent acquittal.

Is it the beginning of a long, hot summer? Will it happen in New York? The ingredients which precipitated the explosion in Miami are clearly manifested in urban cities across America where Blacks are concentrated. This is true regarding the police.

As I compare Miami in 2011, and Miami in 1980, I am forced to ask the question, "Will things ever change?"

I met Dr. Manning Marable at one of the community meetings in Miami in 1980. He didn't say much most of the time. He always had his head down, taking notes. When he raised his head, his large eyes had a penetrating look as though he was searching for something. He only spoke to ask questions. When he wasn't writing, or looking inquisitively, he was reading and gathering written material.

It was obvious to me that Dr. Marable did not come to Miami to get involved as an activist; he was there as a reporter, a student, an author, a researcher, or all of the above. He was there to gather material for some project. This was not to suggest he wasn't concerned—his concern was obvious—but his major contribution would be with pen and paper. The following years proved my observations to be correct. At the time, I didn't know he had already received his doctorate from Maryland University in 1976. Earlier, he had earned a bachelor's degree from Earlham College in Richmond, Indiana, and a master's degree from the University of Wisconsin.

Across the years, we would meet or interact in workshops, seminars, rallies. To me, he had not changed much. He was still scholarly, intense, inquisitive, and analytical. I always admired his studious demeanor, writing ability, radicalism, and his desire to be at places and gatherings where the more timid scholars would not show up.

I owed him a special debt. Dr. Marable had agreed to participate in—and had encouraged Columbia University to co-sponsor with the New York Theological Seminary—a symposium in honor of my eightieth birthday that was being planned by daughter, the Rev. Leah Daughtry, pastor of The House of the Lord Church in Washington, DC, former chief of staff of the National Democratic Committee, and CEO of the 2012 National Democratic Convention; Dr. Albert G. Miller, the Midwest District Leader of the House of the Lord Church and professor of church history at Oberlin College; Dr. Cornel West, professor of African-American studies and religion at Princeton University; and Dr. Obery Hendricks, professor of biblical interpretation at the New York Theological Seminary. The symposium was scheduled for March 2011, and a publisher was set to release a book of the papers given at the event.

Unfortunately, I encountered spinal challenges that required surgery and an extended stay at the hospital, so the symposium has been rescheduled for later in the year. Hopefully, the symposium will take place, but it will not be the same without Dr. Manning Marable.

Continuing in Walter Rodney's Footsteps[53]

Dr. William Manning Marable was a prolific author. His many books include:
- *Race, Reform, and Rebellion: The Second Reconstruction and Beyond in Black America, 1945–2006*
- *African and Caribbean Politics: From Kwame Nkrumah to the Grenada Revolution*
- *Black American Politics: From Washington Marches to Jesse Jackson*
- *W.E.B. Du Bois: Black Radical Democrat*
- *How Capitalism Underdeveloped Black America: Problems in Race, Political Economy, and Society.*

Dr. Marable was a great admirer of Dr. Walter Rodney, a prominent Guyanese historian and political activist. He styled *How Capitalism Underdeveloped Black America* after Dr. Walter Rodney's monumental work, *How Europe Underdeveloped Africa*. Manning called Dr. Rodney "the personification of praxis, a brilliant intellect, and an uncompromising legacy as the voice of the periphery bound up in world revolution." Similarly, Dr. Manning had a great admiration of Dr. W.E.B. Du Bois, as manifested in the previously mentioned biography he wrote.

Dr. Marable taught and organized at some of the oldest and prestigious universities in the country, including Fisk University, University of Colorado, Purdue, Cornell, Colgate, Ohio State, Tuskegee Institute, and Columbia University. At Columbia, where he remained until his death, he founded and directed the Institute for Research in African American Studies (IRAAS). Dr. Marable was not an incarcerated ivory tower scholar; he was very much the political activist. He was the vice chairman of the Democratic Socialists of America. He was a founding member of the Black Radical Congress.

In his article, "Dr. Manning Marable: A Tower of Intellect, Dead at 60,"[2] journalist Herb Boyd quoted Don Rojas—executive director of FreeSpeechTV.org and former communications director of the National Black United Front (NBUF), and later, Grenada's Prime Minister Maurice Bishop—as saying: "Brother Manning Marable was the epitome of the scholar/activist, very much in the tradition of his hero W.E.B. Du Bois. He was one of the few griots still standing who truly both talked the talk and walked the walk. For him, there was no contradiction, no daylight, between principle and practice."

While many people in the black community were choosing sides between segregation and integration, and socialism and nationalism, Dr. Marable's politics and philosophy have been described as transformationalist. He argued that black Americans should strive to transform existing social structures and work toward a more egalitarian society. He urged coalition building. In the essay collection *Beyond Black and White: Transforming African American Politics*, he wrote, "By dismantling the narrow politics of racial identity and selective self-interest, by going beyond 'Black' and 'White,' we may construct new values, new institutions and new visions of an America beyond traditional racial categories and racial oppression."

Dr. Marable's final work, *Malcolm X: A Life of Reinvention*, was published by Viking. As of this writing, I am presently halfway through the six-hundred-page book. I must say that certain portions of the book are disturbing, and I think will generate widespread controversy.

At this point, I'd rather not discuss my concerns, having not finished reading the book. Significantly, the book was published on Monday, April 4, 2011, the forty-third anniversary of the assassination Dr. Martin Luther King Jr. Dr. Marable died on April 1, 2011.

I add my voice to the chorus of admirers. Dr. Cornel West gave voice to my feelings when he said, "Dr. Marable was our grand radical democratic intellectual. He kept alive the democratic socialist tradition in the Black freedom movement, and I had great love and respect for him."

Dr. Marable's cause of his death was not announced. It has been said that he suffered from Sarcoidosis for many years and received a double lung transplant last summer. Surely, we marvel at his fortitude and perseverance to produce the massive book on Malcolm X while he was physically challenged. He is survived by his wife, Dr. Leith Mullings Marable of New York; three children, Joshua Manning Marable of Boulder, Colorado, Malaika Marable Serrano of Silver Spring, Maryland, and Sojourner Marable Grimmett of Atlanta, Georgia; and two stepchildren, Alia Tyner of Manhattan and Michael Tyner.

Dr. Mary H. Harden Umolu Sanders[3]

Sunrise: November 24, 1927—
Sunset: September 25, 2007—

A Queen in her Own Rights

Dr. Mary H. Harden Umolu Sanders was always regal in her bearing—a brilliant woman, proud to be of African origin. She had a fighting spirit and was committed to the advancement of people of African ancestry. Always, she emphasized education. When I think of Dr. Umolu, I think of Dr. Betty Shabazz, Sisters Ella Baker,

Vicki Garvin, and Fannie Lou Hamer. The qualities that made these women, Dr. Umolo had in abundance.

She cast a long shadow. I was glad that I came within the pale. Whenever I would see her, she was always encouraging and challenging. As she did with all she met, she tried to inspire and motivate me.

Because of an unbreakable commitment, I could not attend the funeral on September 24, 2007, so I decided to attend the viewing at Medgar Evers College. Her viewing was held in the Founder's Auditorium. The large auditorium was packed. A long line of admirers waited to take their turn to tell the world how Dr. Umolu was the greatest and of their association with her.

The funeral was held at St. Paul Community Baptist Church, and its pastor, the Rev. Johnny Ray Youngblood, officiated. Reverends Lula Woods and Richard Honeywell read from the Old and New Testaments. Also appearing on the program, offering brief remarks, were Dr. Edison O. Jackson, Pauline Canady, Gloria Chestnut, Iyafin Omosalewa, Amy Olatunji, Anele Cannon, Mahasin Mais, and Martha Sea. The acknowledgements were read by Renee Riddick, and the obituary was read by Asantewaa Harris. Linda Humes did a poem. There were two songs sung during the program—"Precious Lord" and "Then My Living Shall Not Be in Vain." In his eulogy, the Rev. Youngblood added his voice to the chorus of tributes for Dr. Umolu. He rehearsed her commitment, intellect, compassion, and dedication.

The following is an excerpt of Dr. Umolu's obituary:

There are not many people in New York City, especially in the borough of Brooklyn, who are not familiar with the name Dr. Mary Umolu, and most of them know that she has been a staple at Medgar Evers College of the City University of New York since she joined the faculty in 1972.

Born in Virginia of Southern and Jamaican parentage, Mary Umolu's family migrated to New York when she was a young child. She grew up in Brooklyn and received her bachelor and master's degree from Brooklyn College/City University of New York and a Ph.D. from Union University in Cincinnati, Ohio.

After graduation, Mary became a teacher in Haiti. In the 1950s, she traveled to Nigeria, eventually working as a pioneer radio broadcaster in the Eastern Nigeria Broadcasting Corporation (ENBC), and made such a tremendous impact on the broadcasting industry in Nigeria that many there still remember her. She married Minister John Umolu of the Bendel region of Nigeria. This led to her involvement in the Biafran Wars, where she rescued four children and brought them back to the United States.

Upon her arrival at Medgar Evers in 1972, Dr. Umolu, using donated equipment from the Model Cities Program, she was awarded a grant to establish the Medgar Evers College Radio Station, WNYE 91.5 FM. After its establishment, Dr. Umolu spent long hours and showed unrelenting energy and dedication in coaxing the fledgling radio station into existence, through its infancy, and into its current state as a successful communications vehicle for the students of the college, the Central Brooklyn community, and beyond.

In 1997, Dr. Umolu met internationally renowned musician Montego Joe, a master percussionist and music teacher. "I had heard of Mary Umolu years before, but the first time I laid eyes on her was at a Max Roach celebration. She was flamboyant and exciting," said Montego. They married in June of 1999.

Although born in the United States, Dr. Mary Helen Umolu epitomized the traditions inherited from the ancestors, including the gift of storytelling, folklore, dance, and drama. In fact, she is renowned internationally as a master storyteller, and thrilled children of all ages with her tales of African folklore. Further, she has been an ambassador of African-American and African culture, serving as a bridge between two continents. Dr. Umolu has been a pioneer in many other areas that have allowed her to share her gifts and talents locally, nationally, and internationally, as well as with Medgar Evers College.

Mary Umolu was a great lover of jazz music. Her favorite place was "Jazz 966" at the Fort Greene Senior Citizen's Center held every Friday night. She loved this atmosphere where the community came together, dancing and enjoying first-class music. She told Tom McCartney, "I want this for my people, my community. I want them to experience these first-class musicians too."

Dr. Umolu founded the summer Jazzy Jazz Festival series at Medgar Evers College, which runs every Friday night from mid-June to mid-August, and is now a Brooklyn tradition.

In 2004, Dr. Mary Umolu became a priestess of Shango in the Yoruba tradition. She was also a member of Zeta Phi Beta Sorority for over fifty-seven years.

Mary leaves to cherish her memory, her husband, Roger Sanders, aka Montego Joe; her brother Leevester Harden, (Maureen, wife); daughters Juanita Brown (Tom, husband), Mashasin Muhammad-Mais, Chinyelu Nwobu (Ogugua, husband), and Nanadenna Linton; sons; Madubuko Diakite, Chikonla Ajuluchuku and Kehinde Sanni (Mary, wife); cousins Corrine Jenkins (Edward, husband) and Louise Gary (Allen, husband); nephew Sean Harden; niece Lynnette Harden; 25 grandchildren, numerous great-grandchildren, one grandnephew, and a host of other family and friends.

Dr. Umolu loved and cared for the entire universe and all its inhabitants. She will forever be missed. However, we will always remember her wise words that "everything is in divine order.

So we say, so long again, to a friend, a sister, and to a fellow struggler.

Dr. Thomas K. Minter

Sunrise: June 28, 1924, Bronx, New York
Sunset: May 22, 2009, Bronx, New York

An Incomparable Educator

During the month of May 2009, two giants of the human spirit made their transition within days of each other: Dr. Tom Minter on May

22, and Dr. Ivan Van Sertima on May 25. Both were goliaths in academia. I remember both of them in connection with a couple of major organizing efforts in New York City.

Dr. Minter, I remember, in connection with the New York Coalition for a Just New York (NYCJNY), organized in 1985. The purpose of the organization was to convene black leaders of New York in a concerted effort to bring justice and equality to New York, especially for people of African ancestry. We were really trying to maximize our power to change the political and economic equation in New York because we saw our population numbers increasing but without a significant change in our condition.

The NYCJNY was one of the few times that Harlem and Brooklyn leaders actually coalesced—and it may be the only time that a said coalition was led by a Brooklynite, City Councilman Al Vann, who was a New York State Assemblyman at that time. Harlemites in the coalition included Basil Paterson, Percy Sutton, Charlie Rangel, Carl McCall, Denny Ferrell, David Dinkins, C. Vernon Mason, Bill Lynch, and Rev. Calvin Butts. Brooklynites included myself, Annette Robinson, Roger Green, Jitu Weusi, Al Vann, Velmanette Montgomery, Bill Banks, Job Mashiriki, Charles Barron, etc.

There were three important events in which we were engaged during the relatively brief period of our existence: Dr. Minter's campaign for chancellor of New York City public schools in 1983; Jesse Jackson's run for the US presidency in 1984; and the New York City mayoral race in 1985.

It was during the mayoral race that the coalition became irreparably fractured. Unbeknownst to some of us, a deal had been made with some of the Latino leaders so that Herman Badillo would be our candidate for mayor. Al Vann would be on the ticket for Brooklyn borough president, and, I think, C. Vernon Mason would run for Manhattan District Attorney.

We met on February 8, 1985, at the Astor Place office of the Coalition of Black Trade Union. Union president Jim Bell, now deceased, was a key organizer. When the time came to vote on the slate of officers, Herman Farrell dropped the bomb. He announced that he wanted to run for the mayoral seat. A heated debate followed. Just before the vote, I was asked to pray. Realizing the importance of the vote and holding the coalition together, I prayed that we would make the right decision and that whatever that decision was, that unity would prevail. When the vote was taken, Mr. Farrell won, 28–14. Farrell was accused of deliberately blocking Badillo because Badillo had assured Sutton's defeat in the mayoral race of 1978 by throwing his hat into the ring despite the fact that some of us had supported Badillo's run for City Hall in 1973. Al Vann and Farrell lost their respective races. The wounds were so deep that it took years to produce a semblance of healing.

One morning, former judge and civil rights leader Bill Booth and I met at Brooklyn's Junior's Restaurant, famous for its cheesecake. Booth had asked me to meet to talk about the New York chancellorship. He thought that Dr. Minter was a good choice. I agreed.

We brought the idea before the coalition, which enthusiastically endorsed Dr. Minter. A meeting was held with Dr. Minter. When we asked him if he was interested in the job, he said, "Yes," and we commenced campaigning and lobbying for him. He was not appointed. The campaign never really gained traction or momentum. It was never clear whether the loss was due to something we did wrong or whether it was wise or unwise for some of us to have publicly supported him. Common sense should've told us that Ed Koch, who was our political enemy at the time, wasn't going to appoint a friend of his enemies. Or maybe it was the personality of Dr. Minter. Or maybe it was none of the above. The mayor had his person, so maybe it didn't matter what we said or did.

I remember Dr. Minter as a soft-spoken, quiet, unassuming man. He was very personable and easy to like. I guess he stood above six-three feet tall, and was slender, which seemed to add to his quiet demeanor. He had a large forehead and small eyes, which seemed smaller behind his big round eyeglasses. I have to confess, I wondered at times if he was assertive enough. If he had "the fire in his belly" to seek the office and hold it. All of the people I trusted spoke highly of him. In addition to his impeccable credentials, he was an honest, caring man. There was no question regarding his qualifications.

Dr. Minter earned his doctorate in education from Harvard University in Administration and Government and served as the first assistant secretary for elementary and secondary education during the Carter administration. He was deputy chancellor for instructions of the New York Public Schools from 1981–1983. He was dean of professional studies at Herbert Lehman College until his retirement in 1994. It was said of him, he had two passions—education and music. He was married to Dr. Rae Alexander-Minter for thirty-nine years. She said at the funeral, "I feel privileged to have shared my life with Tom."

Dr. Frank Nathaniel Mickens[4]

Sunrise: June 22, 1946, Brooklyn, New York
Sunset: July 9, 2009, Brooklyn, New York

A Principled Principal

On July 9, 2009, Frank Mickens joined the ancestors. He had been principal at Boys and Girls High School in Brooklyn for eighteen years. Within two months, three renowned educators of African ancestry made their transitions: Doctors Thomas Minter and Ivan Van Sertima, May 22nd and May 25th.

And now, Frank Mickens.

There are some people who come to the stage of life, and upon dying leave behind them "footprints on the sands of time." With our voices, pens, and pictures, we try, in vain, to capture their meaning and contributions. Such a one was Frank Mickens: legend, icon, demigod, mythological. He was bigger than life.

If I were asked to choose some words to sum up his life, I would choose *commitment*, *compassion*, *creativity*, *competence,* and *consistency*. These words, I believe, distilled the essence of his life and extraordinary work as an educator, particularly at Boys and Girls High School. He came to a school that had a wide reputation for failing grades and serious disciplinary problems. Dr. Lester Young, member of the New York State Board of Regents, is reported to have said, "I think Frank is a living legend…. I remember what Boys and Girls High School was like a few years ago. It was like an explosion at the end of the day, with five thousand kids all over the streets.

Now you have kids running *to* school, trying to get here. The key is Mickens. Wherever you go, people are trying to get in this school."

Because he cared and had a commitment, he brought a creativity, competence, and consistency that transformed the school into one of the most highly regarded in the city, maybe in the nation. In a few years under his leadership, by the year 2000, Boys and Girls High School had a graduation rate of 85 percent. Before his principalship at Boys and Girls High School, parents sought ways to direct their children to other schools. Then, a few years after he took over, parents employed every kind of stratagem to enroll their children in the transformed school. He was able to combine academics and athletics into educational excellence.

He had a brilliant mind, a tender heart, and an all-embracing compassion. But he was a no-nonsense disciplinarian. He was a tough love personified. The parents, staff, and students reciprocated with love, gratitude, and appreciation. Mickens is quoted saying:

"I lead from fear of failure…. I had compassion. I don't think I was great; I think I was consistent. I really love kids. I love to see potential. And I love to work with dedicated staff. I was strong, and I could say no to anyone if I didn't think something was good for my kids. I am relentless, and few dare get in my way when it comes to my kids."

He was the recipient of innumerable citations, awards, and tributes. And on top of his twenty-four-seven work schedule, he found time to write two books: *My Way: the Leadership Style of an Urban High School Principal*, and *It Doesn't Have to be That Way*.

There were many ways in which Mickens and I interacted, including in programs, rallies, workshops, panels we did at Boys and Girls High School and other venues. He was always cooperative.

One of his last public appearances was at my church, the historic House of the Lord Church. He was on a panel on the state of education in New York City. It was obvious he was in physical discomfort. Yet he was still informative, forceful, sharp, and clear. When the program was over, after the usual pleasantries, a few of us watched as he slowly, laboriously wobbled out of the sanctuary and down the steps. I kicked myself. I had forgotten to offer him the elevator chair. I'm sure he would not have taken it. Someone who was observing with us, whispered to me, "The brother has serious health challenges. Can't you do anything or tell him anything to help him." Sadly, I nodded without giving an answer. I really didn't know what I could do or say. I had the feeling he wouldn't be with us too much longer.

I remember having the same feeling regarding Ossie Davis. Ossie was very sick when he attended my tribute in January 2005, at the Brooklyn Academy of Music. He could barely move. A few days later, he was gone. I will always believe that both Mickens and Davis made a special effort to participate in the program because I was associated with it. Nor is it unthinkable to me that they knew they were going and wanted one of their last appearances to be associated with my church and me. The contemplation of such a consideration filled me with honor, humility, joy, and sadness. I will take these thoughts with me to the grave.

Thank God for Frank Mickens and all who are hewed from the same rock. They come to bless the human family, and then, one day, they are taken from us. It always seems too soon. But they never die nor do they fade away like old soldiers. On this side of history, they live on in the lives of the people they touched and in the words that are said and monuments erected in their honor. And when they reach the other side of history, God awaits them with eternal life and an imperishable trophy.

Endnotes

1   This is a version of an article that originally appeared in the April 15, 2011 edition of *The Daily Challenge*, published in Brooklyn, New York. Mr. Thomas Watkins, publisher.

2   This article was published in the April 7–13, 2011 edition of *The Amsterdam News*.

3   This is a version of an article that originally appeared in the January 13, 2010 edition of *The Daily Challenge*, published in Brooklyn, New York. Mr. Thomas Watkins, publisher.

4   This is a version of an article that originally appeared in the *The Daily Challenge*, published in Brooklyn, New York. Mr. Thomas Watkins, publisher.

4

Entertainment & Sports

George Larry James[1]

Sunrise: November 6, 1947, Mount Pleasant, New York
Sunset: November 6, 2008, Galloway Township, New Jersey

So Long, Larry—You Ran a Great Race

The following was my presentation at the funeral of George Larry James, an Olympian track and field athlete who was part of the famed US relay team that took a stand for justice for African Americans at the 1968 games in Mexico.

We have come here to this holy place to cry and to celebrate. Our family has been blessed to produce five generations of religious leaders—I am pleased and honored to introduce my nephew Imam Saulih Abdur-Ra'uh Daughtry of Philadelphia. Bear with me and pray for me. For the challenge that God has put upon me is to give Larry his rightful place on the pages of history.

On Tuesday, November 4, 2008, the American people elected its first African-American president—Barack Obama. In cities, villages, and hamlets across the world, the news was greeted with tumultuous joy. On Thursday, November 6, 2008, George Larry James lost the bonds of earthly ties and took his journey to meet his Maker and dwell in the mansion that Jesus Christ his Lord and Savior had promised.

I fancy hearing some of my audience ask, "What is the connection between Obama and James?" To answer that question, we must first ask the question, Who is Obama? This man with a strange name, from whence did he come? And how did he do this—the most powerful position in the most powerful nation in the world? Surely, he didn't come from out of space, nor did he spring from the head of Zeus, as did Athena in Greek mythology.

The president-elect is the beneficiary of the freedom struggle, particularly of people of African ancestry, which had its origin hundreds of years ago when the transatlantic slave trade began its cruel and bloody history—and even before that when the first Africans were captured on the African continent.

Significantly, it should be noted that this year marks the two hundredth anniversary of the abolition of the transatlantic slave trade. It is the 170th year of Fred Douglass's escape from slavery and his landing on the banks of the Hudson River in New York City. And forty years ago, American cities went up in fire and smoke on April 4, 1968, when Dr. Martin Luther King Jr. was assassinated, which was followed by the assassination of Bobby Kennedy on June 5, 1968. It was one of the most turbulent times in US history.

The struggle for freedom and dignity took many forms and enlisted all kinds of people: From the stinking bowels of slave ships carrying their stolen human cargo from the African continent, to distant lands to African Freedom Struggles on the continent and Freedom Struggles in the West Indies; from the Underground Railroad in the United States to the insurrections; from the Civil War, led by gallant Union soldiers, Black and White, to Reconstruction, spearheaded by the white legislators Senator Charles Sumner of Massachusetts and Representative Thaddeus Stevens of Pennsylvania; from the twentieth century protest of the NAACP, to the 1940s Pullman Porter Union organizing, to the Civil Rights Movement in the 1950s. Then came the 1960s.

For two years, conscious, committed youths, growing impatient with the slow progress toward human rights, and with the spirit of their militant ancestors whispering in their ears, sought a more assertive way to express their quest for freedom. In the sultry heat of a Mississippi summer in 1966, while on a March Against Fear, as they called it, to the capital city of Jackson to protest the shooting of James Meredith, a tall, brave, young man of ebony hue, who sought to integrate Mississippi State University, Kwame Ture, aka Stokley Carmichael, gave voice to a desire that was burning in the bosom of oppressed and disadvantaged people of African ancestry when he cried out, "Black Power!"

Hysteria gripped White America, and they called that rallying cry "hatred," "a call to violence," "racism in reverse."

"Nonsense!" responded the young leaders. "It is simply a challenge to our people to look within their souls and communities and develop our potential to achieve power to actualize what America said was our right—to obtain what every successful ethnic group who came to America was able to achieve: power. Power to get what American documents and ideals declared should be the right of all American citizens. Was it not Thomas Jefferson who said, "We hold these truths to be self-evident that all men are created equal and are endowed by their creator with certain inalienable rights. Among these, life, liberty, and the pursuit of happiness?" And added to the Constitution was the Thirteenth Amendment, which ended slavery; the Fourteenth Amendment, which conferred citizenship; and the Fifteenth Amendment, which granted suffrage. Black Power would concretize the American ideals for people of African ancestry, yes. But also for all Americans."

Unfortunately, for various reasons, primarily fear, hatred, and self-interest, many white Americans (yes, and some Black) did not interpret the true meaning of Black Power accurately or fairly. Nevertheless, the young Americans prodded on. There is a German word, zeitgeist, which means, the spirit of the times. Dr. Martin Luther King was fond of using it to describe a movement or an idea that captures the minds of masses of people and inspires them to participate in a great cause. "Nothing is so powerful as an idea whose time has come," said Victor Hugo.

These young people, possessed or driven by a spirit bigger than them, gave themselves to the movement for freedom and dignity. All of them did not fully understand it; did not appreciate the revolution in which they were engaged, and the impact they were making on history. They simply, sacrificially, heroically, gave themselves to the spirit of the times.

This was typified by thousands of young students—Black and white, Jews and non-Jews, Protestants, Catholics, believers and non-believers, boys and girls, gay and straight—who went south with the Mississippi Summer Project to register voters. They were beaten, scorned, ridiculed, ostracized, jailed, and even killed. Andrew Goodman, Michael Schwerner—two Jews—and James Chaney, an African American, were among the martyrs.

A Quest for Gold and Liberation

When the Summer Olympics rolled around in 1968, America sent a group of exceedingly talented young people to Mexico City, Mexico. In the group were young African Americans whose prodigious talent was exceeded by their racial and social consciousness. They were deeply committed to the struggle for freedom and dignity—they were captured by the *zeitgeist*, the *spirit of the times*. Their swift feet ran for a higher award than the gold, silver, or bronze that the Olympic committee offered. They were compelled to express their oneness with the *spirit of the times*. They put on black socks, black berets, and they raised black gloved fists. They were proud and brave. They put their "footprint on the sands of time." And they, and the world, would never be the same.

In the Black communities of the world, and among all freedom-loving people everywhere, they were greeted with admiration and appreciation. Their creative audacity was sung to the cradle. Wherever students of history and conscious observers of social movements gathered, they rehearsed the feats of the young African Americans, whose swift feet carried them into the hearts of millions and into the halls of history. They set new records in the individual 400-meter dash: Lee Evans at 43.86 seconds, and Larry James at 43.97 seconds. In the 400-meter relay, Vince Matthews, Ron Freeman, Lee Evans and Larry James ran 2 minutes, 56.16 seconds. They gathered the gold, silver, and bronze Olympic medals.

But they gathered more. They gathered the immortal palms in the love and respect of their people. They won more than the perishable trinkets of human vanity. They won the eternal trophies of dignity and self-respect.

So in picture frames and huge posters on the walls of schools, offices, gyms, and homes, there they are clad in black attire, bodies tall and strong, faces solemn, heads lowered, arms straight, fist black-gloved, pointing God-war—defiant, proud, serious, determined. When the heroics of Freedom Strugglers are recited, inevitably included are the names of Vince Matthews, Ron Freeman, Lee Evans, Tommie Smith, John Carlos—and George Larry James, the "Mighty Burner," as they called him.

Not all understood or appreciated them. There were those who were so infuriated, they unleashed the hounds of hell, and these brave, talented young men were hunted and harassed down the paths of life. They were denied a comfortable livelihood in the workplace, and the learning institutions were no better. Social engagements, as well as contacts for improvement and advancement, were denied them. They were forced to live like paupers, scrapping for crumbs on the outskirts of an insensitive, ungrateful city. May God forgive those who inflicted such hardship and hostility upon the Black Olympians, but let us never forget what they did to our young heroes. The songwriter was on the mark who wrote, "They can't take away my dignity."[2] They can't take away the dignity of freedom-loving people. No matter what they do to them, they can't take away their dignity, and they can't take away the dignity of the Black youths of the Olympic summer of 1968.

Larry, grounded in his faith in the Lord Jesus Christ, faced the obstacles with undaunted courage, creative genius, hard work, toughness, and perseverance. He took odd jobs, went back to school, and through it all, he continued giving himself to charitable work, especially among youth. To the eternal credit of this marvelous institution, Richard Stockton College, he found a home where his talents, commitment, benevolence, and work ethic were appreciated and allowed full expression. For thirty-six years, he lived, loved, and labored at the school. He also became active in the Olympic movement. He held a variety of positions with the USA. track and field organization. In 2003, he was inducted to the National Track and Field Hall of Fame. In 2007, they came from near and far to pay tribute to him, to give him his due. To the end, his last hours, he was still at work, organizing and emailing, still expanding his mind, still interested in current events. To the end, he had to do it his way, always giving instructions and directions, even on how to move his body. The devastating colon cancer had done to him what no human vengeance or vendetta could do: destroy his once-healthy, fleet body. However, his mind remained clear, and his spirit was buoyant to the end.

So long, nephew, Mighty Burner, mighty man. We loved you. The family's love for you was demonstrated by the way your wife of thirty-seven years and family members kept you at home during your long illness. Countless people loved and will remember you. I am proud and grateful I had the privilege of marrying you to my niece, and so welcomed you into our family. You brought lasting love and high honor, and set a high mark of achievement.

When it was suggested that there should be a boycott of the Olympics, you said you didn't want to be an asterisk, so you went to the Olympics. You were not an asterisk. You were an exclamation point! Whence came your commitment to human rights? Was it when you were fifteen, when your mother took you to the 1963 March on Washington and you heard Dr. Martin Luther King Jr.'s "I have a Dream" speech? You once told a reporter, "I realized there was more to life than just me and my neighborhood. There was a whole world of people that wanted to make a difference." And they made you pay for your idealism.

Surely, you and the Black Olympians didn't get all that you deserved. But somewhere in the distant future, when truth and decency get a hearing, the Muse of History[3] will write the names of Freedom Strugglers: Shaka, Kwame Nkrumah, Jomo Kenyatta, and Joshua Nkomo for Africa; Queen Nanny, Toussaint L'Ouverture, Maurice Bishop, and Michael Manley for the West Indies; Richard Allen, Denmark Vesey, Nat Turner, Fred Douglass, Henry Highland Garnet, and Harriet Tubman for pre-Civil War; Edward Wilmot Blyden, Alexander Crummell, H. McNeal Turner, and Ida B. Wells for post-Civil War; W.E.B. Du Bois, Marcus Garvey, Paul Robeson, A.

Philip Randolph, and Adam Clayton Powell, Jr. for pre-Civil Rights Movement; Medgar Evers, Martin Luther King Jr., Ella Baker, and Fannie Lou Hamer for the Civil Rights Movement; Malcolm X, Kwame Ture, Huey Percy Newton, and James Forman for the Black Power Movement.

And then, dipping her pen in the sunlight, she will write in the clear blue, the name of George Larry James, and when their time comes, she will add the names—Vince Mathews, Ron Freeman, Lee Evans, and especially John Carlos and Tommie Smith. And on behalf of freedom-loving peoples through the ages, she will bow and say, "Thank you!"

Go tell it on the mountain! Shout it in the hood in Harlem; Bed-Stuy; Watts, LA; Hill District, Pittsburgh; Fourth Ward, Newark! Go tell it on Pennsylvania Avenue, Washington, DC! Trumpet it to the world, without the Freedom Strugglers of today and yesteryear, including Larry James, Vince Mathews, Ron Freeman, Lee Evans, John Carlos, and Tommie Smith, there would be no African-American president-elect. Let us hope and pray that Barack Obama will always remember and pay homage to the wings upon which he flies.

So long, Larry. You fought a good fight! You kept the faith. You finished your course. You ran a great race. And God Himself, according to the scripture, will give you a crown of life eternal in the heavens. And not to you only, but to all the Freedom Strugglers who do and have done the will of God.

George Michael Steinbrenner III[4]

Sunrise: July 4, 1930, Bay Village, Ohio
Sunset: July 13, 2010, Tampa, Florida

The Boss is Gone

The following statement was issued by George Michael Steinbrenner's family on Wednesday, July 14, 2010:

It is with profound sadness that the family of George Michael Steinbrenner announces his passing. He passed away this morning in Tampa, Florida, at age 80. He was an incredible and charitable man. First and foremost, he was devoted to his entire family—his beloved wife, Joan; his sisters, Susan Norpell and Judy Kamm; his children, Hank, Jennifer, Jessica, and Hal, and all of his grandchildren. He was a visionary and a giant in the world of sports. He took a great but struggling franchise and turned it into a champion again.

Once again, I debated with myself if Mr. Steinbrenner should be included in my pantheon of giants of the human spirit, but he won the argument for inclusion. He met my six criteria:

- He was a major achiever.
- He contributed to enhance the quality of life for the human family.
- He provided significant effort to lift up those at the bottom of the social ladder—or the least, in society.
- He contributed to the advancement of people of African ancestry.
- There was an absence of colossal evil.
- I personally interacted with him.

His major contribution, as we all know, was to the world of sports, particularly the New York Yankees. He brought them back to the halls of greatness. During his tenure, the Yankees won seven World Series, eleven American League (AL) pennants, and sixteen AL East titles. Later, I'll touch upon his contribution to enhance the life of the human family, the disadvantaged, and the people of African Ancestry.

Mr. Steinbrenner made major blunders and incurred the wrath of many. One of the most notable was when he put out money to dig up dirt on Dave Winfield's foundation. I do not believe his foibles and failures reached the level of what I would define as evil. His hard-driven personality and win-at-any-cost attitude created enemies and alienated people. Still, there is no record that he killed, dropped bombs, started wars, or participated in trafficking human flesh. His sins were redeemable, and his broken relationships were reparable.

But even in his pugnacity, Mr. Steinbrenner was grudgingly admired by some who had differences with him. For example, John McClendon, who coached the Cleveland Pipers, had differences with Mr. Steinbrenner, who had purchased the team. Eventually, Mr. McClendon resigned. However, with tongue-in-cheek, Mr. Mc-Clendon had this to say about Mr. Steinbrenner: "I could never say George's attitude toward me was racial because he treated everybody the same. He treated us all like dogs."

Mr. Steinbrenner, like many other charitable do-gooders, was often discreet with his gifts. Bruce Ratner, the president and CEO of Forest City Ratner Companies, is another undercover giver. I would often say to Mr. Ratner and others, "Your refusal to make a public show of your generosity is praiseworthy, but there must be a balance. The Bible says, 'Let your light shine that men may see your good works and glorify your Father in heaven.'"

In *Magnificent Obsession,* a great book by Lloyd C. Douglas, the generous do-gooders were told not to let anyone know of their good deeds; inevitably, they would be exorbitantly remunerated. Again, as in all things related to life, the road to peace, happiness, and prosperity lies in the balance.

There were a number of times I interacted with Mr. Steinbrenner, including in several negotiation sessions—the most important one, around 2005. One of the Yankee executives made a derogatory remark about the Bronx youths. Under the leadership of Dr. Roscoe Brown (a former Tuskegee Airman), the Honorable Laura D. Blackburne (a judge, and NAACP attorney) and I met with Mr. Steinbrenner and his staff. Our argument was that the remarks of the executive were representative of the New York Yankees' contempt and alienation toward the Bronx community, with its large Latino and African-American population. There needed to be a change.

There was no resistance from Mr. Steinbrenner to our proposal. Rather, his question was, "What are the correctives?" We suggested the following:

- Greater interaction between the New York Yankees personnel, including the players and the community.
- Free tickets to special events for the youths.
- Visits to community programs and events.
- Funding for various community programs.

Then we suggested that we would put together an agency through which the funds would be directed to the community. We suggested that the funds could be shifted from the New York Yankees Foundation to our agency. Mr. Steinbrenner readily agreed. His only stipulation was that the president of the agency would be Bob Williams, who had been an integral part of the New York Yankees Foundation. Obviously, Mr. Steinbrenner was protecting Mr. Williams, and also wanted continuity and some control. I suggested that Dr. Roscoe Brown will be vice president, and we would select additional members. Mr. Steinbrenner agreed.

The only questions left was the amount of funding for the agency, and its name. The amount came to hundreds of thousands of dollars, and Mrs. Blackburne offered the name, *The New York Yankees Community Council*. We concluded on a happy note. Throughout the proceedings, Mr. Steinbrenner was relaxed, cordial, talkative, and even jovial at times. The meeting lasted much longer than scheduled.

I recall a moment when there was a slight tension or pause in the camaraderie. I had raised the issue of race. I talked about my love for the New York Yankees, which went back as the late 1930s. Then Branch Rickey, who was the president of the Brooklyn Dodgers, brought in Jackie Robinson in 1946. Not long after that, the Cleveland Indians signed Larry Doby. Other teams signed black players, but the New York Yankees held fast to its lily-white organization. I came to believe that the New York Yankees were racists—or at the least, biased or color conscious. So I became a fan of the Dodgers. More accurately, I became a fan of Jackie Robinson and Larry Doby.

Mr. Steinbrenner gave me a long stare. I stared back at him. I thought he was going to explode. I didn't bat an eye. Then I said, "But things have changed…somewhat."

Looking back, trying to understand Mr. Steinbrenner's demeanor, I think he admired my honesty and boldness. Tough and straightforward people like those with similar characteristics. Even if they don't always agree, they admire qualities in others that they have or are trying to possess. They live by the scriptural assertion (whether they have ever read the scriptures or not), "Iron sharpens iron" (Proverbs 27:17).

As the conversation progressed, we touched upon many subjects. It was then that I learned of Mr. Steinbrenner's munificence. In particular, I was impressed with his relationship with Grambling University's legendary football coach, Eddie Robinson, and the Black Coaches Association. In an article in the *Amsterdam News*, July 15–21, 2010, Howie Evans, a veteran sportswriter and analyst, wrote about Mr. Steinbrenner: "George provided scholarships and other educational tools to the school as he often did for scores of young people around the country."

In addition to the negotiation sessions, I was invited to New York Yankees' functions. The most important events were the ticker-tape parade when the Yankees won the 2009 World Series, and the groundbreaking of the New York Yankees Stadium 2009. On all of these occasions, Mr. Steinbrenner was friendly, outgoing, humorous, and garrulous. There was no doubt, however, that you were in the presence of a tough "hombre" who felt he was in charge. You understood why they called him "The Boss."

As we were leaving his office after the last negotiation session, on the corner of his desk was an eight-by-three-inch plaque. On it was inscribed the words, "Lead, follow, or get the hell out of the way!"

James Brown

Sunrise: May 3, 1933, Barnwell, South Carolina
Sunset: December 25, 2006, Atlanta, Georgia

So Long, Homeboy[5]

James Brown died in his sleep on Christmas morning, 2007. There might have been a few who could match his superlative talents, but none surpassed him. He was simply the best at what he did. Moreover, his influence wasn't confined to his particular genre of music. It has been said his half-beat influenced R&B, funk, hip hop, and his dance influenced the choreography of other entertainers.

There were those of other races who achieved greater fame and fortune than Mr. Brown, but their talents and abilities were so conspicuously less than his. They stole his acts, but they couldn't steal his soul. Such is the story of American racism. God only knows how much has been stolen from people of African ancestry. We know a little of the physical and material thefts—our bodies, our homes, and our lands—but equal to, or surpassing, the material thefts were the spiritual or mental thefts of our music, inventions, literature, or other intellectual properties.

He was called the Godfather of Soul, Soul Brother #1, Mr. Dynamite, and the hardest-working man in show business. It is only the reference to *Soul Brother #1* with which I have questions. I am concerned that the singling out Mr. Brown as "Soul Brother #1" confines the meaning of *soul* to a certain kind of music and demonstrativeness. I always thought of soul as passion, freedom of feeling, agile, and coordinated physical expressions—great talent or gift that's also primarily a spiritual connection to God, a closeness with the universe from which comes the energy or life force, creativity, rhythm.

Some people say that the soul, or this spiritual connection to God, is due to African people being born near the sun. The Greeks seem to think so; they thought so highly of the Ethiopians that they said their gods vacationed in Ethiopia. They attributed the advanced civilization of the Ethiopians to their being born near the sun's path.

Because of this closeness to God, the sun, the universe—however one chooses to define it—we have soul, life, spirit that manifests itself in creative, vibrant, dexterous rhythmic ways. Since the universe is vibration, rhythm is more than music; it is life or the life force. All people have it, but some people seem to have more of it, or are able to tap into it more than others.

Moreover, the soul also encompasses values such as kindness, compassion, charity. In a word, *soul* means *love*—of one's people, culture, history, features, beauty, and achievement. By my definition, there were, and are, many soul brothers and sisters who could be consider #1—at least, in their field of endeavor. Jackie Robinson, Muhammad Ali, Tupac Shakur, Rosa Parks, Fannie Lou Hamer, Dr. Martin Luther King, Jr., Malcolm X, Lorraine Hansberry, James Baldwin, W.E.B. Du Bois, George Washington Carver, Michael Jordan, and the list goes on. They were all soul brothers and sisters—tops in what they did.

That James Brown was a soul brother is indisputable. His voice and songs, his rhythm perfectly fitted with the gyrations of his body, his artistic genius, all flowed from the boundless energy and super creativity emanating from the universe, or God, that blessed him with an abundance of that indefinable something we call *soul*.

There is another expression of soul. It is resiliency or invincibility. It is what has sustained people of African ancestry through four hundred years (1400 years if you add the thousand years of Arab intervention in Africa) of unprecedented cruelty. It is the will to win and the determination to overcome! It is the perseverance to take the worse and make the best, to transform pain into power.

James Brown was blessed with plenty of the aforementioned qualities. The Rev. Al Sharpton expressed this when he said, "No one started lower and went higher than James Brown." His mother left him when he was three years old, and his father did the same when he was seven. He was raised by his grandmother. He grew up in the racist South which created the conditions of poverty and denials, deprivation, dehumanization that so often leads to the incarceration of young black males. Brown was arrested for armed robbery in his youth, yet he used the years he spent in jail to help himself reach his goal. Even in his adult years, there were encounters with the police and accusations of domestic abuse.

I, along with countless others, can identify with those who suffered the viciousness, humiliation, and impoverishment of the racist South. Before my parents brought me to Brooklyn and Jersey City, I spent my earliest years in Savannah and Augusta, Georgia. Brown was seventy-three; I am 75. Although he was born in South Carolina, his earliest years were spent in Augusta. Our childhoods were similar.

Back Home Again

In Augusta, the street that is now James Brown Boulevard used to be Ninth Street or Campbell Street. During World War II, it was the main street running across town to the Savannah River. We kids shined shoes in front of a little restaurant on Ninth Street where Perry

Avenue ends. My father started his first church on the corner of Tenth Street and Perry Avenue. He is buried in the small churchyard there.

Ninth Street also ran across Gwinnett Avenue (now Laney Walker), another main street. In addition, Ninth Street passed another important site: Lenox Theater, the Black showplace. There were other movie theaters on Broad Street in the downtown area, but they catered to whites and compelled Blacks to sit upstairs and endure other humiliations. This was the South of our youth.

Brown, along with other kids, probably tried to sneak into the movies through the side doors, escaping the pursuit of a man we called "Horse." I never knew if it was his real name, or if it was because of his features, or because he chased us down and threw us out of the movies when he caught us. And after earning enough money from shining shoes, selling soda and milk bottles (this was before cartons containers), Brown probably went further down Ninth Street, past the theater, to a bakery where a bag of cake crumbs could be purchased for a nickel.

I am certain he must have been influenced by the music blaring loud from the jukebox in the Savoy, a beer joint on Twig Street, across the street from my father's restaurant. I know he was influenced by church music like the Swanee Quintet and Wings Over Jordan choir. Twig Street ran into Ninth Street, crossing Wrightsboro Road. It was one of Augusta's longest streets, running all the way to Turpin Hill and beyond, where whites lived and Blacks were forbidden after dark. In fact, it was dangerous to be there anytime unless it could be shown that the reason was because of employment or some other reason that a white person could verify.

But in spite of it all, Mr. Brown fought his way to stardom. So when all things are considered—art, resiliency, and love—James Brown was a soul brother in the best and truest meaning of the term. The Rev. Al Sharpton captured what I mean when he said, "I don't think he ever got his credit because people saw him just as a showman and not the music innovator and social innovator that he was. He changed the perception of regular blacks. He wasn't tall, he wasn't light skinned, and he wasn't polished. He was us. It meant the rest of us could also make it."

So they brought James Brown back to Harlem. It was 11:30 a.m. when Rev. Sharpton and the people who had traveled with him arrived at the new home of the House of Justice on 145th Street. Mr. Brown's twenty-four-carat gold coffin was placed in a white chariot with two white horses ready to move forward. The pushing to get near the coffin was ferocious. Rev. Sharpton kept pleading with the crowd to let the family come up front. It was noon when we started to move. Rev. Sharpton was in the middle, I was on the end, and one of the Temptations was sandwiched between us. Behind us were members of James Brown's band, and his agents and managers.

The crowd was jammed along the sidewalk. From the streets to the building, they screamed, "We love you, James Brown." Occasionally, the crowd yelled, "Thank you, Reverend Al." The people were grateful that Rev. Sharpton had brought the superstar back to Harlem. The expressions of gratitude were like simmering water in a partially closed hot kettle, straining for the opportunity to burst forth. He deserved every bit of gratitude and appreciation. So often, celebrities are taken to other places far removed from the identity, culture, and lifestyle of the very people who made them.

As we walked, acknowledging the greetings of the people, we talked about arrangements at the Apollo and in Augusta, Georgia. I noticed three helicopters above. I thought they were police, and I said to Rev. Sharpton, "When was the last time the police came to watch over us in a friendly way?" He replied, "I don't ever remember." We continued to discuss growing up in Augusta, Georgia, and what it meant to James Brown.

Walking next to a member of The Temptations, one of my favorite groups, gave me an opportunity to ask questions about the two-part television series on the group.

"Was it true?" I asked.

"Somewhat," was the reply. "Melvin didn't die in his mama's kitchen. He died in California. Mama Rose is working on a book that will set the record straight."

I asked about Paul Williams, who committed suicide; Ruffin, who was found dead; Eddie, who died of cancer. He shook his head and mumbled, "What a tragedy. What a sad end to great talents."

The whole scene reminded me of other street funeral processions. For Lionel Hampton, the famous musician, we walked from the Cotton Club in Harlem to the Riverside Church. Johnnie Cochran was alive then. We walked and talked, as we were doing today. For Mayor Glen Cunningham, we walked through the streets of Jersey City. And for Sonny Carson, the last procession I walked was through the streets of Brooklyn.

We rounded the corner at 125th Street to an even larger crowd. People had started arriving at the Apollo at 5:00 a.m., and now an estimated ten thousand circled the Apollo Theater from the front and going uptown. When we arrived at the Apollo, pallbearers, managers, members of the band, Rev. Al, and I went into the theater. Once inside, the coffin was placed on the stage.

Last Date at the Apollo

The funeral director, who had driven up from Atlanta, Georgia, with the body, opened the casket slightly. He made small arrangements over the body. Mr. Brown had on a midnight-blue suit, short jacket, saturated with sequins. It seemed strange that this man, small in stature, who was a bundle of energy, now was so still, so stiff. On both sides of the casket, on tripods, were huge portraits of James Brown, his face perspiring, captured in one of his ecstatic performances. On the head side of the casket was a large wreath, red-trimmed and white-centered roses, with the word "Godfather."

The family came in, and the casket was gently opened. The family moved closer, and a palpable quiet seemed to pervade the entire theater. Deanna, one of his daughters, came first to the coffin. She paused, took out a comb, and combed a strip of hair that folded halfway across his brow. She rubbed his eyebrows, bent over and kissed him.

Next, Yamma, another daughter came and smoothed the wrinkles in his shirt. Charles Bobbit, his manager, who had tearfully followed the carriage with us, was even more tearful as he gazed down at the motionless soul brother. They all stood in silence—daughters, sons-in-law, band leaders, managers, pallbearers, and a few close friends. When they had moved to their seats, news people were allowed to make their appearance, and then entered the VIPs, followed by an endless line of viewers.

At 6:00 p.m., the viewing ceased, and a ceremony followed for a select audience. The executive director of the Apollo opened with a welcome. The Rev. Franklyn Richardson, pastor of Grace Baptist Church in Mount Vernon, New York, gave the invocation and introduced Rev. Sharpton for the eulogy. Mr. Sharpton, who had been standing at the head of the casket from the very beginning, spoke of his father-son relationship with Mr. Brown. "He was the father I never had," he said. "When Teddy, his son, died, I became the son he lost."

After Rev. Sharpton had spoken, though not on the program, Tomie Ray Hymie, the mother of Mr. Brown's five-year-old son, spoke. Emotionally, she confessed her love for Mr. Brown. Pointing to the casket, she said, "I love that man over there."

As Rev. Sharpton was about to close the program, Mr. Bobbit came forward, tears still in his eyes, and in a quiet but steady voice, he related the last minutes of Mr. Brown's life:

"I took him to the hospital. Mr. Brown said to me, 'Bobbit, I'm leaving you tonight.'

"'Don't say that,' I said.

"'Yes,' he said. 'I'm gonna leave you tonight.'

"I bent over to cover him. That's why I was close enough to hear him sigh. He sighed three times, closed his eyes."[6]

It was one of the most moving accounts of the last moments of a dying person I ever heard.

Afterward, Rev. Sharpton called Congressman Charlie Rangel. He expressed appreciation to Rev. Sharpton for bringing Mr. Brown back to Harlem, to the Apollo Theater. Rev. Sharpton thanked all the elected officials, clergy, and civil leaders. He called the clergy to the stage and offered the closing prayer.

Then the viewing commenced again. As I was leaving, I greeted Percy Sutton, who will always be one of my favorite people. The last time I saw Percy was at Ozzie Thompson's funeral in Harlem, and before that it was at Preston Wilcox's funeral, where I did the eulogy. I reckoned it is the experience of aging—you meet old friends at the funerals of old friends.

I looked at Rev. Sharpton. I marveled at his energy. At 8:00 p.m., he was still directing everything—after riding in a car the night before from Atlanta, Georgia, walking twenty blocks from the House of Justice to the Apollo, standing like a sentinel at the coffin, and overseeing the funeral arrangements, including speaking, counseling, and media interviews.

I whispered to him, "I'm leaving now. Are you going to be all right?"

He nodded. "Yeah, I'll be all right."

"Do you want me to go to Augusta with you?"

"No," he said. "I think I'll be all right."

Walking out of the theater, into the night, the crowd still filled the street. Observing this turnout and knowing more was to come in Augusta, I thought, "Somewhere, James Brown must be spinning and gyrating, the broadest of grins on his face, singing across the heavens, "I feel good. I knew that I would."

The next day, Friday, there was a small funeral for family and close friends in South Carolina. Then Saturday, they brought Mr. Brown to the 8,500-seat Augusta Civic Center, now the James Brown Center, for the final ceremony before the burial. It was a celebration. They sang! They danced! There were solos, bands, and smaller groups, and speeches. Rev. Sharpton, still in charge, offered more eloquent reflections. Rev. Jesse Jackson was his usual powerful, mesmerizing self. Michael Jackson gave Mr. Brown credit for shaping his artistic genius. Dick Gregory added his recollection. The daughters spoke, too.

Mr. Bobbit retold the last moments of Mr. Brown's life. He also told the story of how "Say It Loud, I'm Black and Proud" came to be written. They were in California, watching television, and saw violence among Black people come on the screen. Mr. Bobbit explained: "Mr. Brown said, 'How come we can't love each other?' He took two napkins that were on the table, and in twenty minutes wrote the song. 'We are going to record this song,' Mister Brown said. 'Get me thirty children.'"

Mr. Bobbit went to Watts that night and found thirty children, gave them ten dollars each, and Mr. Brown made a record.

As I observed the Reverends Jackson and Sharpton and the body of Mr. Brown—all three, eminently successful, all three forsaken by a parent and rejected by most people in their earlier years—I thought, what an inspiration this should be for countless children, yes, and all people, who have experienced the same thing, or other setbacks or hard knocks of which stuff life is made.

So long, home Boy. I'll see you one day soon.

Lena Horne[7]

Sunrise: June 30, 1917, Brooklyn, New York
Sunset: May 9, 2010, New York, New York

The Life and Times of Lena Horne

For several years, I have been writing articles on the passing of giants of the human spirit to share my reflections on great achievers whom I've either met or had some kind of involvement in the struggle for human rights and self-determination. Upon the passing of Lena Horne, I debated a long time whether or not she should be put into my galaxy of superstars.

Surely, her extraordinary talents would demand recognition equal to, and surpassing, some of the giants of the human spirit included in my pantheon, but talent alone is not enough. One of my criteria requires my knowing or interacting at some level with the inductees. I did not know Ms. Horne, and I cannot recall ever meeting her. Another criterion is that the inductees advanced the causes of freedom, social justice, and the overall enhancement of the quality of life for the human family, particularly people of African ancestry. One can be gifted with superlative talents, but detrimental to self and others.

Claims are being made for Ms. Horne's civil rights activism. That, I think, is a dubious distinction. To show up at a civil rights rally and to fight for one's own advancement does not, in my opinion, make one a civil rights activist. When I think of women civil rights activists—or activists, period—I think of Dr. Dorothy Height, Rosa Parks, Viola Plummer, Hazel Dukes, Ella Baker, Ida B. Wells, and Fannie Lou Hamer.

Ms. Horne was representative of a time in our history when most Blacks, and especially the successful, were striving with everything in them to be white. Everything about them bespoke their burning desire to be Caucasian—from their hair texture (it was a time of straightening combs, wigs, and "conks") to skin color (skin whiteners were popular), to spouse selection. It seemed that in those days—and even today—Black success wasn't complete unless there was a white spouse, sweetheart, or prostitute. It appeared that the ultimate achievement was to sleep with anyone who was white. Even a snowman/woman would have been acceptable if there was a guarantee it wouldn't melt.

Let me state my position on interracial marriages or relationships as clearly as I can: I am not opposed to marriage between two people who are sincerely in love, whatever their national origin or religious background. However, I oppose marriage that is an escape from one's identity or race. I believe that members of oppressed races, whose identity, history, and contributions have been stolen, distorted, and used to marginalize, negate, or emasculate them, have a responsibility to prioritize staying with their own people. Only after serious thought and compelling reasons should they go outside of their race. This is especially true for achievers. I believe they owe it to their people. Their success gives them tremendous influence, especially among the young. When they marry outside of their own kind, the message they deliver tends to confirm society's evaluation of their people as less than the dominant class or race.

From April 2–5, 2010, I was a member of the American delegation who was invited to celebrate the fiftieth Anniversary of Senegal's independence and the unveiling of the African Renaissance Monument in Dakar, Senegal. President Abdoulaye Wade's wife was Caucasian. Some critics of the monument say that the woman in the monument resembles his wife, with a flowing hairstyle, blowing in the wind. From my cursory observation, it seems that most Senegalese women try to resemble Caucasians in their hairstyles. In fact, in a conversation I had with some young Senegalese sisters, I was surprised at how blatant their idealization of the European culture is. One has to wonder what influence Ms. Wade has on their thinking. If the president, and the presidents before him, could not find a suitable mate among the innumerable African women, surely some African women must reason that, "There must be something wrong with us. Let us strive to emulate Euro-Americans."

Let me be crystal clear: I have never, and will never, reject anyone, no matter who they marry. Some of my heroes, past and present, married outside of their race. At least Lena Horne was honest about it and said she married her second husband in 1947 to promote her career. "It was cold-blooded and deliberate," she once told *The New York Times*. "I married him because he could get me into places a Black man couldn't. But I really learned to love him. He was beautiful and just so damned good."

However, I think my ambivalence, shared by most African Americans, is deep and relentless. Growing up in the South where attempts to dehumanize African Americans were blatant and pervasive, we, especially the youths, were sensitive to racial inequities and desperately needed validation of our Black worth, and too many of our achievers of every field of endeavor let us down or disappointed us.

On the other hand, what were they to do? Arab and Euro-American unprecedented barbarism and cruelty—not the least was to rob or distort African people's identity and history—had succeeded in taking control of Africa by killing, raping, exploiting, colonizing, and enslaving Africa's sons and daughters. Lena Horne's generation faced a world shaped into the image of dominant Euro-Americans, as it is the custom of those in power to make everything of worth in their image.

Black Power [7]

Thank God for the concept, idea, and philosophy of Black Power—a major turning point in our history—and the struggles of the late 1950s and the early 1960s that paved a way for this to arise. However, in those days we were still "negroes" and "coloreds," and still showing signs of the arrested development that such appellations connoted.

In 1966, Kwame Ture, aka Stokely Carmichael, shouted "Black Power!" at a Mississippi rally, and it thundered across America and leapt oceans to reach black people everywhere. We became proud of our Africanness and blackness. We cried out, "I'm Black and I'm proud!" We openly expressed our rage, anger, and resentment. We threw out the wigs, straightening combs, and conks. We threw away the skin whiteners. We changed our names and apparel to assert our Africanness and the love of self and our people. Yes, some relationships were fractured. Misunderstandings and misrepresentations emerged, just as Dr. Martin Luther King, Jr. and others predicted. However, I believe history proved that whatever the price, it was worth it. But if achievements and relationships come at the cost of self-rejection, we are the losers. Malcolm X used to say that the greatest crime the white man has committed was to teach us to hate ourselves.

There was a white professor with whom I used to have honest, candid conversations on a range of topics. One day, he boldly told me that he had no difficulty getting black women, especially the professional types, to sleep with him. (He might have been exaggerating—at least, I want to believe he was.) When the Black Power movement came, he said he couldn't get close to these black women. In fact, they viewed him with disdain, contempt, and resentment.

Let it be clearly understood. The Black Power movement was more about Black people coming to the truth of their identity, history, achievement, and potential than it was about Euro-Americans. No matter how the proponents of Black Power would have expressed themselves, it would have elicited anger, fear, hostility, and misunderstanding from most whites. For in the final analysis, it was, and is, about power, human rights, and self-determination. Those in power, the privileged class, will always resist those who struggle for their place in the sun.

This is not to suggest that everybody wanted to be Caucasian or anything but African. There have always been courageous and brilliant teachers, parents, leaders who have proudly asserted their true identity and love of their people. but they struggled to enlighten and empower their people. I'm far within the mark when I say, sadly, that the overwhelming majority of people of African ancestry wanted to be other than themselves.

Lena Horne personified this ambivalence. Because of her light complexion, she encountered hatred and bitterness from Black people, which suggested sentiments of "Yes, I want to be white, but yes,

I hate you because you are near white." This ambivalence is another one of the agonies that Black people must endure, living in a racist and hostile Euro-American world.

My current feelings toward Lena Horne and her generation, especially the achievers, are a mixture of pride in her prodigious talents and the commendable gestures she made to strike a blow against racism; of disappointment that she did not do more to assert her blackness and help her people; of anger at the racism that forced people to make decisions and behave in ways that were/are contrary to their self-respect and dignity; of sadness for the hatred, bigotry, and intolerance that bedevil the human family that would not accept as equal this beautiful, super-talented, kind, and sensitive woman, and would not allow her the freedom to be herself and vouchsafe the opportunities to which she was entitled.

Honesty compels me to say that my feelings toward black achievers have not been changed. As I have said many times, I don't have a lot of respect for most Black achievers, especially today's rappers, although their artistic talents may be great. There have always been Black super entertainers and athletes, but their contributions to their people have been minuscule and pervasively detrimental. Lena Horne had to face obstacles that are not present to contemporary achievers, and therefore, more should be expected from them. In the absence of self-love, self-hatred abounds and will manifest itself in all kinds of destructive and negative ways toward individuals and their people.

I subscribe to the proposition that oppressed people need a cultural revolution in every generation. We are forced to ask, "Where are the cultural revolutionaries?"

As of this writing, CNN is doing a study on race relations. Various shades of painted children's faces were placed before other children. When asked which one of the children they liked, they pointed to the ones with a lighter shade. When they were asked why they liked that child, they answered, "Because they are white." When they were asked about the dark-faced children, they disliked them. When they were asked for a reason, they said, "Because they are black."

Of course, there's nothing new about this experiment. Dr. Kenneth Clark argued a similar experiment before the Supreme Court, which helped to persuade the justices to overturn the 1896 *Plessy v. Ferguson* decision that legalized segregation. The decision set the stage for the Civil Rights Movement, starting with the Montgomery Bus Boycott in 1955, when Rosa Parks refused to give up her seat for a white man.

My immediate reaction to the CNN study was: "We've been over this before. Do we need repetition?" After a few seconds, my response was: "Yes, not only do we need to see this again, but we need a lot more teachings on race relations."

To repeat, every generation needs a cultural revolution.

Maxwell Lemuel Roach[8]

January 10, 1924, Newland, North Carolina
August 16, 2007, New York, New York

Taking It to the Max

"My point is that we must decolonize our mind and re-name ourselves.... In all respects—culturally, politically, socially—we must re-define ourselves and our lives in our own terms."

—**Maxwell Roach**

"I will never again play anything that does not have social significance."

—**Maxwell Roach**

The huge gothic structure that is the Riverside Church in New York City can be seen from far away. It is the church that Rockefeller built. It is the church where Dr. James Forbes, its first Black pastor, recently resigned. I wonder why decision makers for Black celebrities, more often than not, choose to have their funerals at the Riverside Church. Is it the size, convenience, availability, or prestige? Are there no Black churches that can accommodate the occasion?

Whatever the reason, it was here that we gathered for the funeral of famed jazz

— drummer Maxwell Lemuel Roach.

After entering the VIP entrance, I went to the chapel and greeted the family. Maxine, Maxwell Roach's eldest daughter, was delighted to see me and profusely thanked me for attending. "Where else would I be? There's only one place for me to be today, and that is here," I said. Ayo, who is one of the twin daughters—Dara being the other—stepped forward and introduced me to the rest of the family, including Daryl, Keith, Raoul, and Kyle Roach, who also served as pallbearers. Even in their sadness, they all were gracious and polite. They reminded me of their father.

I first met Max Roach during the early 1950s at Birdland. The old jazz spot was the mecca for innovative musicians. A new sound had hit the scene. It was Bebop. The leaders included Dizzy Gillespie, Miles Davis, Bud Powell, Max Roach, Art Blakely, Thelonious Monk, and of course, the Bird—Charlie "Yardbird" Parker.

During the funeral, someone quoted Max Roach, saying to Dizzy, "Soon as we learn how to play fast, Bird is gone." A group of us Brooklynites would stay at Birdland until the program was over and drive him back to Brooklyn. We shared the various substances that were popular at the time. He was always friendly, approachable, and unusually humble, with a great sense of humor.

Terrie Williams, who heads one of the largest Black public relations firms in the country, handled the funeral arrangements, and I assisted in officiating. She was superb. The church was packed in the sanctuary, as well as the three-tiered balcony.

I could not help comparing Max's funeral with Mzee Moyo's since they died on the same day, and given the proximity of their final services. At Riverside, the audience was well-dressed, mostly Euro-American style. At the House of the Lord, where Mzee's service was held, African apparel was scattered across the church, and the motif was African, including libation, apparel, language, greetings, and music—mostly drums. The audience was more demonstrative, relaxed, emotional, humorous, with spontaneous interjections and an open mic for community expressions. At Riverside Church were the Black achievers, the superstars, and the acceptable to mainstream America. At the House of the Lord Church were primarily the radicals, revolutionaries, activists, nationalists, pan-Africanists, socialists, grass-rooters, hood dwellers, and the working class. Mzee's funeral was more diverse than at the Riverside Church, involving different religions and political views. Although the ceremony was structured, it allowed for open expressions. After the viewing and the ceremony, the casket was opened for another viewing. The two funerals demonstrated the full range of African people, from black to almost white in complexion, creative words and music, uniquely colorful in every way from body wear to body motion.

Dr. James Forbes opened the Max Roach's ceremony with welcome, scripture and prayer. He said, "We have come to bid farewell to a gifted genius. We shall have sorrow and laughter." How right he was!

Renowned mezzo soprano Elvira Green rendered "A City Called Heaven," her operatic voice singing, "I've been tossed and driven, got no place to call my home, but I've been hearing of a city called Heaven. I'm trying to make it my home."

Maya Angelou spoke, remembering how James Baldwin, Max, Roach and another person whose name I don't recall, adopted her as a sister and kept telling her she was a genius. Jazz pianist Randy Weston followed. He played softly, sweetly, and brilliantly. Then came poet activist Amiri Baraka. He spoke of the days he idolized Max Roach, and how he loved him, not only for his musical genius, but also for his commitment to the Black Liberation Struggle. He said Max had asked him to do his biography, and that he spent many days with Max and family. He concluded with a poem he had written not long after meeting Max. When he was finished, he received a boisterous standing ovation. I thought, "No disrespect, but we can all go home now."

Next was Bill Cosby. He was, as usual, hilarious. He said Max Roach was the reason he became a comedian, paused for effect, and then related the story. He wanted to be a drummer. He paid for drumming lessons. He studied the drummers, including Art Blakely. He went home and he copied their style. He was doing okay until he heard Max Roach. Then he put up his drumsticks. Years later, when he had gained some fame, Max Roach came to him and introduced himself. He said to Max, "Pay me my money for my drum lessons." All during his presentation there was pervasive laughter. He, too, received a standing ovation.

Congressman Charlie Rangel read a letter from the former President Bill Clinton. Then he quoted from *The New York Times*: "To call Max Roach a jazz musician is like calling Shakespeare a strolling player." I'm not sure what was intended by that quote. It can be interpreted as a put-down of jazz.

Jazz singer Cassandra Wilson sang "Lonesome Lover" with a bluesy touch. Sonia Sanchez stepped forward and said, "I was told to be short. I am short." In her poem, she spoke of the genius of Max Roach. "We tried to catch them in mid-flight," she said, "and swallow them whole."

Jazz legends Jimmy Heath and Billy Taylor played beautifully together. Heath played the clarinet. I guess he chose it rather than the sax because it has a more soothing, mellifluous sound. But whatever instrument Jimmy uses, the sound is always mesmerizing.

New York Lieutenant Governor David Paterson remembered how Max Roach had protested the Newport Jazz Festival in the 1960s. He, too, praised Max for his commitment to the Black struggle for freedom. Phil Schaap remembered the annual Max Roach birthday celebration on his radio program. Other music makers on the program included Gary Bartz, Odeon Pope, and Reggie Workman.

The children of Max Roach came forward, with Maxine as the spokesperson. She thanked everyone. Then speaking quietly and lovingly of their father, she said, "Yes, he was a genius of a musician, but he was more. He was a cultured man who taught us music, art, cooking, reading, and above all, love. And he taught us how to move as one. Bye-bye, Daddy. We love you."

The Rev. Calvin Butts, pastor of Abyssinian Baptist Church, did the eulogy. He spoke with pathos and humor. It is true that wherever black people gather, whatever the occasion, there must be humor. He reminded the congregation that Max Roach had his roots in the church. "He used music as an instrument of struggle. And when the saints go marching in, Max Roach will be in that number," he said.

The ceremony concluded with Elvira Green singing "Precious Lord, Take My Hand," and Dr. Forbes saying the benediction.

There were two pieces in the ceremony that provoked a ripple of uneasiness. One was when Stanly Crouch, whose name was not on the program, made remarks. It was hard to reconcile his conservative views, and what seems at times, his demeaning of people of African ancestry, with the likes of Max Roach and the tone of the ceremony. The other piece of uneasiness was a film showing Max in Israel during the bombing in 2001. It seemed that it was blatant propaganda and inappropriate for this funeral ceremony.

Slowly, we moved out of the great sanctuary, into the vestibule. Old friends had to greet each other. Idolizers had to shake hands or get close to their idols. Clusters of individuals blocked the aisles or conversed in between the pews. It seemed no one was in a rush. Outside, it was the same, as groups stood around talking, hugging, and backslapping.

The sun was brighter and hotter as I drove back to Brooklyn to tend to the business of living on this side of history, but the words of David Paterson stayed on my mind: "May heaven welcome its newest drummer."

Ossie Davis[9]

Born: December 18, 1917, Cogdell, Georgia
Died: February 4, 2005, Miami Beach, Florida

Unimpeachable Integrity

"He had no contradictions"

—Haki Madhubuti, publisher, Third World Press

"He couldn't say no."

—Earl Graves, publisher, Black Enterprise Magazine

"He was always available."

—Susan Taylor, editor, Essence Magazine

"He was free."

—President Bill Clinton

I knew sad news awaited when my wife, Dr. Karen Smith-Daughtry, received a telephone call. Her voice became quiet and solemn. She furtively glanced in my direction.

"Mmm, Mmm" she kept mumbling. Then, "Where did you hear it?" she asked the caller, who I learned later was one of the daycare employees. More, "Mmm, mmm, mmm…. Goodbye."

We drove for a while in silence.

"I have something to tell you when we are on the plane," she said.

"Yeah, I know," I whispered to myself.

I knew somebody had died. I started wondering who. A relative now in the intensive care unit? A member I just visited in preparation for a serious operation? A relative of a member who I just prayed for the day before? Or was it a tragic accident?

We made our flight just in time, because as always, I wanted to cram in another meeting. This was the monthly meeting of the African American Clergy and Elected Officials, a group I helped to start in 1991. Dr. Gardner Taylor, then-assemblyman Al Vann, and I co-chaired a meeting to achieve the election of David Dinkins to the mayoral seat. After the election, we saw the need to keep it alive. It was, and still is, the only organization where clergy and elected officials meet monthly. I was elected its first president. The Rev. Joe Parker, pastor of Wayside Baptist Church, is the current president. I had not attended the meeting for a long while, so I wanted to make an appearance.

When we were comfortably seated on the plane, I braced myself for the bad news. First, I went into a melancholy guessing exercise with my wife. I went through a process of elimination until I had exhausted all my guesses.

"Ossie Davis is dead," she said.

So brief. So startling. So final. So unbelievable. *Ossie Davis is dead.* I've heard the words a thousand times since, but I've never gotten used to them.

As the plane climbed skyward, carrying us to our quarterly National Board of Elders meeting in Washington, DC, my mind began to roam back through the corridors of history, in search of the times that Ossie and I had interacted.

I believe the first time we had significant interaction was at an anti-Koch rally on Broadway and Barclay Streets in Manhattan in 1978 or 1979. Many of us believed at the time that New York City mayor Ed Koch was anti-Black, anti-poor, and anti-working people.

Ozzie had readily agreed to participate in the rally. Not only did Ozzie show up, but he made a great speech, endorsing the rally and its objectives, and embracing me on the stage before the world.

He won me that day forever. I'm sure he was severely criticized for participating in the rally, by blacks and whites. I headed the National Black United Front, which had gained the reputation of being the pre-eminent activist, mass-based, independent pan-Africanist organization in the country. Consequently, I was demonized by most white opinion makers who exerted significant influence over many black leaders. But since we had the capacity to organize thousands of people at any given time, we had to be dealt with. Too many black leaders whose very existence depends on white benevolence, live a spineless, two-faced kind of life. They don't want to anger their white masters, so they try not to get too close to white-rejected black leaders—but they can't get too far away either. They fear the wrath of effective activist Black leaders and alienation from the masses whom the activists represent.

There is another side to this spineless game. It is locking the activist, or the white-rejected leader, into a stigmatized image. All authentic leaders want the ability to maneuver or to have tactical flexibility, but it serves the interest of white-controlled leaders to keep the activist fixed in a demonized image so that their position with their white masters isn't threatened. Malcolm X complained in his last days that the negroes wouldn't let him turn the corner.

White-controlled leaders want to negotiate in the suite while the activist raises hell in the streets. They call this the "good cop-bad cop" approach to negotiation with the government or corporate America. Whenever I've been in a meeting and this tactic is discussed, I've always made it abundantly clear that I could be both a good cop and bad cop. If I can shake the apple tree, I can make the jelly. Therefore, cowardly "in-betweeners" are not necessary. If you can't march in the streets, we don't need you to negotiate in the suites.

To Ossie Davis's eternal credit, he didn't have a membership in that spineless double-dealing, two-faced crowd. He was straight and principled, a man of integrity, courage, and decency. What you saw is what you got at all times, and with everybody. He was at home in all circles and among all people. Comfortably, he walked among kings, and he kept the common touch. His progressive politics was never hidden. His activism and identification with activists, reformers, and revolutionaries was never undercover. His anti-war posture was never a secret. During the McCarthy era, he refused to denounce Paul Robeson, even when such stalwarts as Jackie Robinson and Langston Hughes were forced to do so.

Osse's befriending of Malcolm X when he was persona non grata, and his delivery of one of the most memorable eulogies, was no sudden departure from his character. He truly believed that Malcolm was our black shining prince.

A Prince in his own right [10]

There were many other occasions on which Ossie and I interacted. There was the fundraiser for the now deceased Leon Bogues, a New York State assemblyman from Harlem; and Ossie seemed to be always available for anti-apartheid activity.

I remember a rally in Central Park where Jesse Jackson and I were among the speakers in the 1980s. Jesse asked me to look over his speech, then gave it to Ossie to read. Jesse wouldn't speak until Ossie finished reading his remarks, making changes and giving his approval. So high was Ossie regarded by Jesse. In fact, after that rally, we—Jesse and his sons—journeyed to Rome, where we met the Pope, and among other issues, raised the apartheid issue with him.

Ossie and Ruby were there when we did our fundraising luncheon at Vincent's Restaurant in Harlem for Zimbabwe African People's Unity headed by Joshua Nkomo, the godfather of the African Liberation Movement. My daughter, Sharon, and her double Dutch team had won the citywide Double Dutch Championship, and performed at the luncheon. I remember how Ossie related to my children, making sure he had something to say to all of them.

Ossie and Ruby were there in 1982, at the disarmament march and rally at the United Nations and Central Park. We had organized over a million people, according to the police count, from across the world to demand worldwide disarmament, especially nuclear disarmament.

Indeed, Ossie seemed to be ubiquitous. Any program or activity for justice, peace, for racial and religious harmony, equal opportunity for the downtrodden, Ossie Davis was there. No matter what you asked him to do, no matter how small or how large, no matter how prestigious or non-descript the participants, Ossie Davis was there.

When four cops shot and killed twenty-three-year-old Guinean immigrant Amadou Diallo[10] for standing in front of his home, and we began organizing a civil disobedience campaign at the police headquarters, I called Ossie. He knew what I was calling him about and had already made up his mind he was going to jail. We met at our church—Ossie, Ruby, my wife, and I. We had arranged for Councilman Charles Barron to be in that group. I shall never forget seeing him and Ruby, standing there unflinching, head high and proud, as the police placed handcuffs on them. They were placed in the paddy wagon. I followed them to the booking precinct, which was in Harlem. Throughout the whole ordeal, which lasted into the evening, he and Ruby remained strong, brave, and humorous. I should add, early on, he went to jail long before it became popular to do so.

On my fortieth pastoral anniversary in 1998, he came to speak at the church. His book had been published, and we were proud to do a book signing at our church. As always, he was in high spirits. I cannot say how he was around other people, though I suspect he was always the same. But I know that when we met, wherever it was, we had the grandest time. I think I know, from my side, that we had a unique admiration society between us. We literally enjoyed every moment we spent together, except the last time we were together which was at the tribute. For I discerned that he was not his usual buoyant, humorous self. But he was trying hard.

He and Ruby were present seventeen years ago when my wife and I celebrated our twenty-fifty wedding anniversary. Ruby and my wife were so beautiful. Ossie was handsome and buoyant— he was beaming with happiness. He and Ruby were so happy for us. One of my favorite pictures I have of them is at that wedding anniversary.

When I called him to ask if he would attend the anniversary, Ruby was on the other line. He said, "Wait, let me get Ruby off the line."

"Oh no!" I said.

"I can call back"

"No! No! That ain't nobody but Ruby. I can talk to her anytime," he said facetiously.

When the January 8, 2005 tribute was planned for me, one of the first persons I called, as always, was Ossie. I told him what was being planned and asked if he would participate.

He said, "To the bone. To the bone."

If I live to be two thousand, I will never forget his words. He always had some witty affirmative to anything I asked him to do.

And he did participate "to the bone." As the date of the tribute approached, he became very ill. We were told that he may not be able to make it. Then we were informed that he and Ruby would be present. They *were* present, and it was an unforgettable time. First, we had agreed that he and Ruby should open the tribute with the Lord's Prayer. Second, I remember how slowly he was moving— obviously he had summoned all his strength and determination to be present. I felt so grateful throughout the evening.

From the moment Ossie and Ruby entered the portals of the Brooklyn Academy of Music (BAM) and moved toward photo ops in the vestibule, he was a different Ossie. His face was sunken, his eyes had a faraway look. He seemed elsewhere—and perhaps he was. Maybe he heard his name being called. Gone were those joyful greetings, the hearty embrace, the zestful, "Let's go do it."

Above all is the memory of my giving him a special award. It was my intention to give an award to three persons for whom

I have the highest admiration—Jesse Jackson, Percy Sutton, and Ozzie Davis. I wanted to give the award publicly. This is my practice whenever I'm honored, to honor someone else. It is my way of saying, whatever I've achieved, I stand on somebody's shoulders. The award was a five-by-eight-inch disc made from the plank that lowered our ancestors in the ground at the re-interment ceremony at the African Burial Ground in 2003. But my family decided this was my evening. The awards should be given in private. It was a wise decision. We had a quiet, solemn moment in the back dressing room. I gave each an award. I cited one of the most memorable experiences I had with each one.

It was the last time I saw him. After that, we went our separate ways to do what was asked of us.

I shall treasure forever the memory that the last act we shared together was my giving him an award from the burial of our ancestors. I had the opportunity to express my love, admiration, and gratitude. And what could be more fitting than to give him a relic that linked him to our African forbearers.

So now, in the words of the Bible, "He is gathered unto his fathers." His eyes are closed. His body is still. His voice is silent forever more. But I will always see his laughing face. I will always feel the loving embrace. I will always see him and Ruby at the BAM, and I will hear them intoning from the stage, The Lord's Prayer:

Our Father which art in heaven,
Hallowed be thy name.
Thy kingdom come,
Thy will be done in earth,
as it is in heaven.
Give us this day our daily bread.
And forgive us our debts,
as we forgive our debtors.
And lead us not into temptation,
but deliver us from evil.
For thine is the kingdom,
and the power, and the glory,
forever.
Amen.

So long, old artist, warrior. You have left us a rich legacy, and we shall do all we can to measure up.

A Versatile Genius

Ossie Davis was a phenomenal actor, artist, and activist. But more than that, he was a man of profound humility and superlative sensitivity to the pain of others. I'll share a story that illustrates the truth of this assessment.

Through the tail end of a snowstorm, I drove up to Sullivan County Correctional Facility to be the keynote speaker at a program organized by the lifers and long-timers at the institution, on March 12, 2005. It was an all-day program featuring speakers, poetry, workshops, panel discussion, and an awards ceremony. I was overwhelmed by the goodwill, admiration, and appreciation toward me. They were amazingly knowledgeable on events, issues, personalities, and my work.

What impressed me deeply, and I told the men so, was that they were asking the right questions—including the question of maturity: "What can I give back?" They wanted to know what they could do for our community. They expressed remorse for the harm they had done. Now they wanted to make it up, to give something back. I promised I would work with them.

On the way back home, I could not keep my mind off prison—the prison we had just left, and the prison system. What a beautiful group of brothers—and they were representative of countless others locked behind prison walls, a terrible loss to themselves, to family, to race, and to society. Tragically, there is no plan to address the problem.

On April 4th, I went to the Urban League's state-of-the-race press conference at the JP Morgan Chase building at 270 Park Avenue. We had learned that JP Morgan Chase had profited from slavery, was caught lying about it, and now it was ready to pay $5 million for student scholarship programs in New Orleans.

Sitting up there, surveying the New York City skyline, thinking about slavery and its legacy and the profits made from that demonic institution, I could hardly focus my mind on what Urban League President Marc Morial was saying about the conditions of Black people. Still, I knew from the tenor of his voice and the expression on his face that whatever it was, it was bad. Among all the bad things that were happening to us, one area captured my attention: incarceration— Black incarceration in particular, but incarceration in general. The April 26, 2005, Daily Challenge featured the article, "Prison Population, World's Highest, Up Again," by Allen Elsner, who quotes Department of Justice statistics:

- Twelve percent of Black males in their late twenties were behind bars, compared with 3.6 percent of Hispanic males, and 1.7 percent for whites.
- The United States had incarcerated 726 people per 100,000 of its population, seven to ten times as many as most other democracies. The rate for England is 142 per 100,000 of its population; for France, 91 per 100,000; and for Japan, 58 per 100,000.
- Women were the fastest growing segment of the prison population, increasing by 2.9 percent over the year to over 103,000. In 1980, the United States imprisoned 12,000 women.
- 283,000 mentally ill persons were in US prisons and jailed, and 92,000 foreigners.

By any yardstick, those figures indicate there is a crisis regarding the increase of prisoners. If Euro-ethnic incarceration rates equaled that of Black incarceration, I'm sure it would be treated differently. I offered my assistance in the prison program the Urban League was developing.

Mr. Morial made another significant point: When Italian and Irish immigrants came to this country at turn of the twentieth century, they moved up the social ladder by working on parks and the transportation system projects. Now, the massive construction projects proposed for West Side Manhattan and the Atlantic Yards in Brooklyn can open opportunities for Blacks to improve their condition.

I shared all of that to show how focused I'd been on Black incarceration and its related issues. As the universal law goes, what our minds are focused upon, we will attract to us related material. So it's no wonder to me that I came across a presentation on the issue that Ossie Davis made when Link, an organization that works with prisoners, invited him to receive an award and make remarks.

Here is what Mr. Davis said:

Ladies and gentlemen, brothers and sisters, and my sons, you're almost on the verge of seeing an old man cry. I am deeply touched, happy beyond the telling of it, to be in your presence this morning. You graduates! Stalwart warriors! You builders, you makers of the future, you redeemers of the dream! I represent more than myself as I speak to you. First, I represent my mother. I'll be glad to tell her what I saw this morning: the realization of her dream and mine. I also represent my wife. I should have encouraged Ruby to come with me. On this happy occasion, I can't express in mere words what it means to be here. I do congratulate all of the institutions and persons and organizations involved in bringing us to this moment. I'm glad you gave me the opportunity to be a part of it. This gives me the ammunition that I need to continue what I consider my life's mission to be.

A couple of weeks ago, I was at Howard University, talking to another set of students. I felt the same pride then as I do now as I look you in the eyes. There is no difference; there is no separation between you and them. As an elder of the tribe, I welcome you into the service of the greater community. We are all involved desperately in finding our way out of this wilderness, out of this rock, to create a thing that we will one day call America.

And it will be the miracle that God intended.

We're a long way off. Much remains to be done. But if we believe that education is a tool, and that change is possible, then what I see in your face, what I feel in your handshake, reassures me that one day we will build that dream. I am a happy man. I've lived a long time, and I, too, have looked into the valley of despair—when I thought that hope had died—with war, crime, disease, AIDS, and all we do to pollute the environment. Sometimes I asked my God, 'Why hast thou forsaken me?'

I, as an old man, I may not be here when America recognizes itself as the true home of democracy for all people, but you will have helped to make it so by just what you did today. I thank you for the gift. You enriched the end of my life. For that, God bless you. Do good work!

Some people think his remarks equaled his eulogy for Malcolm X. Whatever one may say to that, these remarks reveal a man of profound humility and superlative sensitivity to the pain of others—a giant of the human spirit.

Wesley "Wally Gator" Watson[11]

Sunset: September 3, 2010

Give the Gator Some!

Wesley (Wally Gator) Watson was a renowned drummer and artist par excellence, who toured the world with the greats of jazz, R&B, and rock.

But he was so much more.

The love and appreciation of Wally were evidenced by the un-precedented traffic outside of the church and by the overflow of crowds that packed into our church for his homegoing services. People were everywhere. Every seat was occupied in the sanctuary, including the balcony. Three- and four-deep crowds stood against the walls. Downstairs in the fellowship hall and out on the sidewalk, throngs of people stood around and moved about in solemnity. Eyes flooded with tears, and heads sadly nodded. Grief-stricken, stooped shoulders characterized practically everyone. There were whispered conversations in the sanctuary as old friends hugged and shook hands. With forced smiles, they greeted each other. There were also sounds—loud, quiet, and soothing sounds. The music continuously played from during the viewing, which became a "jam session" of musicians playing tribute to their friend. As they used to say in my youthful days, "the cats were wailing."

For over 24 years, Wally was a faithful and consistent member of our church. He eagerly and humbly served our church in any ca-pacity. Nothing was too big or too small for him. To see this superb and internationally renowned musician do menial tasks at the church humbled, challenged, and inspired all of us. For over three years, Wally was a musical director and the overall supervisor for one of our church's singing groups called Dedication, which was headed by Senior Minister Renaldo Watkis.

Wally was a multi-dimensional genius, and he played many roles in life. He was an Emergency Medical Technician (EMT) at the scene of the destruction of the Twin Towers on September 11, 2001, arriving with an ambulance shortly after the second tower collapsed and continuing to work there for more than two months. Wally was also a licensed pilot, animal trainer, mentor, teacher, singer, and instructor. He was a versatile renaissance man. He rightfully belonged in the ranks of the legendary Jack-of-all-trade.

Perhaps, I say, it was his curiosity and interests that compelled him to know, try, and fix everything. His equanimity was proverbial. In all of the years that I knew him, I never once saw him disturbed, "out-of-sorts," or frustrated. We were in some tension-packed situations. At some of our marches, rallies, and demonstrations, Wally assisted with security. He actualized Rudyard Kipling's staggering challenge: to keep your head while people around you are losing theirs and blaming you, and to make allowances for their weaknesses. Wally was balanced and even-tempered. He was serenity personified.

Wally was a kind man, too. He was a big man—big in physical size, but surpassing his outward size was his inner size. His kindness far exceeded his girth. His kindness, compassion, and courage were beautifully manifested in his care of Lionel (Hamp) Hampton in his waning years. It reminded my wife, Dr. Karen S. Daughtry, and I of how her brother, Earl (Buster) Smith, Jr., who was also a professional drummer, cared for Sun-Ra, the legendary musician. Wally's courage was revealed when he went into a burning house to pull Hamp out of the swiftly engulfing flames.

Wally's enduring tenderness and sensitivity to Hamp's every need were too wonderful to behold. Wally was a gentle giant. He walked softly through life. He called to mind what was said of Brutus in Shakespeare's *Julius Caesar*, "His life was gentle, and the elements so mixed in him that nature might stand up, and say to all the world, "'This was a man.'"

Wally loved to laugh, and he loved to make others laugh. He smiled easily and often. Humor was his trademark—he was a practical jokester. He loved telling funny stories. There was one act that always brought forth laughter. Whenever he was late to a meeting, he would throw his hat into the room. Then, he would boldly follow and say with a serious tone, "The hat is late. I'm on time."

He gave freely of his resources and talents. He taught many—young and old—how to play the drums. Two of his prized students were his son, Ayinde Watson, and Tariq Washington. Ayinde was our church drummer from the time he could sit on the drum stool. (He played for Winnie Mandela when the Mandelas made their historic visit to the United States of America. It was at our church that Winnie made her first public statement.) Tariq has been the church's drummer since he was 4 years old. He is the youngest son of Paul and Peggy Washington, who are longtime members of our church. Paul is a scholar, and Peggy is a performing artist. They are also veteran activists.

I knew Wally's family well. The church membership of his wife, Elise, preceded his own. Wally was a family man. He married Elise on September 4, 1980. They stayed together to the end. They celebrated their 30th wedding anniversary with friends and relatives on Sunday, August 22, 2010. They had three sons. Everyone knew how much Wally loved the boys. But above all, he left the testimony that he was a born-again child of God. He gave his life to Jesus Christ in 1980. Thus, we share this hope that we shall meet again one day soon. In that day, there will be no more suffering and sorrow, and no more parting of the ways for eternity will have begun.

Endnotes

1   This is a version of "1968 Olympic Gold and Silver medal winner, dead at 61," an article that originally appeared in the Nov. 25, 2008 edition of *The Daily Challenge*, published in Brooklyn, New York. Mr. Thomas Watkins, publisher.

2   This references a line from "The Greatest Love of All," a song originally recorded by George Benson for the 1977 biopic "The Greatest,"

about the life of Muhammad Ali, and later re-recorded and released in 1985, by Whitney Houston.

3   From the lecture "Toussaint L'Ouverture" by Wendell Phillips, 1861.

4   This is a version of articles that originally appeared in the September 1, 2010, and September 3–6, 2010 weekend editions of *The Daily Challenge*, published in Brooklyn, New York. Mr. Thomas Watkins, publisher.

5   This is a version of articles that originally appeared in the January 3, 2007, and the January 5–7 weekend edition of *The Daily Challenge*, published in Brooklyn, New York. Mr. Thomas Watkins, publisher.

6   In Augusta, Mr. Bobbit added: "I called for the nurses. They worked on him frantically, but he was gone."

7   This is a version of an article that originally appeared in *The Daily Challenge*, published in Brooklyn, New York. Mr. Thomas Watkins, publisher.

8   This is a version of an article that originally appeared in the September 5, 2007 edition of *The Daily Challenge*, published in Brooklyn, New York. Mr. Thomas Watkins, publisher.

9   A version of this article originally appeared in the April 27, 2005 edition of *The Daily Challenge*, published in Brooklyn, New York. Mr. Thomas Watkins, publisher.

10   Amadou Diallo was an unarmed twenty-three-year-old immigrant from Guinea who was accosted by four plain-clothed police officers as he stood in front of his Bronx home. The police claimed Diallo looked suspicious, and that they thought his wallet was a gun, so they shot him forty-one times, with nineteen of the bullets hitting and killing him. The officers—Sean Carroll, Richard Murphy, Edward McMellon, and Kenneth Boss—were all acquitted in a trial that was moved from the Bronx to Albany, New York.

11   This is a version of an article that originally appeared in the September 24–26, 2010 weekend edition

of *The Daily Challenge*, published in Brooklyn, New York. Mr. Thomas Watkins, publisher.

5
Family and Friends

Alberta "Bert" Bernice Franklin[1]
Death of the "Golden Child":
A Study of the Impact of Race on a Black Southern Family

Just when I thought I had respite from deaths and funerals, I received word that my first cousin, Alberta "Bert" Bernice Franklin, had gone the way of all flesh. "Would you do the eulogy?" I was asked. So off to the sunshine state I flew.

Following are excerpts from my eulogy. The readers may find interest in the life and the times of a black family in the segregated South of my youth. I am sure that countless Black families will readily identify with our family.

We were first cousins, children of sister and brother. Emmie, my mother, and Cleare, Bert's father, were the children of Grandpa Emmett and Grandma Henrietta Cheatham. We lived together in a white house—it seemed large to me at that time—on West Forty-Fourth and Florence Streets in Savannah, Georgia. My older brother, Bob, and I spent the first ten to twelve years of our lives there—years that helped to shape what we would become.

There were dirt streets, except West Forty-Fourth Street going south. Starting at Florence, which ran east to west, the street and the sidewalk were paved. It was the white part of the neighborhood. We could only pass through that area during the day. Even then, the risk of being insulted or attacked was always possible. The lawns were neatly cut, houses were gleaming white, and everything was clean and orderly. The Black part of the neighborhood, that part of the street on which we lived, was trashy and had plenty of garbage. The rainwater always remained for long periods of time. There were lots with debris strewn. Dilapidated houses saturated the streets. There were some homeowners who struggled to maintain cleanliness and order. They planted pretty flowers, cut their grass, and did the renovations when necessary.

Even in those early years, I would stand in the middle of the street, study the contrast, and wonder why. I still wonder why the contrast across the nation. Now, I understand why. Obviously, the street on which we lived was representative of a thousand streets across America. I have often wondered whence this race consciousness came. It seemed that all my life, or as far as I can remember, I have been conscious of race. I have pondered and agonized over the racial differences. Even in my youth, the race question was always with me. I am not suggesting I always acted in ways that promoted our race. I am saying that I have always been aware that race mattered.

When I went to Augusta to live with my father for a while, I worked at a grocery store owned by a Chinese. I tried to steal everything I could to give to the poor black families. Looking back, I wondered where I got this Robin Hood venture. I was eventually caught and fired, as I knew I would be. The person who spied on me was a Black youngster my age. But he looked Chinese, acted Chinese, worked for the Chinese, and so, in the interest of Chinese, informed me.

It was clean and neat around our house—Grandma saw to that. Everything was fixed and working properly—Grandpa saw to that. If ever there was a man who loved work, Grandpa was that man. He was tall, kind of bent over, with a keen face that was always serious. He had a reddish-yellow completion. The rumor was that his mother had been raped by a white man. Bert's color and work habits probably came from Grandpa. Grandma was just the opposite. She was dark complexion, short, and a ball of fire that always seemed to be fussing at something or someone. It was she who wheeled the strap or switch. (For the Northerners who do not know, *the switch* was usually a thin and long limb taken from a tree and used to employ punishment. It was very painful and would leave welts.) But the ultimate punishment was the electric cord. It was only used in extreme situations.

Bert got her size and motor mouth from Grandma Cheatham. She was always eager for talk. The more animated the conversation, the better she liked it. Her voice could always be heard above the rest.

There were others in the house. In the early days, there was my mother, who had separated from her husband, my father, before she left for points North; Aunt Natalie, my mother's buxom, light-complexioned sister; and her husband, Uncle Riddick, a tall bony man who talked out of the side of his mouth; and Bert, Bob, and me. Not many years separated us. Bob was two years older than Bert. Bert was two years older than I. I can truly say it was a home of love, laughter, discipline, order, cleanliness, and plenty, or so it seemed to me. And it was a place of work. Mother and Aunt Natalie worked at a dry cleaner called The Modern Hat Shop on West Broad Street. Uncle Riddick worked at "the plant." I am not sure what or where that was, but he must have earned a good salary, for he bought a new Chevrolet, which was the talk of the neighborhood. Grandpa worked on everything and everywhere, and Grandma worked in the house and on us.

While there was ecstasy at times, there was also agony: family separation and deaths, especially the death of my Aunt Natalie. She died mysteriously during or post-childbirth. They never told us kids the real reason for her death, but it was conveyed that the death was not necessary. We lost a dear member of the family. The grieving was deep and long, but we gained a baby, Isaac Jr. They called him Icky, and even then, he looked like his father, except for the light complexion of his mother.

Bert was special to Grandma. She called Bert, "My Golden Child." Years later, I came to understand why Bert was special:

- Bert was a fatherless and motherless child, but for different reasons. Her father had died suspiciously in a car accident in Florida. He was a big-time gambler and wheeler-dealer. My oldest brother, Alonzo, named after my now deceased father, Bishop Alonzo Daughtry, lived with Bert's father. He maintained to his dying day that Uncle Cleare was murdered. Bert probably got her innovative approach to life from her father. She was good at what she did, which was primarily in the medical field.
- Bert was special because she was a girl. Long before there was any women liberation movement, Grandma ruled the house and women were first.
- The third reason was that Bert was of light complexion, "high yella." In those days, and to a significant degree today, color mattered. We were/are so Europeanized that the closer we were to European skin color, facial features, and hair texture, the more beautiful we thought we were. Thus, Bert was Grandma's "Golden Child." She was the favorite.

My brother Bob vividly could recollect all that old stuff and could never forget. Poor Bob, he had nothing going for him. Bert was the favorite for reasons already expressed. Bob, brown-complexioned, could not lay claim to color. Bert had that locked up. He could not lay claim to age. There were two older brothers, and I was the baby—at least I had that going for me. But among us it was understood that Bert was the Golden Child.

When the grownups were out of the way, we had fun times. We played games, like hopscotch, jump rope (I do not remember jumping double Dutch) hide and seek, and marbles. In fact, my brother and I won the citywide championship shooting marbles. But because of our strict religious teaching, which forbade marble shooting, we could not bring the trophy home. We went to the park together— Can't Park on West Fifty-Fifty Street, and we played on the swings, sliding board, and ran races around the park. We slept together, fought together, and ate together. We celebrated holidays together— Easter, Thanksgiving, and oh yeah, Christmas and Santa Claus.

We were convinced that we were honorably favored with a visit from the North Pole by that roly-poly, cherub-cheeked, gift-bearing man with the red-and-white-fur-trimmed hat and suit. Our parents went to great lengths to convince us. They put fire ashes around the fireplace to prove that Santa had come down the fireplace. We were too young and excited to ask, "How could a fat man get down the chimney?" What a strange exercise! Our parents would work hard, make sacrifices for us to have good things for Christmas, or to make sure that our desires, which we would write on a paper, would be fulfilled, then point to a peculiarly dressed, funny-looking white man and say to us children, "He brought you these things," and would spare no ends to convince us that the lie was true. It was bad enough that they gave credit to another, but the other was a European who was subjecting us to all kinds of cruelties. It was another grave mistake our innocent parents made in teaching us the glory of white people and denying themselves what was due them. Thus, the love and appreciation, which should have been directed to our parents, was directed to a white man.

There were toys and fruit, raisins, bags and boxes of stuff. My mother, who had now moved northward, made sure we had enough. She would send us boxes of secondhand stuff from "up North." And there were skates. We never had a bicycle, but skates we had from Santa, so we were told. We went to Forty-Fifth Street where part of the street was paved and there was a little hill to skate. Bert took great care to make sure I would not fall. She could not enjoy her own skates; she was too busy watching me

Finding a Solution [2]

We also had our chores: raking the garden, running errands, cleaning the house and the dishes. I almost forgot about the dishes. That chore to us was the supreme punishment. Early on, Bert and I found a solution to this unpleasant task. You simply got rid of the food-stained pots, pans, and dishes by throwing them out of the window. Obviously, in time, the missing utensils testified against us. Bert's punishment was light. Always we thought she and Grandma had a contract. Grandma would hit her or tap her lightly, and she would scream, wallowing in the floor. After all, she was Grandma's Golden

Child, and you are not supposed to demean or punish gold. First Bob, then I, received the harshest punishments.

And there was school. I did all right, Bob did better, and Bert was the best. She was always smart. She always knew everything. She even knew what she didn't know, but she was good at pretending she knew. And if you didn't know that she didn't know, she would convince you that she knew. Then came Jacob, my baby brother. I was eight years old when he arrived.

Sadly, they all went away. Bob and Jacob, then Bert, went north to Jersey City. My mother was already there, and then followed Grandma after the death of Grandpa. I was sent to Augusta, Georgia, to live with my father, and later I, too, ended up in Jersey City, after first living in Brooklyn. I spent the rest of the years bouncing back between Jersey City and Brooklyn. My father lived in Brooklyn, where he had started a church in 1940, at 2024 Fulton Street.

What a contrast. In the South, we had our own big house and yard and chickens and two pecan trees in the backyard and plenty of space to play. Now, we were in a small high-rise apartment with multiple dwellers and neighbors who seemed hostile and seldom spoke. The impact was too much for some of us. We got lost in the asphalt jungle. We were separated, distant from each other in a strange land. Some of the family members never recovered the formal family solidarity and law-abiding ways. We started getting married, and there were children.

All in all, those were precious times. Long have been the hours, even more so as I grow older, that I have spent thinking about what used to be. The inevitable gallop of time widens the distance and makes those days even more delightful to contemplate.

We were inseparable: Bob, Bert, and Herbie, children whose mothers and fathers, at given points and times, were far away, children raised by their grandparents. Bert grew up to be so much like her grandmother. Occasionally bossy, she was demanding, commanding, feisty, forward, audacious, and fire breathing. And then she was sweet, mellow, loving, caring, embracing, and always playful. Like all intelligent people, she had a sense of humor. She loved fun times and was funny in a positive, healthy way. The Bible says, "A merry heart doeth good like medicine." She had a rare smiling face; she always seemed to be smiling. I cannot remember a time when she was not smiling. It was as if she was born with this smile. It was in her genes. When we were young, Frank Sinatra used to sing about "Nancy with the laughing face." The song could have been written for Bert. When I look back on our years in Savannah, Georgia, what stays constant in my mind is her smiling face. Oh, we got into scrapes and arguments. We fought, as children do, but those memories are forgotten or faded beyond recognition. The smile and the laughter, however, are still very vivid in my mind.

Another thing about her face, it seemed tilted, ever so slightly, as though she was looking at you sideways. Her eyes were always full of curiosity, questioning, looking straight at you. But there was fire, too. She could become angry. Again, it was anger inherited from her Grandma, a little lady who was frequently in a rage.

She was always a fast talker, probably encouraged by her love of chewing gum. Grandma used to scold her often about "smacking that gum." Grandma thought it was uncouth and sounded "like maggots in a beef bone." So when Bert became irate, the words spurred forth from her lips like a machine-gun fire. She was industrious, always busy, always working at something.

Bert was creative and meticulous about her appearance. She was friendly and independent. She was profoundly sensitive to the hurts and pains of others. It came as no surprise when she pursued the medical profession. In our childhood, we shared each other's hurts. When one of us was punished, we huddled together. We hurt each other from time to time, but we did not want anybody else hurting us. She loved her family. Coming out of our Savannah experience, family was everything.

They are all gone now, except for Jacob, Icky, and me. Grandpa and Grandma, Mother, Aunt Natalie and Uncle Riddick, and Bob, and those who came by Forty-Fourth and Florence Streets are gone, too. My father, my brothers—Alonzo Jr. and William Emmett (W.E.), Uncle Baby and Aunt Trudie, who lived on the eastside of town, and now Bert, my first cousin—Bert the Golden Child—are gone.

So we come here today to say so long to the "Golden Child." Not goodbye, but so long for a while. For we will meet again one day soon. And we have come to declare our faith and hope that death does not make an end. No! The few brief years that we sojourn in this valley of tears and sorrow are not all there is to life. Beyond the grave, we shall live again. "The grave can't hold our bodies down," as we sing in our church. The Bible teaches us that it is all right to have sorrow, but not as others who have no hope.

When the shadows of the cross loomed across the path of Jesus, and sorrow engulfed the disciples, Jesus turned to them and said, "Let not you heart be troubled; you believe in God, believe also in me. In my father's house are many mansions; if it were not so, I would have told you. I go to prepare a place for you. And if I go and prepare a place for you, I will come again, and receive you unto myself; that where I am, there you may be also" (John 14:1–3). Thus, Jesus was reassuring his disciples, and us, that there is a place being prepared for us.

It is necessary for us to go through the grave to get home. Like the old lady who confused everybody as she would alight from the bus and go into the cemetery. They thought she lived there. Upon closer examination, they discovered she lived on the other side of the cemetery. She had to go through the cemetery to get home.

We say to the "Golden Child," we will not look for you in the cemetery, but we will look for you in your new home. And when we meet again, there will be no more parting of the ways, no more parting of the family, no more hospitals, no more pain, no more dialysis machine, no more pill taking, medicine prescription, no more surgery—all those things will have passed away. In your new glorified body, in the place that Jesus has prepared for you, you will live forever. And one day soon, we will see you again. And what a day that will be, when we all get to heaven.

Bernard E. Brooks[2]

Sunrise: 1935, Camden, South Carolina
Sunset: October 27, 2007, Spartanburg, South Carolina

A Respected Friend

We were neighbors once upon a time. We were never close friends, but Bernard E. Brooks and I had a friendly mutually respectful relationship. I participated in his fundraising when he ran for mayor and was elected Teaneck, New Jersey's first black mayor from 1983 to 1988. The only other Black mayor in Bergen County, New Jersey, at the time was the Rev. Walter Taylor in 1971. Rev. Taylor also was pastor of the Galilee Methodist Church in Englewood, New Jersey. He officiated my wedding to Karen Smith in 1962.

Mr. Brooks was tall, dark, with flashing eyes. He was brilliant and forward thinking. He was tough, but always respectful to everybody.

Teaneck's former mayor Paul Ostrow said, "Bernie was one of those people I tried to emulate in the way he treated people. A true legend."

Councilwoman Jacqueline B. Kates, another former mayor, said, "He was stern at council meetings and disliked a lot of talk during public sessions. He always addressed residents as *Sir* and *Madame*. He wanted to treat everybody the same way, with dignity and respect. Bernie transcended race. He was our first black mayor That was a very proud achievement for him, and a proud moment for Teaneck."

Mr. Brooks's quest for dignity and respectful interaction among all people motivated him to start a Friendship Day Program. He encouraged black and white families to visit each other's homes.

He was a true professional in his politics and in his business as a finance and management consultant. He tried to move to Teaneck Council into the computer age. Another former mayor, Frank Hall, recalled, "When he joined the Council, he tried to make it more professional. That's where his management and expertise came in. He was a big help."

While his business and political responsibilities kept him busy, he still found time to volunteer in many organizations and activities. He was a member of the Bergen County NAACP and the Urban League of Bergen County. He was active in Little League Baseball, senior housing, and the Bergen County Girl Scout Council. He was a trustee of Holy Name Hospital in Teaneck. He served on the advisory board at the School of Management at the New Jersey School of

Technology, and was a member of the New Jersey's Supreme Court Ethics Committee.

In October 2003, Teaneck expressed gratitude for Mr. Brooks's character and contributions when the township dedicated a park in his honor—the Bernard E. Brooks Park on Intervale Road.

One evening, as I passed his home, an ambulance was parked out front. I went inside. There was a heavy, sad silence. People spoke in hushed voices. I knew something strange and traumatic had happened. He was seated in the living room, his body, his aura, his face, especially his eyes, told me what I knew in my spirit. I had been to this place many times before. Death had entered the house. I sat beside him. He said, "My wife just died."

We sat in silence for what seemed a long time. In times of staggering sorrow or trauma, I hesitate to speak. Always I remember Job and his friends. Job's suffering and loss has become proverbial: His children were killed, he lost his wealth, his body was afflicted with a painful disease, his wife told him to curse God and die, and it seemed that God had forsaken him. His friends came to comfort him, and for three days sat in silence with him. Then they spoke and said all the wrong things. Job angrily said to them, "Miserable comforters are ye all."

After a while, I spoke to Bernard about faith and hope. Then I prayed for him. We sat for a little while longer. Then I took my leave. Not long after, he moved back to Spartanburg, South Carolina.

And now he has moved to his eternal home.

He was survived by his wife, Julia Lyons-Brooks of Spartanburg; four daughters: Sharon Brooks of Thousand Oaks, California; Karen Brooks of Gwynne Oak, Maryland; Susan Brooks of Newark, New Jersey; and Theresa Brooks of Atlanta, Georgia; and three sisters, Martha Brooks and Ruth Webster, both of the Bronx, New York; and Vivian Bracey of Mount Vernon, New York.

Richard "Dick" Gidron

Sunrise: October 10, 1939, Chicago, Illinois
Sunset: October 11, 2007, Scarsdale, New York

"He was a giant, in size and charity"

He was a big man. His generosity was equal to his physical size. He was community minded in special ways. There are many testimonies of his munificence. Two in particular that stand out are quoted in *The Positive Community* magazine.[4]

His pastor and *close* friend, the Rev. Dr. Gregory Robeson Smith of Mother AME. Zion Church in Harlem, said, "For over thirty years, Dick Gidron has been my close friend, confidant, elder brother, Masonic brother, who inspired me and countless others to live, give, and strive for the best in life. Dick Gidron was a friend to the community by supporting programs uplifting the community, remaining in his roots, and showing us all entrepreneurship is a reality. The word *no* did not exist in his vocabulary. So many people always turned to Dick for help. His influence, professionalism, and dedication stretched far beyond New York. He was a champion, a trailblazer, my friend, my brother. Dick Gidron, I will miss you. Your impact will never be forgotten."

The other glowing tribute was paid by the Rev. Al Sharpton, who said, "My longtime friend Dick Gidron was a pioneer, and I will miss him dearly. He supported us through every one of the civil rights struggles in the past twenty years, and there was not a time I could not call on him for support and friendship. His breed was a rarity, and his accomplishments profound. In 1972, he became the first African-American Cadillac dealer in the New York area, and only the second in the nation. For him to endure through constant scrutiny, in spite of all the naysayers, proved that he was one of the great business leaders of our time. In fact, the only thing Dick Gidron was guilty of was being Black and successful in America. He was one of a kind, and his family and friends not only knew him as the 'King of Cadillacs' but as a loving father and husband. He was also the Black folks' bank. When you did not have credit, you could still get a car from Dick Gidron—and I speak as one of his noncredit customers many years ago. Mr. Gidron had faith in his people and a love for helping people of all walks of life. He was a philanthropist and always one to do a good deed. The whole community looked up to Mr. Gidron, and not a day shall pass that I will not miss his friendship. On behalf of my family and me and the National Action Network, you will forever be missed, Mister Gidron!"

It was in the late 70s when I first met Dick Gidron. I had heard about his philanthropic outreach through many people who had had dealings with him. On two occasions, I had been the direct beneficiary of his generosity. I had an old car that had broken down beyond repair. In the meantime, I needed transportation. I asked Dick Gidron for help, and he gave me a gray Cadillac. It was not new, but it was clean and running smoothly. It served me well until I was able to purchase a new car. He never asked for a cent.

The second instance of his charity was during Jesse Jackson's run for the presidency in 1988. It was time for Jesse to focus on New York for the Democratic primary race. It meant an entourage of staff, media, party leaders and well-wishers. I had been traveling with and organizing for Jesse across the country. Now in New York, I wanted to make sure that we had sufficient vehicles for the entourage. I called Dick Gidron for help. He supplied six vehicles for the duration of the New York City campaign, and a special car and driver for me.

Adrian A. Council, publisher of *The Positive Community Magazine,* cited this history in her tribute to Dick Gidron in the November issue of *The Positive Community:*

> *Gidron was the ultimate go-to guy and team player. One day, during the 1988 presidential race, Jean Wells and I were meeting with Mr. Gidron to discuss his advertising on the radio stations. The meeting was interrupted with a phone call from the Rev. Herbert Daughtry. He called to say that the plane of presidential candidate Jesse Jackson would be landing in two hours. Mr. Gidron dispatched six cars with drivers to aid the Jackson campaign.*

During his battle with General Motors (GM), I was eager to answer his call for help. With some of the most influential leaders in New York, we commenced meeting periodically to strategize to secure justice for Gidron. In the meetings were Rev. Dr. Calvin Butts; Rev. Dr. Gregory Smith; Rev. Al Sharpton; former New York City mayor

David Dinkins;   Rev. Dr. Franklyn Richardson, pastor of Grace Baptist Church; Hazel Dukes of NAACP; and others. We held a press conference in front of GM's office to demand that General Motors honor its agreement with Dick Gidron. At our last meeting, held at Abyssinia Baptist Church, we decided we would use our influence with the Black members of GM's Board of directors, hopefully to gain their support or direction. If that failed, we were ready to call for a boycott of GMs products. A couple weeks later, I learned he'd had a stroke. The next news I received was that he had died.

His problem with GM revolved around property that Mr. Gidron said GM had agreed to sell him. He put a lot of money into the building. Then a fire that destroyed the building. GM reneged on the deal, leaving Mr. Gidron holding the bag and losing his money. Because of the cash flow challenges, Gidron began to have tax problems, which eventually landed him in jail. I am certain all this tension contributed to the deterioration of his health.

I was in Chad, Central Africa, when the viewing and funeral occurred at Abyssinian Baptist Church. I wished I could have been there. Everything seemed to have happened so suddenly. It was hard for me to believe he was gone. It seems that we had just had a meeting, which we had just spoken on the phone. During the troubles with the GM, he would call me often. He would say, "I need you, Doctor Daughtry. I need all of my friends. The GM has done a terrible wrong to me. I need your organizing skills."

Every time I see a Cadillac or a GM car, I think of Dick Gidron. Maybe God had a special chariot with a special driver to take him home. Or maybe Jesus came for Gidron and took him to Heaven Himself.

Fred Willis

Sunrise: February 12, 1932,
Sunset: September 11, 2008,

Friendship from the Cradle to the Grave

The passing of Fred Willis brings home to me again the fact that, according to my knowledge, all of my generation has gone into oblivion. There are two of us left—Sunny Rowe and myself. Fred was one of the first persons I met when I came from Georgia in 1942. Guy Worthy Jr. introduced him to me. Guy and Fred had been friends almost from the cradle. We all remained friends throughout our teen years. I wonder who remembers Fred. Who remembers that he had a mother and father and two sisters named Shirley and Bernice? Both of whom I had a teenage crush on; neither of them paid me any mind. The youth of our time played punch ball on Prospect Place, where Fred lived. It was called "The Market" in those days because the streets were lined with pushcarts—another enterprise that has disappeared. Once upon a time, pushcarts pervaded the streets of New York. We played handball on Howard Avenue and Prospect Place at PS 144, where my son, Herb Jr., is now a principal. We played basketball in the schoolyard and gym at PS 178 on Dean Street and anywhere else there was a basket and a ball. If there was none, we made our own.

We played softball in the park bounded by Dean and Pacific Streets and Ralph and Howard Avenues. We named our team the Tomahawks, and we were good. As far as college was concerned, it never crossed our minds. We were programmed for vocational schools: in Brooklyn, Automotive High School in Williamsburg, and Lane High School for Morticians; and in Manhattan, the Needle Trade for Tailors. College was like a distant country that you only heard about, but nobody you knew traveled there. In a real sense, we were programmed for mediocrity and failure. Without the proper educational background, we were disposed to criminal behavior, and therefore doomed to the penitentiaries.

However, as his later years proved, Fred was a genius. Still, he was programmed for vocational occupation. Because of his determination, he did succeed in earning a Bachelor of Arts degree from Hunter College as the years went by. He was a professor at New York Technical College, where he taught calculus. They called him "The Professor," but when we were growing up, we all recognized Fred's brilliant mind, and we called him, "Mr. Education."

There were two things Fred could do exceptionally well: he could fight, and he was a scholar. He was way ahead of his class. One of the most memorable fights in the neighborhood was between a peer we nicknamed B., and Fred. B. was flamboyant, a fancy Dan. We had waited long for this matchup. We even tried hard to instigate it. Finally, the showdown arrived at the PS 178 gym. I don't know how it started, but it was sudden. There was an argument, and somebody said, "Get out of my face!" Then hands went up, and finally, Fred and B. were at it. It didn't last long. B. danced around, showboating. Fred stalked methodically, almost as if he had paper and pencil in his hand, working through a complicated mathematical problem. Or it was a like a cobra and mongoose. Fred was the mongoose, staring confidently, moving slowly; B. was more colorful, swinging and circling. And then, like a bolt of lightning, Fred landed a punch into B's stomach. B. doubled up and ambled away into a corner, where he remained for the rest of the day, quiet, embarrassed, and defeated.

I know I may be repetitious, but it is always on my mind that the dominant society failed us, and then blamed us because we did not succeed.

Mayor Glenn Cunningham[5]

Sunrise: September 16, 1943, Jersey City, New Jersey
Sunset: May 24, 2004, Jersey City, New Jersey

A Major Mayor

Flying home across a Houston, Texas sky, after a few days of rest in the Puerto Vallarta sun, my wife turned to me and said, "I don't know how to tell you this, but I've got to tell you before you hear it on the radio."

Oh God, what is it now?

"Glenn Cunningham is dead," she said.

"Dead?!"

"Yes, he died while riding his bike. A heart attack, I think."

"When?"

"Maybe Wednesday morning. I received the call from the church. We didn't know how to tell you."

At least, I think that's what she said, since my mind was racing back through time to the Jersey City of my youth.

I knew Glenn as a little boy. His older brother Lowell and I were running buddies. Our lives were less than honorable, but we vowed to keep Glenn straight. I would always say, "We didn't do a good job on ourselves, but I'm proud of Glenn. We must have had a positive influence on him."

We were proud of him. Glenn had worked hard, maintained his integrity, and never forgotten his past and his people. He started as a patrolman and became captain of the Jersey City Police Department, serving twenty-five years. He was appointed head of New Jersey's US Marshal's Office by President Bill Clinton and served for five years. He was elected mayor of Jersey City in 2001, and Jersey City State Senator in 2003. (In New Jersey, you can hold both offices— mayor and state-elected offices.)

The last time I saw Glenn was in 2003, at a Kwanzaa program organized by the Veterans activist Khybili Tyariri at City Hall in Jersey City. Glenn appeared hale and hearty, and was with his lovely wife, Sandra. We reminisced about old times, and he shared with me what he wanted to do for Jersey City. After I finished my keynote speech, he gave me the keys to the city.

I spoke with him a few weeks later and asked him to do something about the construction blocking up the street where Queen Latifah had her office, interrupting her business. A few days later, his deputy mayor, Drayton, called back to say it was done.

I also asked him to co-chair a gala being planned in my honor. I told him he would be the only elected official I'd approach for the job. I had so many friends who were elected officials that if I had started down that path, I wouldn't have known where to stop. But because of our special relationship, I felt justified in making this exception.

My mind came back to the plane. I heard my wife say, "I just spoke to him. I called his secretary to tell her to convey to Glenn the gala scheduled for June eighteenth, 2004, was postponed to December eleventh, 2004, but he came to the phone. He sounded upbeat. He said he was looking forward to the gala. He was prepared to do whatever I wanted him to do."

Life is so fragile.

We seem sometimes to swing on a gossamer thread, yet we are made tough and can endure almost anything. Life is made of such apparent contradictions. "Boast not thyself of tomorrow, for thou knowest not what tomorrow shall bring forth," says the Bible.

I thought of my oldest brother, Alonzo Jr., who had been found dead in his home in Philadelphia just a few weeks before Glenn's passing. I reflected on my own recent experience with a heart problem.

My doctor called me one morning, urging me to come to his office before noon. I had just returned from my morning exercise program, stretching, walking, running, and shadow boxing. I felt fine.

When I arrived at the doctor's office, he directed me to go downstairs for an EKG. Why was this necessary? I had my annual physical. Blood work was okay, "perfect." Why was another test necessary? I completed the exam and returned to the doctor. He read the markings, looked up, trying to remain calm.

"I have to put you in the hospital," he said.

"When?" I asked, startled.

"Now."

"What's the problem?"

"Heart flutter, a form of arrhythmia."

"What does all that mean?"

"It means your heart isn't pumping properly. The blood from the top chamber isn't flowing properly to the lower chamber. The remaining blood can clot. If the clot reaches the brain, you die or have a stroke. We have to keep you under observation for a while."

"How long?" I asked.

"I don't know. We have to see."

As it turned out, it was five days.

I pondered if Glenn had had the same problem I'd experienced.

I thank God because it was only through my intervention to get my wife to make an appointment for her physical that I nonchalantly asked the doctor about my EKG exam. Had not my wife been having some discomfort, I would have never called the doctor, and who knows what would have happened?

After the doctor examined me, my wife's discomfort disappeared. It was as if God was saying, "I've got to get somebody's attention in a hurry. Let me allow discomfort to Mrs. Daughtry to get things moving." The doctor informed me that the condition could have come from genetics since my family has a history of cardio-vascular problems. Or it could have been aging, or stress or other unknown factors. He did say my health program probably saved my life. I have been a vegan for twenty years, and I vigorously engage in physical exercise, including full-court basketball. Health is a major part of my ministry, and after this experience, I increased my emphasis. I've said to all, "Take care of yourself. If you lose your health, all else matters little. Get your periodic physical examination and be consistent."

The pilot's voice interrupted my thoughts: "Fasten your seat belt. We are encountering turbulence."

About a week before Glenn died, I visited Jersey City just for a walk down memory lane. One of the places I visited is my old barber shop on Edge Avenue, now a landmark. "Larry" was still cutting hair in the place where I'd gotten my first cut six decades earlier by Mr. Johnson, the owner. As was our custom, we discussed events and personalities from long ago. Then Larry said to me, "Mayor Cunningham was here a few days ago. He is doing a book on Jersey City. He will be back next week to interview me." We expressed our admiration for him.

Glenn loved Jersey City. He was always talking, writing, and taking pictures about Jersey City.

In a conversation about a week after his passing, Glenn's wife explained to me all that had happened. I felt deep sorrow for Sandra. She was a perfect complement to their public service, perfectly handling public ceremonies, including the Jersey City station of the historic African Burial Ground procession to lower Manhattan or the Kwanzaa Celebration at the Jersey City City Hall. I prayed with her and wished her well.

Glenn died at 10:45 p.m., May 24th, in Greenville Hospital in Jersey City, an hour after he arrived. It is the same hospital where my brother Bob died twenty years before, of heart problems.

Harvey L. Smith, president of Jersey City's city council, succeeded Glenn as mayor. In 1953, his father, Stan Smith, and I both committed our lives to the Lord and vowed to become ministers.

So long, Glenn. We will miss you. But I know your brother Lowell, and all our generation who have gone before, are happy to greet you, and so is the entire heavenly host. Hopefully we who remain will be inspired by your life and make our contributions, too.

Glenn Cunningham, mayor of Jersey City, died at age 60. Long live the spirit of Glenn Cunningham and all our people who struggle to move us toward the Promised Land.

From the armory, we traveled south on Jordan Avenue to South Monticello Avenue. The twenty or so blocks brought us to Communipaw Avenue. We passed Saul's bar, one of the famous hangouts. A block before Communipaw was Lou's pool hall. Here, I would sneak in at age fourteen and learn to shoot pool. Around the corner was the bowling alley where I did the backbreaking work of setting up bowling pins. The long working hours earned me a few dollars and distaste for backbreaking work

We crossed Communipaw, where half a block east was the police precinct where Glenn Cunningham worked. We entered Martin Luther King Jr. Drive, which used to be Jackson Avenue.

MLK Jr. Drive once was a well-kept street with comfortable attractive homes and apartments and thriving businesses. It was the street we "walked" and assembled. If you wanted to meet someone, chances were, if you walked up and down the street long enough, you would meet that someone.

Soon, we were passing "The Club."

The Club had an interesting history. It started further up MLK Drive, between Kearney and Ege Avenues, as the Viking Club. Most people thought it was named after the Jersey City Vikings, a highly regarded semi-pro football team. But once the club became a gambling place, some people didn't want the Vikings name associated with it. I sharpened my gaming skills at the Viking Club, and at sixteen became the "houseman" responsible for collecting the owners share, a cut after each game. It even had a couple of pool tables there.

The name issue was resolved when the owners moved the club—first down MLK Drive, between Union and Atlantic Avenues, and later beyond Bramhall Avenue—and renamed it the Colored Independent Civic Association (CICA.)

It was the all-purpose hangout. Everybody who was anybody came by The Club, as it was called. There were all kinds of gambling, horses, numbers, sports and all kinds of deals being made. There was a large room with the card tables and different kinds of games—rummy, poker, Georgia skin, coon can, even dominos. The games changed from time to time. There was a smaller room in the back for more private games.

The Club was also an information center, a barber shop, street corner, bar room, and classroom rolled into one. It was a political center, too, offering voter education and registration opportunities.

One of the major political victories demonstrating The Club's influence was the defeat of Frank "I Am the Law" Haque. He had been mayor for more than thirty years, and people thought he was invincible. Then leaders of The Club supported Haque's opponent, John V. Kenny, in a mayoral election and achieved the impossible: Kenny won. It was unbelievable the way The Club leaders were able to involve reefer smokers, gamblers, number writers, pimps, prostitutes, and liquor drinkers in the electoral process. Vivid in my mind was this reefer seller standing on the corner, eyes half-closed, swaying to and fro, urging everybody to get out and vote.

It was at The Club that I stumbled upon a plot to beat the number bankers. "The numbers," in New Jersey, was a gambling enterprise based on guessing the number of trades at the stock market in New York. There was an elaborate scheme being formulated to have relay teams, starting with a person at the stock market who would relay the number as soon as it appeared, before it became public. Another person would relay it to the next person, and so on, until it got to the number writer, who was also a part of the scheme.

It was a dangerous business. If caught, death or physical mayhem was inevitable. An old hustler said to me, "Son, this is dangerous stuff. You know what will happen if we are caught." I nodded. "You shouldn't be in this. You are too young. I'm an old man. If I'm caught, it won't matter all that much to me. But you're young."

I insisted on being a part of the scheme. The old hustler said, "Okay, son, it's your funeral." We proceeded to rehearse the plan. For various reasons, the whole thing collapsed. Thank God!

Occasionally, I still visit The Club. Just about everybody I once knew is gone, but the atmosphere and activities remain the same. The smoke is thick, the talk is loud, and the booze abounds. I sit and wonder where I would be had not Jesus Christ came into my life in 1954.

Now we were passing Union Street where PS 14 is located. This is the public school I wanted to attend when I arrived from Georgia. It was predominantly black, but I ended up at PS 15 on Stegman Street, which was predominantly white. I recall the principal at PS 15, Dr. Bannerman. She was a frail little white woman with a southern accent. She loved to talk about the "darkies" and their habits. I hated her. Today the school is a primary and middle school named after the late Whitney Young Jr., former head of the National Urban League.

PS 14 was later named after Flip Wilson. I was there for the naming ceremony. I was good friends with Flip's brother, Clifford, whom we called "The Fox."

Nearing Forest Avenue was Caruso, another infamous liquor store and watering hole. Across the street was the 418 Club, a more upscale watering hole. Not far from the 418 Club was "the cut," a known gathering place above the railroad track. On any evening, reefer smoke filled the air. In addition, fiery arguments and tall tales were exchanged.

At that time, nobody paid much attention to reefers or any form of dope. The only treatment center that we knew about was in Lexington, Kentucky. A man named Sonny R. was given credit for bringing heroin—also known as *horse*, *white lady*, and *junk*—into the community. Before we knew it, another destroyer had taken hold of our community. Innumerable persons, old and young, became hooked. Whole families were destroyed.

But nobody seemed to care—until 1948, when young white women were caught getting high with Black musicians at the famed Birdland jazz club. Then society became aware and alarmed. An outcry erupted, and a demand that something be done. How many times has that happened? As long as an ill is contained in the Black community, it's not a problem. This reflects how society esteems Black humanity.

The next block up was Ege Avenue. On the corner was Marie's restaurant, where a portly black woman was owner and cook. I can't remember what was on the menu, but with our heads swimming from marijuana, our stomachs demanded sweets and liquids, we would keep Marie's open late into the night, making endless orders of sweet potato pie, coconut cake, milk, and sodas. We ate and laughed the hours away. One of the persons among the nocturnal crowd was Danny W., the brother of Red W. He had won the reputation as being one of the biggest potheads in Jersey City.

One night, he went to a church and "got saved." He went home and flushed all his reefers and tobacco down the toilet. He, like Sluggo, wanted everybody "to be saved" immediately. His conversations had one subject matter: Jesus Christ.

They nicknamed him Mr. Bible because every time you saw him, he was carrying a Bible. Months later, Danny died suddenly. We never knew why. The whole town was shocked. In his coffin, they placed a Bible in his hand. It was hard to believe he was gone.

We turned west on Orient Avenue, where Glenn once lived. We went up to Bergen Avenue and turned south. Looking northward on Bergen Avenue is the Millers' library, where monthly lecture series sponsored by the TAP the Power Within forum are held.

The procession continued past Grant Avenue where I had lived between MLK and Ocean Avenues. There, on the corner of Bergen and Grant Avenue, was Snyder High School. Vivid in my mind was the black and orange uniforms and the name of Covella, a white football player whose exploits were compared to Aubrey Lewis of Montclair High School, who became the first black football player at Notre Dame University. Years later, I took some kids from my church in Brooklyn to see Lewis. We went into the wooded area around his house, and he cut some branches and made a wooden cross. It hangs in my pulpit today.

The funeral process continued on Bergen Avenue, turned east on Bidwell Avenue, not far from the Greenville Hospital where Glenn died an hour after arrival, and where my brother Bob died twenty years before, amid many unanswered questions.

Then we turned south on MLK. Drive, to east on Warner Street, to south on Ocean Avenue, to Chapel Avenue. All along the way to the Bayview cemetery people were lined up. Some of them must have been waiting for hours. Some had brought chairs and benches to sit on. I said to the ministers who were riding in the limo with me, "It is great to have VIP's attend your funeral. But it is greater to have the people show their love by lining the streets the way they have done."

We entered the cemetery, winding through the narrow curvaceous streets. It was an old cemetery. The bronze casket was placed above the ground, atop a grass-green carpet. The immediate family sat in chairs. The weeping now became audible. Family members buried their heads in their hands. Ms. Cunningham fell over on the shoulders of Glenn's brother.

Dr. Maize and I moved closer to the casket, and he read the familiar burial litany, concluding with "ashes to ashes, dust to dust…" As he spoke, he plucked the petals from the white rose flower I held in my hand, and announced that I would do the closing prayer.

I paused to gather my composure, and prayed:

Oh God, our help in ages past ,our hope for years to come, our shelter from the stormy blast, and our eternal home. We are gathered here in this hallowed place with hearts mixed with sadness and gratitude. We are sad because our loved one, Glenn Cunningham, mayor and state senator, is no longer with us on this side of history. But we are not as sorry as others who have no hope.

We are grateful, too, for the time Glenn was with us, and all the good he did. He put his footprints on the sands of time. While we place his body in the ground, he will never die. His spirit will live as long as the sun shines. We are grateful that one day, we shall meet again, and on that day, there will be no sorrow, suffering, death, or parting of the ways. For the former things would have passed away. Till then, comfort the family, inspire us all to do your will.

After the prayer, there was a pause, and the military ceremony began. When the ceremony concluded, the clergy in a line marched past the family. I had an eerie feeling as I greeted one of Glenn's brothers. He looked so much like Lowell, now deceased, with whom

I used to "run" with. When I reached Ms. Cunningham, I bent over to embrace her. Tears were rolling down her face. She was sobbing as she thanked me. I whispered to her, "You will always be in my prayers. Stay well, stay strong. God will take care of you. Let's carry on."

A little distance away, the ground was open to receive the coffin. Rev. Maize and I walked with the family to the burial ground, paused for a moment, and then returned to our cars. The reception was held at Tavern Restaurant in Lincoln Park. The place was packed. It was whosoever will, let him come.

One person present who was dear to me was Bernice Lawrence. She is the wife of the renowned, deceased evangelist John Lawrence. In 1953, and for many years thereafter, John had had a powerful influence on my religious conversion and development. Innumerable lives were changed through his ministry.

The drive back home seemed short. I lost track of time as I pondered my Jersey City days, the life and times of Glenn, the days' events, and the cause of death. Again, I vowed to redouble my effort in urging people to take care of their health and get their physical checkups.

As I neared home, I started humming Dion's melancholy melody (pardon me, Dion, for changing the names):

Anybody here seen my old friend Glenn?
Can you tell me where he is gone?
He freed a lot of people.
It seems the good die young.
I just looked around, and he was gone
Anybody here seen my old friend Sonny?
Anybody here seen my old friend Malcolm?
Didn't you just love the things they stood for?
They tried to find some good for you and me
So we would be free soon
One day it's gonna be
Anybody here seen my old friend?
Can you tell me where he is gone?
I think I saw him coming over the hill
with Martin, Sonny and Glenn

I was up at 4:45 a.m. and arrived at the church a 6:15 a.m., with Glenn and memories of Jersey City still on my mind. Sleep didn't come easy the night before. I'm not sure if it was because I couldn't sleep, or didn't want to. I can usually sleep anywhere, at any time under, any condition. But I think I just wanted to rehearse the events of the past few days and try to interpret their meaning.

I headed to my first meeting at 9:00 a.m. It was with the Downtown Brooklyn Clergy, which had been organized to have major influence in the downtown Brooklyn area. My next meeting was at 10:00 a.m. with the Downtown Brooklyn Leadership Coalition, formed of clergy, elected officials, community activists, and businesspeople.

Both meetings were held at the Christian Life Center on Atlantic Avenue in Brooklyn, where the Rev. Dennis Dillon is the pastor. And both meetings focused on the $18.2 billion development plans for downtown Brooklyn. The development plans include everything—shopping mall, housing, retail and commercial space, even a sports arena.

Downtown Brooklyn offers the space no longer available in Manhattan, and so Downtown Brooklyn would undergo dramatic changes in the next five to ten years. The changes have had a major impact throughout Brooklyn.

Our organizations had been meeting for several months, and had developed a twelve-point community agreement document. The document was endorsed by more than seven hundred people in a community meeting at Hanson Place United Methodist Church.

Our noonday prayer from 12:00 to 12:45 p.m. was the next item on my schedule. Every Wednesday, we have weekly prayers, at which time I deliver an inspirational message. At 1:00 p.m., I attended Donna Brazile's book signing at the Yale Club in Manhattan. Donna, who cut her political teeth in the Jesse Jackson presidential campaign, was promoting her new book, *Cooking with Grease*, published by Simon and Schuster.

I remember when Donna came into the campaign. I was impressed with her audacity, diligence, and acumen. She later became a campaign manager during Vice President Al Gore's presidential run. I had started with Jesse from the beginning. I was in the crowd that was urging him to "Run, Jesse, Run." We held a most important meeting at our church in October 1983. The major black leaders were present. I remember Jesse saying, "I need three things to run. I don't want 'Run, Jesse, Run' to become 'See Jesse run.' The three things I need are money, machinery, and the masses." Those years with Jesse were some of the most exciting in my life.

At 2:00 p.m., I was interviewed in front of the Yale Club with John Noel of Channel 4 TV, the NBC flagship station in New York City. The subject was the release of Limerick Nelson. He was the young man convicted of killing Yankel Rosenbaum during the 1991 Crown Heights unrest sparked by the killing of Gavin Cato, seven years old, by a car in a caravan escort for Hasidic Rabbi Menachem Schneersohn.

The following is a paraphrasing of the interview:

TV 4: Lemrick Nelson is released. What do you think?

Me: Good. He paid his debt. Now let's give him a chance.

TV 4: But the Rosenbaum family is angry and feels that an injustice was done.

Me: If I were the Rosenbaums, perhaps I would feel the same. I don't think so. But let us not forget Gavin Cato. His killers were never brought to justice. They disappeared almost immediately after the event. Cato's father has apparently moved on. I've been told he is friendly with the Hasidic community.

TV 4: Relationships are better now, a community leader said.

Me: I don't know. But the problem, as I saw it, wasn't cordiality; it was about power. Arrangement—who receives the goods and services coming into the community, and in what proportions. It's wonderful to say hello passing each other in the street, but the question still remains, *Is the majority population receiving its fair share?* My guess is it isn't. Therefore, tension still exists. No self-respecting people will allow that kind of situation to exist forever.

Let me be clear, I'm not blaming the Hasidic community. Not where they have legally, aggressively developed their community to get all they can. Substantial fault must be placed on the black community. If the majority population—the overwhelming majority in this instance—allow themselves to be contained or to be powerless, especially where there is no military might deployed, then they should blame themselves. 'It is not in the stars that we are weaklings, but in ourselves,' said Brutus in Shakespeare's Julius Caesar.``

After the interview, I returned to the church for more planning, praying, counseling and telephoning. At 5:00 p.m., we held the Randolph Evans Memorial Scholarship reception for those who had received the scholarship. In November 1976, fifteen-year-old Randy, for no reason, was killed by Police Officer Robert Torsney. November 1977, the jury sentenced Torsney to psychiatric treatment with weekends at home.

The community was furious. We organized Black Christmas 1977. We had three objectives:

1.   To perpetuate the memory of Randolph Evans.
2.   To create a movement
3.   Political and economic empowerment.

After a year of boycotting Brooklyn stores, a ten-point agreement was consummated. One of the items was the establishment of the Randy Evans Memorial Scholarship in which each year, ten college-bound students would receive $1,500 each. Two hundred sixty students have received scholarships as of 2004.[6]

I spoke to scholarship recipients about the history of our struggle in general, and Randy Evans in particular, and challenged them "to give back to their community."

My next meeting was at the church, at 7:00 p.m., with the board of directors of the Mo Better Jaguars, a sandlot football program and more. Chris LeGree and Ervin Roberson started the program after their return from the Million Man March in Washington DC, Oct 16, 1995. They were football men, so they reasoned that they could make a difference in that sport. The program encompasses more than football. It is parenting, mentoring, and tutoring, with a heavy emphasis on schoolwork and discipline.

The football program consists of five teams, ages seven through fifteen, in addition to cheerleaders. On Saturday practice sessions during the football season, over two hundred kids, with their parents, assemble at Betsy Head Park. It is a great opportunity to reach youngsters at a most important age, as well as their parents and spectators, who come to watch them play. They are excellent football players, too. The Midgets, the oldest age group, consisting of thirteen to fifteen-year-olds, won the national championship in Orlando, Florida, in 2001. They are in the National Pop Warner League, in a way comparable to Little League Baseball.

I became involved in 2001. I went to watch my grandson play. I was so impressed with the team's discipline and skill. I know somebody was spending a lot of time with them. Later, I met the coaches, Chris and Irwin. The more I stayed around, the more involved I became. In the year 2002, I was elected president of their board of directors.

The meeting focused on:

• Recruitment
• Staffing
• Fund Raising
• Addition to the Board of Directors
• Relationship to the National Organization

The meeting started at 7:00 p.m., and lasted until 10:00 p.m. It had been a long day, and as usual, profoundly satisfying. The demands of the day were also helpful in that they required my energy and concentration, and so gave me respite from the past several days of deaths and funerals.

One of the telephone calls I received during the day informed me that the Rev. Harvey P. Jameson's wife, Carolyn Evans Jameson, had died. The wake would be Thursday, June 3, 2002, from 4:00 p.m. to 7:00 p.m., and the funeral at 7:00 p.m. I put it on my schedule. I was going to be with the dead again.

Endnotes

1   This is a version of the eulogy that ran as an article in the September

14–16, 2007 weekend edition of *The Daily Challenge*, published in Brooklyn, New York. Mr. Thomas Watkins, publisher.

2   This is a re-edited version of the article "A Black Mayor Ahead of His Times," that originally appeared in the November 14, 2007 edition of *The Daily Challenge*, published in Brooklyn, New York. Mr. Thomas Watkins, publisher.

3   *The Positive Community* magazine, November 2007, p. 34.

4   This is a version of several articles titled "Mayor Glenn Cunningham Dead at 60,"and "Memories, Memories," which originally appeared in the June 4–6, 2004 Weekend Edition of *The Daily Challenge*, published in Brooklyn, New York. Mr. Thomas Watkins, publisher.

5   As of the publishing of this book in 2019,have received this scholarship.

6

Gone Too Soon

Brent Dwayne Duncan[1]

Sunset: June 19, 2010, Brooklyn, New York

Another Youth Killed by Violence

Brent Dwayne Duncan was only eighteen years old. On Saturday, June 19, 2010, he was awakened from his sleep at his home in Brooklyn, by two friends who invited him to a party. As was the story of his life, aiming to please, he dressed himself and drove to the party in a car that his father had just purchased. While he was at the party, an altercation erupted amongst the partygoers. The details are sketchy, But as it is often the case, the cause could have been minor, such as a certain look, a meaningless gesture or word, or a past misunderstanding. It doesn't take much to incite some people to violence. Brent was trying to ward off the escalating confrontation by leaving the scene. He waited in his car, trying to get his friends and relatives inside the vehicle.

Then he was shot and killed.

When his mother, Dionne Vincent, received the call from the hospital about her son, she could not believe it. She replied that her son was sleeping in his bedroom. She then discovered the reality that her son was not in the room. His grandmother Bernadine was the one who called me to ask to do the eulogy. She is the aunt of Michael Griffith, who was chased to his death by a white mob in Queens, New York, in the infamous Howard Beach Case, in 1986.

That is often how I become involved in such violent deaths—a call from a family member or friend. And sadly, young people were killed around this same time. One of the clergy of my church, Minister Zakia Russ, informed me that the son of her co-worker had been killed and connected me with the family. On June 2, 2010, another member of my church, Cathy Moore, called me to say that there had been a family dispute where one brother killed the other. Not since the days of my youth had I been close to fratricide.

I attended the funeral, and it was one of the saddest I have ever participated in. And on May 28, 2010, Nicholas Heyward—whose eleven-year-old son, Nicholas Jr., was killed by a police officer on September 22, 1994—called to inform me of a sixteen-year-old girl who was killed.

I heard myself pray, "Oh Lord, how long? How long, oh Lord, before violence will cease in the land? And the weeping of loved ones for their slain children can be heard no more?"

Young People Showed Up

On June 25, 2010, young people packed Schenectady Avenue between Avenue D and Foster Avenue in Brooklyn, for a prayer vigil for Brent. And the following Monday, the beautiful and spacious Bethesda Healing Center was jam-packed for Brent's viewing and funeral service, with attendees standing in the vestibule, against the walls, and outside the center as well. Seventy-five percent of the crowd was young people.

Soloists and one of the church's small singing groups sang comforting and inspiring music. Family and friends offered scriptures, prayers, and reflections. A long candlelight procession followed the eulogy. The funeral director gave instructions for the viewing. A long line filed pass the casket as "Gone Too Soon" played. Michael Jackson sang that song at a memorial for Ryan White, a child who died from HIV. Pop star Usher Raymond sang the song at Michael Jackson's funeral in 2009.

Brent was a model young man. The thirteen-page booklet containing his obituary, photos, quotes, and comments by family and friends testified to his charitable spirit and how much he was loved. Excerpts from his obituary read:

> *Brent was a family person. He was the glue that kept everyone and everything together. He idolized his father and loved his mother. Brent did whatever was needed to ensure that everyone was happy and safe.*

> *Whenever he met an older auntie, friend, or cousin, he would hug them and play with their face, always telling a joke. He was always respectable, always smiling. He always had some advice to give. He loved posting inspirational quotes online, and he was a very persuasive person.*

> *Brent cannot be summed up in one word, or even on this page, but if there was one word to describe him, it would simply be "AMAZING!"*

His mother said, "Brent, you are loved. You brought love to every single person you met. You were the peacemaker in our family, the dresser, the person that would say what nobody else dared to say. I had to share you with many people because you refused to let me keep you to myself. You loved freedom, and your heart was always singing. I'm proud of you, son. My heart will always bleed for you, until we meet again."

His father wrote, "Brent, you are my world and my heart, and I wish I could take your place."

Throughout the ceremony, the casket remained open. The parents, grandmothers, and siblings of Brent sat in the front row. Occasionally, the sobs of his mother became audible. His father, Peter, sat motionless as if transfixed in pain. His grandmother Bernadine appeared to be absorbed in seeing that everything went well.

My Eulogy for Brent Duncan[2]

When word reached me that another young brother had been killed, I could hear the melody of the song "Gone Too Soon." Flashing across the screen of my mind were the many other young brothers and sisters who were killed by other brothers and sisters. I can still hear the sweet, sad voice of Usher Raymond singing the song at Michael Jackson's funeral.

Like a comet
Blazing 'cross the evening sky
Gone too soon.
Like A Sunset
Dying with the rising of the moon
Gone too soon.

We gather this evening in this beautiful, holy place, and we echo the mournful melody, "Gone Too Soon." We view the strong, handsome face of Brent, and we say, "Gone Too Soon." In our minds, we see him again, and we mourn. Gone too soon. We see him joking, laughing, and playing. Gone too soon. We remember how strong and brave he was. Gone too soon. We remember the hugs, kisses, and the I love you's. Gone too soon. We recall his favorite quotes:

- *"I'm not afraid of dying. I'm afraid of not trying."*
- *"Promise what you can deliver, and deliver more than what you can promise."*
- *"The sky is not the limit 'cuz there's footprints on the moon," and*
- *"Everything is OK in the end. If it's not OK, then it's not the end."*

But has Brent really gone too soon? Do we really go too soon when our lives have counted for good, when we have lived for others? When we have lived as Brent has lived, it is never too soon. As Dr. Martin Luther King Jr. had taught us, the essence of life is not how long we live, but how well we live.

Jesus lived approximately thirty-two years. When he was crucified, those who were around him might have said, "Gone Too Soon."

But to see from a distance and to note the global impact of His life across the centuries, who would now say, "Gone Too Soon"?

We have just concluded the thirty-second anniversary of the Randolph Evans Memorial Scholarship. Randy was a fifteen-year-old black youth unjustifiably killed by police officers. I used to say to his mother, Missus Annie Brannon, as I used to say to Missus Griffith, the mother of Michael Griffith, who was chased to his death by a white mob; and to Missus Diallo, the mother of Amadou Diallo, unjustifiably killed by police officers; and to Mister and Missus Bell, whose son, Sean, was also unjustifiably killed by police officers. All of these young men were still in their early twenties. I used to say to these families, "Take comfort that your sons did not die in vain. Songs, books, movies, scholarships, organizations, street marches, and demonstrations, boycotts, workshops, lectures, speeches, and essays have all been done in their memories. Countless lives have been changed and made better because of them."

An old friend, the late Doctor William Jones, former pastor of Bethany Baptist Church in Brooklyn, used to say, "I don't want to die in shallow waters." I understood Doctor Jones to mean, "I don't want to live my life doing small, meaningless, or mediocre things, and die leaving no record of doing or even attempting to do something significant."

Brent did not die in shallow waters. In the years that he lived, he touched innumerable lives for the good. Thus, he has put his "footprints on the sands of time."

"Too soon" is a human evaluation of time. For God, it is never too soon or too late. God is always on time. I think we all know the popular saying, "He may not come when you want Him, but He's always on time." God's time is not our time. The scriptures say, "A thousand years is as a day to the Lord." There is what is called Kairos time, which means the Lord's time—a time pregnant with meaning, a momentous time.

"Too soon" might mean it is too soon to avert a greater loss or a greater pain. Who knows what awaited Brent down his path of life? Now, his mother, father, and all of his loved ones and friends can be proud of him, and they can cherish his memory for as long as they live. But who can say what awaited around the bend? It may not have been his "Huckleberry friend," but a catastrophic end.

Too soon? Nay, he lived a full life! Gone? Yes, but gone where? Has he gone from our minds? Has he gone from our memory? Has he gone from our yesterdays? Gone? Really gone? Nay!

Not in Shallow Waters [74]

The day after Brent's funeral, we reassembled at the church to prepare for the burial. The family was already present when I arrived. The casket was open. I stood at the casket with Grandmother Bernadine looking down upon the handsome young man with a tan suit and shirt that seemed to have been accentuated by his smooth ebony face. His hair was braided. Ms. Bernadine whispered to me, "He's such a handsome young man. He was a good boy."

I made brief remarks and prayed. The funeral director gave instructions for the final viewing. The last to view was the immediate family, including the parents, grandmothers, and siblings. When everybody had departed to their cars, the father and the pallbearers stood around the coffin. The father tucked the interior blanket alongside his son's body as if Brent was asleep in bed, making him comfortable for the night. When the lid was lowered by the director, the body was carried out to the "black coach of sorrow."

We drove away from the church. An endless line of cars followed the hearse through the streets. We paused at Brent's home. The funeral director carried a bouquet of flowers and placed them beside the door. The mother disembarked from the family car. She walked to the hearse, placed her hand on the back of the vehicle, bent her head forward to the glass window, and quietly wept.

The casket was placed at the open gravesite. Again, I uttered brief remarks. I called attention to the huge gathering, especially of young people, and I sought to console the parents by saying, "It is a show of love that these young people have gathered in such great numbers to bid farewell to Brent." I did the committal with the traditional words, "Ashes to ashes, dust to dust." The sad ritual of the grave diggers commenced. The casket was lowered into the ground. When the lowering contraption was removed, the green blanket around the casket was neatly folded and tucked away in the truck.

Grandmother Bernadine orchestrated a flower gathering. Each person placed a flower into the gravesite over the casket. Then a small truck with an attached hydraulic shovel full of dirt moved forward to the grave and dumped its load onto the casket. This was done three times until the dirt was a small mound above the grave. The gravediggers with the rakes began to level out the dirt until it was smooth. All the while, Grandmother Bernadine led a medley of songs: "Farther Along," "This Is My Story," and "Going Up Yonder."

When the gravediggers were finished leveling the ground, a long white cross-shaped wreath was placed on the grave. During the whole ritual, sobs and wails could be heard. I was motioned to do the benediction. Afterwards, I went up to the top of the gravesite, where Grandmother Bernadine stood. I embraced her and whispered a prayer. She pointed to a tombstone near the site where Brent had been buried, and she said, "That is my daughter. She was killed in a car accident five years ago."

I looked back as I drove away in the blistering sun. The crowd was still standing, weeping, leaning on each other and drying each other's tears. It seemed as though they had no plans to leave anytime soon.

Damon S. Allen[3]

Sunrise: October 17, 1973
Sunset: September 4, 2006

Eulogizing Damon S. Allen

On the morning of September 4, 2006, Damon S. Allen, a sanitation worker once cited for his heroism in saving a child's life from a burning building, was killed by stray bullets. I officiated the wake at the Frank R. Bell Funeral Home, and later eulogized him on September 9th, at the Christian Culture Center, where the Rev. A R. Bernard is pastor. The following is my eulogy:

Fellow workers from BK 17 had glowing things to say about Damon when they gathered for the candlelight vigil Debbie Griffith organized in front of his mother's St. Marks Avenue home:
"He was a giver."
"He was a straight-up brother."
"He was a mellow brother."
"He was a true brother."
"He was a hardworking brother."
"He was a non complaining brother, even about the twelve-to-eight shift."
"He was eager to do any job."
"He was happy to be working."
He said, "I never knew garbage could smell so good."
"He was always pleasant."
"He was always humorous, with a peculiar laugh that caused other people to laugh."
"He was always friendly, and we loved him at BK Seventeen."

But they loved him, too, where he lived. He was the DJ man. He was a joy bringer. He was happy to see other people happy. He was the protector, always concerned about other people's well-being. He was a loving, obedient son and grandson. Outside of the door of his mother's home, there sat two boots. They are the boots of a man who respected his mother's home. He would not wear his work shoes inside the house. Even as a big old grown man, he still honored his mother's wishes. He was a loving and caring father. He was Damon S. Allen, born October 17, 1973, and crossed over September 4, 2006.

Yes, he was all the aforementioned, and he was more. He was a hero. Destiny or Deity had so ordered his life that he was always there when he was needed by endangered human beings. About a year ago, as fire raced through an apartment house—a father with his little girl, standing in the window, frantically screaming for help. There stood Damon, yelling to the father, "Let the child go!" He assured the father that his arms were strong enough to catch the child. Damon was right. His arms, like the arms of God that protect us, hold us, embrace us, held fast the child. Yes, he saved the life of a child, and the father, too. For once his child was safe the father navigated himself to safety.

In the early morning hours of September 4th, bullets were sprayed into the street. People scattered for safety. Not Damon. He stood tall, urging everybody to get down. There is something magnificent, heartwarming, as we visualize a man, with a hail of bullets flying around him, resisting the instinctive urge to duck, to get down, and to take care of himself. There he stood, courageous and concerned, driven by a deep urged to ensure the safety of others. There comes to my mind the poem by the English poet Alfred Tennyson, immortalizing.

Charge of the Light Brigade
Cannon to right of them,
Cannon to left of them,
Cannon behind them
Volley'd and thunder'd;
Storm'd at with shot and shell,
While horse and hero fell,
They that had fought so well
Came thro' the jaws of Death,
Back from the mouth of Hell,
All that was left of them,
Left of six hundred.

Another picture comes to my mind—the day President Anwar Sadat, president of Egypt, was killed in Egypt. The shooter saturated the stage where Mister Sadat was seated. Instead of diving for cover, he stood up, straight and tall. And the bullets cut him down.

Yes, the bullets cut down Damon, too. In the mean streets of Brooklyn, before the sun came up, perhaps old Sol couldn't bear to watch. He, Damon S. Allen, stood up, and because he stood up, other people now stand in the land of the living, while he, Damon, lies before us, never to be seen again on this side of history. Yes, he was a hero! He was a man! It could be said of Damon what Mark Anthony said of Brutus in the Shakespearean play Julius Caesar:

"His life was gentle, and the elements so mixed in him that nature might stand up and say to the world 'This was a man!'"

Yes, he was a hero. But what is a hero? From whence do they come? The debate still abounds, whether heroes are born or made. Take it from me, heroes are not born. All living creatures are born. Heroes are made. They are the sum of the many things that shape their lives, especially the teachings of parents, schools, religious institutions, etcetera.

When Damon was ready for school, his mother released him to find the way by himself. She followed from an unobserved distance. She was teaching him to be brave and independent. Then, when he had his first confrontation, his action was a forerunner of how he would behave in the future in the time of crisis. He was just a child when a bully came upon him, took his hat off, and cut it with a razor. He stood face-to-face with the bully. Later, his mother asked him what was the nature of the conversation that he had with the bully? Damon related to her, the bully said, "What are you going to do? And Damon said, "I ain't running."

Heroes don't run. They don't run away from danger. They run to danger, especially when others are in danger. That is the story of Damon's life: "I ain't running."

When people are in trouble, "I ain't running."

When a father and child are threatened by a consuming fire, "I ain't running."

When bullets are flying through the morning air, "I ain't running."

Say to his mother and father and grandmother and grandfather, "Your son, your grandson, was a hero."

Say to his children, "Your father was a hero."

Say to his friends, "Your friend Damon was a hero."

Say to the world, "Your citizen was a hero."

Say to generations yet unborn, "Damon S. Allen was a hero."

Tupac Shakur[4]

Sunrise: June 16, 1971, Harlem, New York

Sunset: September 13, 1996, Las Vegas, Nevada

Who Will Weep for Tupac Shakur?

September brings many significant events. Two of the most memorable were 9/11 and the death of Tupac Shakur on September 13, 1996. When I learned of Tupac's death, I was emotionally devastated, although he had told the world he wouldn't live long. Early in the morning, when I received the call that he was dead, I sat up in my bed and began writing the following:

> *It is now 3:15 a.m., and I am driven to put to paper some thoughts about Tupac Shakur, gone from this life forever—at least, in the flesh. What shall I say of this young man who lived such a flamboyant, violent, tumultuous life, and who died at 25 years old on September 13, 1996?*

Let me speak first to his membership in church. Tupac's mother, Afeni, brought him and his sister to this holy place. The three of them stood right there at the altar and united with this congregation. He was a lad of about ten years. When I asked him what he wanted to be, he replied, "A revolutionary." Needless to say, I was surprised. I ought not to have been. There is a saying concerning "a chip off the old block," or "the twig doesn't fall too far from the tree." Afeni Shakur, who was pregnant with him while incarcerated for allegedly plotting to bomb something, and later found not guilty, was a revolutionary. She was a member of the Black Panther Party, a group of young black men and women who, from 1966 to 1982, created enormous fear between some whites and a certain kind of black person.

Afeni was committed to making things better for the masses. If revolution means complete change, she wanted that. Afeni wanted a complete change for the better, and she thought that could happen with the Black Panthers. Later, she was to fall on hard times, but we are not here to tell her story. We're here to remember Tupac—Tupac the revolutionary. He said, "I want to be a revolutionary," and maybe that explains his life.

He wanted change. I know there are those who will say he went about it the wrong way. But that is not for me to judge. I will leave that to God and others. I confess, I'm not good at that sort of thing. But let us remember, we shall be judged by the judgment we render, says the scriptures, and again, "Let the one who is without sin cast the first stone." Indeed, "The evil that men do lives in them; the good is often interred with their bones," said Shakespeare's Mark Anthony, at the death of Julius Caesar.

To say that Tupac wanted to be a revolutionary—that he wanted to change things—but that he didn't know how, is not harsh. We disagreed with how he went about it, and I think that those of us who loved him, in spite of everything, told him so. And if we would be criticized for that, then criticize God, too, for that is where we learned it. The Bible says, "God so loved the world that he gave His only begotten Son—"

Those of us who loved him can accept the criticism of his method. We wanted better from his behavior and words, and we told him that.

He had such prodigious talent. He was more likeable than he wanted to be. Tupac had such fierce determination. He went from the gutter of extreme poverty and devastating rejection to reach the mountaintop of success.

After he joined the church, he played as any normal child. He laughed. He cried. He played with other children. And then Afeni took him to Baltimore. They told me he did well in school. He was smart. In performing arts school, Tupac was an exceptional student.

After moving out West, they said he hit bottom. He was constantly looking for a place to stay and something to eat. It seemed nobody liked him in those days except his mother, who, as we all know, was struggling with her own problems.

Finally, he made it. He became a star. He was a success.

I would see him from time to time when he would come back to New York. His mother would call me and ask me to talk to him, but those were fleeting, superficial visits. When he was shot, back in 1994, he sent for me. I visited him in Bellevue Hospital. He had just been operated on. His head was bandaged, and he seemed to be semiconscious. I said to him, "Son, I'm going to pray for you, and you are going to be all right." I put my hand on him and prayed for him—a brief prayer—then I departed. When I returned to my church about a half-hour later, I was told that Tupac had gotten up and was gone from the hospital. We were to have many belly laughs about that later.

During the time when he was incarcerated on the sexual assault charge, I visited with him often at Rikers Island—as least once, sometimes two or three times, a week. I went to court with him on the day he was sentenced, and would have spoken on his behalf if I were asked to do so. During those visits, while I was in the private, steeled, enclosed room, we talked about many things and made many plans. At first, he would complain that he was being mistreated. I carried his complaints to the higher authority. Things became better. We talked about religion. I would remind him of his membership and his revolutionary aspiration, and would challenge him to live up to the ideals of those ideologies. I would speak to him of others who used the jail time to produce great goods.

There were times when he seemed depressed, angry with the system. He maintained his innocence, but accepted the fact that he was guilty of other things, and so maybe he was paying for those things. Tupac said he would be and do better. He admitted that his head had not been clear for many years. He was thinking more clearly now, he said.

We talked of plans to help our people, especially our youth. I tried to get a commitment from him to help our prison program. He talked of his plans to have a retreat center in Atlanta where youth would be brought from inner cities, and while there, they would learn a trade, enhance their schoolwork, and would be exposed to celebrities who would come and share their experiences with them.

We talked of his proposed marriage to Jada. He wanted me to do the ceremony. The wedding would be in Atlanta. He had it all planned. We talked about the plays, movies, songs he was writing. Tupac told me of one play in particular. A young man was running away from some men and ran into this house, where he hid out, and on and on it went. When he was through, I said to him, "Why not have the young man go into a church and have a minister help him?" He paused, he thought, he looked at me and said, "That's a good idea. You see, I have to write what I know about, what I have lived. I don't know anything about the church or religion."

To return to religion for a moment, he was confused and troubled by religion. He told me the Muslims were trying to convert him, but he was not moved by their efforts. Tupac couldn't accept Christianity or the Bible, for that was too closely associated with the white man. I remember one visit in particular— he was extremely agitated. He had been humiliated by certain acts of the prison guards. As was my custom, whatever else we discussed, I would bring the conversation back to ideals and challenges of God, religion, and the Bible.

On one occasion he said to me, "Reverend, I don't want to hurt your feelings, and I don't mean any disrespect, but it's hard for me to believe in the same book as the white man. This system that beats you, me, and my people, that does all kinds of evil things all over the world and claims the Bible as its book, how can I believe in the same book?" My response was, "Listen, I know how you feel. I went through the same thing. I have felt the same way."

Maybe that's why I strayed from the church for many years. For all of my youth, in fact, although I came from four generations of black preachers. But when I found the Lord—or when God found me after I hit the bottom—that's when my life changed. I began to study the history of our people and the history of religion. I discovered that the Bible teaches that Blackness is the origin of civilization, that the so-called major Western religions, including Judaism, Islam, and Christianity, have Black roots, and that Christianity was shaped and influenced by African people.

I continued with my history lesson of African people and religion. I said, one of the reasons that I believed God saved me was to send me on this mission to teach our people that the Bible and

Christianity have African roots, and to encourage the struggle for human rights and self-determination, especially for oppressed people. When I finished, he stared at the floor for a long time. He looked at me and said, "I didn't know that, Reverend." I said, "I know. This truth has been kept from us by both white folks and Blacks who benefitted from our ignorance."

On one occasion, he told me something startling that revealed his toughness, tenacity, his fierce determination, and his intuitiveness. He said, when he wanted to achieve something, he would find a picture of the thing desired or draw a picture. Then he would put this picture on the wall over his bed, and he would stare at the picture long and often. He would not sleep in the bed until he had achieved his goal. Now we know why he rose like the Phoenix Bird of Greek mythology, from the ashes, to soar to dazzling heights.

I will weep for Tupac, and I will weep for all the rebels—some we like, and some we don't. I will weep for Malcolm and Martin. Yes, and I will weep for this society, too, for all of us. And if we can't weep for Tupac, let us weep for ourselves, for our society, for what we are, that we have not prepared a better society for all our children.

Endnotes

1   This is a version of an article that originally appeared in the July 16–18, 2010 weekend edition of *The Daily Challenge*, published in Brooklyn, New York. Mr. Thomas Watkins, publisher.

2   This is a version of an article that originally appeared in the July 30–August 1, 2010 weekend edition of

   The Daily Challenge, published in Brooklyn, New York. Mr. Thomas Watkins, publisher.

3   This is a version of an article that originally appeared in the September 13, 2006, edition of

   The Daily Challenge newspaper, published in Brooklyn, New York, Mr. Thomas Watkins, publisher.

4   This is a version of an article that originally appeared in the September 10–12, 2004 weekend edition of

   The Daily Challenge, published in Brooklyn, New York. Mr. Thomas Watkins, publisher. It includes excerpts from the author's book, *Dear 2Pac: Letters to a Son.*

7

Parishioners

Deacon Betty Brazell[1]

Sunset: September 10, 2006

The Passing of Two GiantsDeacon Betty Brazell and Mr. Oswald Thompson

On September 10, 2006, Deacon Betty Brazell made her transition. She was sixty-eight years old. Her name may not be as recognizable as some of the giants about which I have written. But her family, friends, and especially her church, know she was a giant of the human spirit.

Those who were around during the welfare rights and community control of school struggles will probably remember her. Ms. Brazell, along with women like Helen Marshall, Georgia Ware, and Mae Mallory, were in the thick of those battles and other efforts to make Brooklyn, particularly Black Brooklyn, a better place.

She is best remembered in the church world. In our church, The House of the Lord, she was everything. She served faithfully for thirty-five years, holding many titles and performing many tasks.

She was funeralized at The House of the Lord Church September 15, 2006. In my eulogy, I said:

She was there for everybody, and she made everybody feel special.... She had the answer to every question, the solution to every problem. She was the original magic woman. Mysteriously, what was not there, she could suddenly make it appear.... Yes, she was always there for us. She was always worrying about us. She seemed to love us more than she loved herself. She would do for us when she would not or could not do for herself.

She was a wounded healer—hurting and healing. And that, I submit to you, is one of the qualities that makes us most like Jesus the Christ. To heal while hurting, to touch others when we need a touch, to feed when we are hungry, to give drink when we are thirsty, to comfort when we need comforting are the attributes of Deity.

She exemplified Saint Francis Assisi's prayer:
Lord, make me an instrument of Your peace.
Where there is hatred, let me sow love.
Where there is injury, pardon,
Where there is doubt, faith,
Where there is despair, hope,
Where there is darkness, light,
and where there is sadness, joy.
O Divine Master, grant that I may not so much
seek to be consoled, as to console;
To be understood, as to understand;
To be loved, as to love;
For it is in giving that we receive,
It is in pardoning that we are pardoned
And it is in dying that we are born to eternal life.

Alas! Betty Brazell is gone now, but will never be forgotten. We will remember her in our memory, in our ceremonies of remembrance, and in our churches. We will have sorrow and joy. Sorrow because we will miss her, but joy because we will see her again—on that day that God brings all things to perfection.

Eloise McConnell Rabb

No Time To Mourn

On December 4, 2009, Eloise McConnell Rabb made her transition. She was a member of my church for nearly fifty years. Her death was sandwiched between so many pressing obligations—a press conference announcing Charles Barron's run for City Council Speaker, mentoring engagements, a meeting of Governor David Paterson's task force on police shootings, and a meeting on immigration reform. Such is the life of an activist pastor. It seemed there was no time for mourning. But on December 9, 2009, my wife and I caught the 10:00 a.m. US Air flight to Columbia, South Carolina, the home of Sister McConnell. The rest of the day was spent conferring and counseling with family members. The wake was in the evening.

December 10, 2009, we funeralized Sister McConnell at Reid Chapel African Methodist Episcopal Church. The program lasted over four hours, and reminded me of the funeral for Coretta Scott King in Atlanta, Georgia. Sister McConnell wanted a long program; she got her wish. From the church, we carried her to the family burial ground in Jenkinsville, South Carolina.

Thus, the death of my long-time member was sandwiched between a myriad of demands, but through it all, day and night, no matter what the involvement, I could not get Sister McConnell off of my mind. I reckoned my involvement was a kind of blessing in disguise. I really didn't have time to seriously mourn. Perhaps it will all come down on me later.

I would like to share with my readers the eulogy of a magnificent, magnanimous woman. I do so to express my profound gratitude to Mrs. Eloise McConnell Rabb and the entire family. The least I can do is perpetuate her memory in this eulogy.

My Eulogy for Sis. McConnell[2]

She was ready. That is what Sister McConnell said when Old Death came a-creeping in her bedroom. She said, "I am ready." She had made her plans. She told us what she wanted, how she wanted her homegoing to be. She was ready. That's my subject. That's what I want to talk about. It sums up my theme, and it sums up her life. She was ready.

Turn to your neighbor and ask him or her, "Are you ready?"

Readiness is a word that brings excitement and anticipation and joy. Whenever you are ready for whatever awaits, you are filled with eagerness and gladness. It means you have done all you could to prepare for whatever awaits. So when time comes to make the ultimate transition, to leave behind loving family and friends, and to go meet our Maker, if we have prepared, if our lives are in order, we should be able to say, "I'm ready."

There is another aspect of readiness: It brings joy to the heart of the prepared person—and it brings joy to the hearts of loved ones. When parents know their children are ready for the tests of school and life, they sleep at night. We come again to this sad and joyful time. Sad, because a loved one has been taken—no, not taken, but is gone from us. She left because she wanted to leave. She left because she wanted to go. She was ready. Nevertheless, it is a sad and joyful time because she has left us. It is joyful because of where she has gone.

The Bible says, "I would that you sorrow not as others who have no hope." Yes, it's all right to cry. But remember, beyond the tears, there is heaven, where the wicked cease from troubling, and the weary are at rest.

The Bible tells us that "the eye has not seen, and the ear has not heard, neither has entered the hearts of man, the beautiful things which God has prepared for them that love Him." Jesus said to His disciples, "Ye therefore have sorrow, but I will see you again." While we weep and mourn, we can still say, triumphantly, "Oh, death, where is thou sting? O grave, where is thy victory?"

Our Lord Jesus Christ has gone and prepared a place for us that where He is, there we will be also. How many more of these occasions we will have to attend before they come for us? And on that day, we shall not ask for whom the bell tolls, for the bells will be tolling for us. Aging ones whose sun is sinking ever so rapidly, we remember the lines from the poem "Childe Harold's Pilgrimage," by Lord Byron:

What is the worst of woes that wait on age? What stamps the wrinkle deeper on the brow? To view each loved one blotted from life's page.

Every blot leaves a scar. Tears and time will bring some healing. Faith and hope will bring some comfort. The rolling years will bring some sweetness of memories. But the scar tissue will always remain until they come for us, until the glad day of reunion beyond the clouds.

It seems but yesterday we were here, in this church, for Baby Joe, Sister McConnell's first born. We cannot escape the question, "Who shall they come for next?" We need not fear dread, or even try to circumvent or hide from the inevitable. For whether it is good or bad depends on how we live. If we have lived our lives according to the scripture, we have nothing to fear, neither on earth nor in heaven.

When the Greek philosopher Socrates was condemned to death by drinking hemlock poison, he gathered his students and friends around him. He was accused of importing an alien philosophy and corrupting the youth. It is true he imported his philosophy from Africa, as did most of the Greek scholars and thinkers. As he breathed his last breath, they heard him whisper, "A good man has nothing to fear in this life nor in the one to come."

Who lies before us on this afternoon on the fourth of December in the year 2009, so cold, so stiff, so lifeless? Who lies before us is not what you see—this physical, material body is not who lies before us. What we see is the tabernacle of clay that housed who it was, who lived amongst us, and who now has gone beyond us, but who is and will always be present among us. Her body may be there, but her spirit lives on. Soon, we will put this body into the ground, but no grave can keep it there.

Who lies before us? Way back on August 5, 1922, her parents named her Eloise. Yes, that's what they named her, but who was Eloise? She was a wife, mother, grandmother, aunt, cousin, co-

worker, neighbor, friend, and member of The House of the Lord Church. All these she was, and more.

Let me tell you how I came to know Sister Eloise McConnell Rabb. Over forty-five years ago, in addition to my pastoral duties, I was on the evangelistic trail. I had just concluded a revival at a church in Montclair, New Jersey. As I came out of the door and headed toward my car, a young woman stopped me and asked me if I would visit her sister in the hospital in Brooklyn, New York, where my church was. The following Sunday, after service, I went to the hospital. Crowded around the bed of Maxine, the young woman's sister, were family members, and among them was Sister Eloise. I continued to visit the hospital frequently. When Maxine went home, we started having Bible classes in her home. When Maxine died, we came to Jenkinsville for the funeral and burial.

The Bible studies continued. We moved to different homes: Eloise on Park Place; Leone and Jerry de Lima, a sister and brother-in-law, in the Thompkins Housing Development; and Tee and Roger Turner, a sister and brother-in-law. From these Bible studies, Roger became a preacher and then a pastor at Victory Baptist Church on Howard Avenue in Brooklyn. Their daughter Cookie became a minister, too. Eloise and family, including her three daughters Yvonne, Barbara, and Sandra, became members of my church. And not just members, but the bedrock of our church. It is hard for me to think of The House of the Lord Church apart from the McConnell family in general, and Sister Eloise McConnell Rabb in particular. She was there in every capacity. Wherever the church needed her, she was there. She was there through all the trials and tribulations of our early church years:

She was there when we started our choir. Her children, especially Sandra, were the voices of angels. They helped to make the music of our church.

She was there when we started our day care center, which has grown to three. We have achieved national accreditation under the leadership of Dr. Karen Daughtry.

She was there in the marches and demonstrations and boycotts for our social, economic, and political justice, which made our church different. Through our church, she was a part of the Civil Rights Movement, the Black Power and the African Liberation movements. And she was there for the movement of political empowerment. In a word, she was a part of the struggle for human rights and self-determination for all people.

She was there when members were sick, lonely, hospitalized, and homebound.

She was there when we needed hospitality. And she seemed to always be there with her special culinary skills.

She was there when the children cried, when they were christened and baptized.

And she was there when members died. She was at the burial ground when the bodies were lowered into the earth.

Yes, she was there for the weddings, the banquets, the birthday parties, the fellowship times, the Sunday dinners after service in the Fellowship Hall, and coffee and cake around the kitchen table, picnics in parks, and backyard cook-outs.

She was there for anniversaries, conventions, conferences, and celebrations for one thing or another.

She was there for workshops and seminars, and the long bus rides to Georgia for the annual memorial ceremonies.

She was there for the hallelujah times we had at other churches, and the shouting, singing, jumping, running, crazy Holy Ghost services at 415 Atlantic Avenue.

She was always there for everybody and everything—gentle, kind, caring, smiling, all-embracing. I wonder sometimes if we were there for her as she was there for us. God knows.

No, there was no way we could match her tenderness, compassion, sensitivity, self-giving, and her concern for others. The truth is, I don't know how many of us really tried to be like her, or were even grateful to her for who she was and what she did for all of us. We were too caught up in our own worlds. Too enthralled with our own needs and desires. Too self-absorbed. Lord, forgive us.

The Challenge of Leadership [3]

Leadership is a towering challenge. With the exception of, maybe the president of the United States, pastoral leadership tops the list, and even here we face some of the same challenges. The major difference is the pastor deals with eternal realities that reach beyond the grave, death, and dramatic earth changes.

The challenges we, as pastors, face are the stuff of everyday life and must be encountered by all who still hold membership in the human race. However, I believe that the most difficult of all the challenges we must bear are the frailties of human beings: the betrayal of trust; the summertime friendships; vocal supporters who love you today and hate you tomorrow; gossipers, backbiters, liars, infiltrators, Judases, murderers of character. All these are among the professed supporters, friends, and yes, even family members whom we meet as we attempt to do the ministry to which God has called us.

I often wondered why Jesus would even receive the adulation of the crowd, with their palms and branches, knowing that in a week they would join the crowd crying, "Crucify him." I've come to believe that Jesus was teaching us a lesson: to not be overwhelmed by the adulation of the crowd. Yes, Jesus had his Judas, Caesar had his Brutus, and Othello had his Iago. And every pastor has, among his or her flock, wolves in sheep's clothing.

But eternal thanks to God, who does not leave us alone. God is always with us.

And God does not leave us without faithful supporters. God knows that while we trust Him, it is so comforting and encouraging to have humans with us, too.

I count myself to have been exceedingly blessed to have friends who "sticketh closer than a brother," rare, special people who were sent by God to perform special services at special moments of history. For God has blessed me with the likes of Minister Josephine Madison, Deacon Betty Brazell, Deacon Leroy Applin, and now, Sister Eloise McConnell Rabb.

Across four generations of terrifying tragedies, painful illnesses, and untimely deaths, Sister McConnell never changed. She remained gentle, caring, loving, self-giving, and she remained the rock for the family and for the church. She was the grandmother, the mother, the aunt, the friend, the superlative parishioner to us all. I watched and prayed with her as we carried her mother and father to the burial ground; when she buried one husband and then another; when sisters Maxine and Jerry made their transition; when her children Yvonne, Barbara, Sondra, and Baby Joe, and granddaughter Zakiya, went the way of all flesh.

Through it all, Sister McConnell never lost her composure or her concern for others. If you didn't know her, you would think she didn't have a care in the world. Her smile and friendliness never left her. She was Christ-like—a wounded healer, hurting and helping. A nurse with a bleeding heart, broken and mending, crying on the inside and bringing laughter on the outside. And now she's gone.

But is she really gone? What's gone? The body? The body has been going from the day of its birth. We started dying when we are born. What remains?

Memory and spirit.

We should keep her name ever before us. There is an African proverb that goes, "As long as a loved one's name is mentioned in the village, they never die." Yes, God called her home. The body, the flesh, we will put beneath the soil, but her spirit will live on.

We tried so hard to keep her here. We prayed. We fasted. We prepared health programs, but to no avail. Her time had come. She was ready.

We must let her go. She is where she longed to be. The reunion has begun with her mother and father, children and grandchildren, and sisters.

Who would bring her back? Who here would say, "Come back to the trials and tribulations of this life"? To the pain and sickness, hospital beds and doctors, tubes and medicine? Who here would say, "Come back," if we truly believe she's in a better place? If we truly believe she's with the Almighty and her loved ones? And if we say we would bring her back, who are we bringing her back for? For ourselves. Surely not for her. Who here would be so selfish as to say," Come back because I need you?" Nay, but let her go. She has been around for us for so many years. It's time to let her go.

Let us remember that we weep not for Sister McConnell; we weep for ourselves. She's in a better place, but we must go on facing the challenges of life without her physical presence. Now let us say, "Farewell, Grandmamma, Mama, Auntie, Cousin, Friend, Parishioner. We would not bring you back, even if we could, but we will see you one day."

Let us go forth from this holy place, to the burial ground, return the body to the soil from which it came. And when the day is done, let us look back and remember the good times and cherish the sweet, delightful memories. Be grateful for the years she sojourned with us. Be grateful that God gave her to us, and be grateful for what she gave to us.

Then, looking forward, let us remember our day will come, too. So let us live our lives that we might land where she is, where the final reunion will be consummated. There will be no more tears, no more pain, no more parting of the ways. For the former things will have passed away; all things will be made new, and God the Father, Jesus Christ the Son, will reign forever and forever. Hallelujah!

Endnotes

1   This is a version of an article that originally appeared in the September 20, 2006 edition of *The Daily Challenge*, published in Brooklyn, New York. Mr. Thomas Watkins, publisher.

2   This is a version of an article that originally appeared in the January 6, 2010 edition of *The Daily Challenge*, published in Brooklyn, New

York. Mr. Thomas Watkins, publisher.

3   This is a version of an article that originally appeared in the January 8–10, 2010 weekend edition of *The Daily Challenge*, published in Brooklyn, New York. Mr. Thomas Watkins, publisher.

8

Politicians

Geraldine Anne Ferraro[1]

Sunrise: August 26, 1935, Newburgh, New York
Sunset: March 26, 2011, Boston, Massachusetts

The First Female Vice Presidential Candidate

I first met the Honorable Geraldine Anne Ferraro at the conclusion of the Democratic Convention in San Francisco, California, in August 1984. The Rev. Jesse Jackson had captured the imagination of people of African ancestry, other minorities, and the youth in his run for the presidency of the United States of America. Preceding the convention, thunderous cries of "Run, Jesse, run!" had followed his campaign across the country.

That historic campaign started earlier. In October 1983, New York City councilman Al Vann (who was a New York State assemblyman at the time, and one of the most powerful politicos in New York) and I (then-chairman of the National Black United Front, the most potent and influential mass-based, independent, pan-Africanist organization) pulled together top-ranking black leaders and met with Rev. Jesse Jackson at The House of the Lord Church.

"I don't want 'Run, Jesse, run!' to become 'See Jesse run!'" Rev. Jackson said to us. "If I am going to run, I need three things: the masses, the money, and the machinery."

And he did run! It was one of the most important runs for the presidency of the United States of America by any African American up to that point. Other African Americans, such as Shirley Chisholm—the first Black woman elected to the US Congress—also ran for presidency, but no one came close to having a similar impact as the Rev. Jesse Jackson.

Rev. Jackson has not received the credit due to him for making the contributions he has made to Black progress, especially in the political arena. Somewhere in the distant future, truth will get a hearing, and the story of his contribution will be told. It will become indisputable that President Barack Obama was a direct beneficiary of Rev. Jackson's remarkable campaign.[2]

At the aforementioned convention, Walter Frederick Mondale, the former Senator from Minnesota, won the nomination to be the Democratic Party's standard bearer for president. He picked New York congresswoman Geraldine Ferraro as his running mate. It was the first time a woman had been given the honor. It didn't help. He lost forty-nine of the fifty states to Ronald Reagan.

Among African Americans, there was widespread controversy as to whether they got all that they deserved. There were criticisms of Coretta Scott King, the wife of Dr. Martin Luther King, Jr.; and Andrew Young, the former US Ambassador and aide to Dr. King. Both had supported Mr. Mondale and Rev. Jackson. It was heartbreaking to hear and see Mrs. King and Mr. Young booed by the people of African ancestry. Black people had invested so much in Rev. Jackson's campaign. Their expectations were riding high, and to come away empty-handed, as many perceived it to be, was painfully frustrating.

At the last meeting of people of African ancestry at the Democratic Convention, Rev. Jackson announced that he would be meeting Mr. Mondale. This implied that he would be negotiating our piece of the action. Rev. Jackson chose four of us to accompany him to the meeting: Ronald Vernie "Ron" Dellums, the former US congressman from California; Walter Edward Fauntroy, the former US congressman from Washington, D.C., and aide to Dr. Martin Luther King Jr.; Maxine Waters, the US congresswoman from California; and me.

When we arrived at the presidential suite at the hotel, Mr. Mondale came out to greet us. He was all aglow. Fresh from his victory at the Convention, he enthusiastically shook our hands. Rev. Jackson and Mr. Mondale retired to another room. All of us were disappointed that we were not invited to attend the meeting, but no one said a word. After about thirty minutes, Mr. Dellums expressed his concern that the meeting was lasting too long, and that we were still waiting outside. He said, "I am uncomfortable waiting outside of the meeting. This is not good." All of us nodded in agreement.

After about forty-five minutes, Jesse returned from the meeting. As we were getting ready to depart, Geraldine Anne Ferraro came out of the room to greet us. I wasn't sure if she was in the Mondale-Jackson meeting.

A Fantastic Ferraro[3]

Ms. Ferraro was all smiles as she embraced everyone. "This is a tough lady," I said to myself, as I scrutinized her demeanor. Her attractive face couldn't mask the ruggedness and the steel in her eyes. She was very pleasant, but beneath the gentility, it was obvious that we were in the presence of a smart and tough woman who could hold her own in any circle.

As we discussed the political landscape and evaluated the Democratic Party's chances of winning, I was impressed with her knowledge on a wide range of subjects, and her honesty regarding the Democratic Party's chances of winning. She admitted it was going to be an uphill battle, but she was confident that the Democrats would be victorious. She was also candid about the opposition she would encounter as a woman, but then again, she was confident that she could handle it.

We wished her much success. I never got a chance to meet Ms. Ferraro again. As I studied her from a distance, my first impression proved to be accurate. She was sharp, intelligent, tireless, and articulate.

She made a favorable impression on all of us. We promised to be supportive, but we thought Rev. Jackson should have been chosen to be the vice presidential candidate. He had run a superb race. He brought a multitude of new voters into the Democratic Party. He generated great excitement. Again, we resigned ourselves that this was America, and racism still ruled. Looking back, Walter F. Mondale could not have done any worse with Rev. Jackson. On Election Day, voters went for the Republican ticket: 59 to 41 percent, including 55 percent of the female voters. The 525–13 Electoral College win was the largest margin in US history.

In the 2008 election, Ms. Ferraro was a senior fundraiser in Hillary Clinton's campaign for the Democratic presidential nomination. She was forced to resign after being quoted as saying that President Barack Obama's popularity was attributed to the media's infatuation with the idea of a Black man running for high office. "If he was a woman—of any color—he would not be in this position," Ms. Ferraro said.

Ms. Ferraro was born in Newburgh, New York, where her father ran a restaurant and a bar called the Roxy Club. Before she reached the age of ten years, her father died of a heart attack. He was indicted for running a numbers racket. The family relocated to the Bronx in New York City, where Ms. Ferraro's mother worked as a seamstress, sewing beads and sequins on fancy dresses.

During her school days, Ms. Ferraro skipped grades, and she attended college on a scholarship. She studied law at night, and she was an elementary school teacher during the day. She married John Zaccaro, a real estate agent. She raised three children in Kew Gardens, Queens, while she practiced law part-time. In 1974, she was sworn in as an assistant district attorney in the Queens County District Attorney's Office. In Congress, she was a protégé of former Speaker of the House Tip O'Neill. This association surely played a significant part in landing her the vice presidency candidacy.

In 2008, she was supportive of Sarah Palin, who was selected to be the vice presidential candidate by Sen. John McCain, the Republican presidential candidate. On NBC's Today Show, Ms. Ferraro said of Ms. Palin, "I want her to do well. I think it's important for little girls to see someone who can stand toe-to-toe with a guy who has been in the Senate for thirty-eight years, and run for vice president." Significantly, she could understand the inspiration that Ms. Palin's presence provided for little girls, but she could not understand the inspiration Mr. Obama supplied for little Black children—indeed, all children. However, Ms. Ferraro did support Mr. Obama after the primary.

Ms. Ferraro died on Saturday, March 26, 2011, at the age of seventy-five, after years of suffering multiple myeloma.

Maurice Bishop[4]

Sunrise: May 29, 1944, Aruba, Netherlands Antilles
Sunset: October 19, 1983, Saint George's, Grenada

Remembering Maurice Bishop

The December 24, 2008, *Caribbean Life* newspaper carried a front-page story on Maurice Bishop, former Prime Minister of Grenada, whose killers were scheduled to be released. On December 18, 2008, at the recommendation of the Grenada Mercy Committee, Governor General Carlyle Glean authorized the release of three former associates of Mr. Bishop. These three persons were among a group of seventeen imprisoned in 1983, for the murder of Mr. Bishop and several members of his cabinet who were killed October 19, 1983.

The recommendation to Mr. Glean asked him to forgo the balance of the sentences of Hudson Austin, Colville McBarnette, and John Ventour. In 2006, Andy Mitchell, Vincent Joseph, and Cosmos Richardson were released after spending twenty-three years in prison for firing the fatal shots at Mr. Bishop. In 2000, Ms. Phyllis Coard, the only female member of the group, was released on medical grounds. She is the wife of Deputy Prime Minister Bernard Coard, the alleged mastermind behind the coup. In 2007, three other members of the "Grenada 17"—Lester Redhead, Christopher Stroude, and Cecil Prime—were released from Richmond Hill Prison in Saint George's, Grenada. The other seven members of the assassin group, including Bernard Coard,[6] were scheduled for release in 2010.

Mr. Austin, the former Army general who led the People's Revolutionary Army, is quoted as saying, "I am happy to be out. I'm looking forward to going home to my family to straighten out some things, like the complete rebuilding of my home." Ventour, who was diagnosed with prostate cancer in January 2001, said prison had changed his life. He said, "You can imagine how overwhelmed I am." He said that day was "undoubtedly, the darkest day in the history of Grenada," referring to the day of the assignments. He was very remorseful as he spoke.

I will always remember the moment when I got the news that Mr. Bishop and members of his administration had been killed in an attempted coup led by Bernard Coard. It was in the early morning hours when I received the call. I kept trying to unravel and make sense of the information. Was I dreaming? Surely it was a nightmare. I thought if I returned to sleep, in the morning I would awaken to the reality that Mr. Bishop and his associates were intact. This was all a bad dream. Sadly, tragically, it was all too real.

My relationship with Mr. Bishop and members of his government, including Mr. Coard, went back to 1979. In March of that year, Mr. Bishop, who headed the New Jewel Movement, succeeded in taking power from Eric Gairy. During this time, I was chair of the Metropolitan Black United Front (BUF). In June 1980, we convened a National Conference in Brooklyn, where the National Black United Front (NBUF) was formed. I was voted chairman. Jitu Weusi was appointed chief of operations. Adeyemi Bandele was appointed director of international affairs. It was he who suggested to me that the NBUF should send a communiqué to the US government, urging recognition of the New Jewel Movement as the legitimate government of Grenada. In March 1980, we were invited to the New Jewel Movement's first anniversary commemoration. We were given royal treatment and spent considerable time with most of the leaders of the new government, the people of Grenada, and other world leaders. We were very proud that at the ceremony held in the Queen's Park stadium, our NBUF banner was hung conspicuously across the gigantic score board, clearly visible near and far. In fact, it was photographed and appeared in some of the media.

Our friendship with the leaders deepened as we occasionally visited Grenada. We made it our oasis. It was such a beautiful, restful island with friendly, wonderful people. We were always given red-carpet treatment. In the United States, we enjoyed the same genuine friendship with Grenada Ambassadors Dessima Williams, Caldwell Taylor, and Kendrick Radix.

New York City councilman Charles Barron, who was our church's youth leader at the time, led a delegation of our youth, including my two daughters, Sharon and Dawn, to Grenada, where they met with Mr. Bishop. He fondly remembers the prime minister taking time from his demanding schedule to meet with the delegation in Carifta Cottages where they were staying. Mr. Bishop spent forty-five minutes with the delegation, cordially interacting with them and patiently answering their questions.

I remember one particular call I received from Mr. Bishop. He was deeply concerned that the United States was going to invade Grenada. Tension between the two countries had grown progressively worse. The Reagan administration thought that the Grenadian government was too cozy with some US government enemies, and claimed that they showed signs of "leftist leanings." The US Government also believed the Grenadian International Airport was primarily being built for military purposes, and would be used by US adversaries. It meant nothing to the Reagan administration that Grenada had only a small airport, which did not accommodate large aircrafts. Grenadian leadership had entertained plans to build an airport large enough to handle all kinds of air transportation prior to Mr. Bishop taking office. The plans for the new airport were in keeping with the growth of the island as envisioned by the people of Grenada. So it is no wonder that rumors began to circulate that President Ronald Reagan was looking for a pretext to invade the island.

The US Army was conducting maneuvers on a small island named Vieques that bore striking similarities to Grenada. Eventually, during the coup, Mr. Reagan did invade Grenada on the pretext of protecting US students. There was, however, never any evidence that the students were endangered. In fact, they were enjoying themselves and were in no way affected by what was happening in the country. After the US invaded, they discovered some old unused rifles in a warehouse, and Mr. Reagan announced to the world that the US Army had arrived just in time.

After receiving that call from Mr. Bishop, I began to campaign, traveling across the country, informing the world of the possibility and likelihood of an invasion of Grenada. Several months before the coup and the invasion, I organized a congregational delegation to visit Grenada with the leadership. During our visit, we met with Bernard Coard. We had our usual, friendly time. He was always jovial. My interaction with Mr. Bishop was serious and business-like most of the time. During this time, Mr. Coard was very profuse in his praise of Mr. Bishop. He spoke of their long friendship and the time they had spent together in the United States, studying the Civil Rights Movement. Never in a thousand years would I have suspected that there was any animosity, or even distance, between the two men. On the contrary, all outward signs confirmed a friendly, mutual admiration.

We also had a memorable meeting with Jacqueline Creft during this visit. She was reported to be the lady friend of the divorced prime minister. Ms. Creft was responsible for education on the island. As she elaborated on the success they were having, I said, "Wow, you all are really doing great work! Let me give you a big hug." We threw our arms around each other, smiling and laughing to the delight of all who were present. It was a proud moment, and I will always remember it. In fact, I have a photo of that moment, including our embrace.

Ms. Creft was representative of the intelligence, commitment, and excitement of these young revolutionaries who were determined to create a model of government in Grenada with the people, by the people and for the people.

On one occasion, we had visited the island with the intention of meeting with Mr. Bishop. However, because of emergencies, the meeting could not take place. While we waited at the airport, preparing to return home, there was a sudden stirring, which always meant a VIP—usually a government official—was in the vicinity. Sure enough, it was Deputy Prime Minister Bernard Coard, with his entourage. He was concerned that we were disappointed about not meeting with the prime minister. He wanted to make sure we were all right, and that we understood what had prevented the meeting.

Now, a phone call early in the morning was telling me that all this had been destroyed—not from afar ,but from within.

Ronald Reagan

Sunrise: February 6, 1911, Tampico, Illinois
Sunset: June 5, 2004, Los Angeles, California

Reagan Passes On

When I arrived in Augusta, June 5, 2004, I learned that Ronald Reagan had died. It was a Saturday, and all day the media was consumed with the life and times of Ronald Reagan. Significantly, throughout the day, and even up to Monday, June 7, I saw only three black persons interviewed. US Secretary of State Colin Powell, and a woman from the Hoover Institute, both had nice things to say about Reagan. Powell was Reagan's National Security Advisor from 1987 to 1989. The third person was Jesse Jackson. Jackson explained how Reagan related to the idea of him going to Syria to free Lieutenant Goodman. (I missed that trip, but I was in Washington, DC, when his delegation returned.) When the reporter asked Jackson for his personal opinion of Reagan, he said they had different points of view. He was trying to be nice and tell the truth at the same time. He pointed out that Reagan went to Philadelphia, Mississippi, where civil rights workers Andrew Goodman, James Chaney, and Michael Schwerner were killed during the Freedom Summer campaign in 1964. Reagan also paid a ceremonial visit to the military cemetery in Bitburg, where Nazi's were buried, during his 1985 trip to Germany.

Reagan opposed civil rights. Jesse put Reagan in perspective. Truly, Reagan was not our president; he was president of Euro-ethnics. He was given credit for what came to be called the Reagan Revolution. Yes, it was a revolution, but going in the wrong direction: backward. He moved the nation back toward its slavery, segregation, racist, lynching, and terrorist past.

When he became president, every negative element that had been driven back into the shadowy cages of America came crawling out. No, he wasn't a man who inspired the best in America, contrary to the popular notion. If there is any doubt, one need only look at his record and the people who were his closest friends and the causes he supported. The record is stark and unmistakable.

The biblical way of judging greatness is through the eyes of the oppressed, the excluded, the exploited, those at the bottom of the social ladder. That is the way God judges greatness. It is not just what you do for your own kind, the elite or the upper classes, or the powerful, but what you do for members of the outcasts, the least in society.

When we judge Reagan by God's standard, his presidency leaves much to be desired. He is weighed in the balance and found wanting.

I landed back in Newark, New Jersey on June 9, 2004, at 8:30 p.m. It had been eight days since I started this autobiographical sketch. It has been a fascinating and instructive experience, even in writing an abbreviated edition. Former president Bill Clinton said in reference to writing his autobiography: "It was a great experience. Digging into one's past gives new insights into one's life and times. Everybody should write an autobiography." Amen.

Senator "Ted" Edward Moore Kennedy[6]

Sunrise: February 22, 1932, Boston, Massachusetts
Sunset: August 25, 2009, Barnstable, Massachusetts

It was 6:38 a.m. when I learned Senator Ted Kennedy had passed. Returning from the beach at one of my favorite getaway places, I paused in the reception area to pick up a bottle of water, and there it was on CNN. I moved closer to the television, mumbling—or more accurately, mourning. My eyes had not deceived me: Ted Kennedy was dead.

I'm a year older than him, and I'm still here, I thought. Many friends, associates, relatives, and enemies of my generation are gone or in a deteriorated physical, mental, or emotional state. I had been up since 4:30 a.m., stretching, walking, running, praying, meditating, and swimming, feeling healthy, vibrant, and euphoric. I breathed a prayer of gratitude. Twenty-five years ago, I heard the voice of God direct me to change my eating habits and overall unhealthy lifestyle. I became a vegan. And after having serious bouts with urinary tract, heart, and prostate, I'm certain it was my vegan lifestyle and the grace of God that has kept me alive.

As I walked to our rooms, I tried to compare my sadness with the sadness I felt when Teddy's brothers were assassinated—Jack in 1963, and Bobby in June 1968. To the best of my recollection, my sadness for them in no way compared to what I felt for Ted Kennedy. I wondered why? Maybe I'm older now, and I know more about Teddy. Maybe I had interacted with Teddy in some way, either in person or on issues we both cared about. Maybe it was because he was around longer. He had been in the Senate forty-seven years, almost as long as his brothers had lived—Bobby was forty-two, Jack was forty-six. Whatever the reasons, I felt a deep sadness, not just for Teddy, but for the entire Kennedy family. They had given so much to this country and had suffered so much. In the last half-century, the Kennedy family and America seemed so intertwine, it's hard to think of one without the other. Rarely has a wealthy family involved itself in public service with a particular concern for the poor and disadvantage as has the Kennedy family. I felt something else too: that in some strange way, I had lost something with this passing. That a part of my history was gone, too.

I debated whether to tell my wife. I waited a while, walking around aimlessly. Then, when she was awake and able to grasp the news, I conveyed sad information.

"Oh, no!" she said. Shaking her head, she sat up in bed, located the remote control, and flipped on the television as if she needed to hear it for herself. She saw what I had seen earlier. But by now, more information was coming forth regarding his death and his life, with an announcement that coverage would be provided throughout the day with a special program: "Ted Kennedy in His Own Words" for the evening. How are they able to put together so much information in such a short time? Then I remembered, they had been preparing for this day since the announcement that the Senator had brain cancer.

At the height of Jesse Jackson's presidential run, a Black reporter explained to me that the media's extensive coverage of the campaign was, in part, an effort to be ready should one of the many known threats against his life actually happen. I felt piqued as I pondered that the media had already prepared for Jesse's assassination. It seemed so cold and callous. But the media is the media, and the media has to survive, too, in this capitalistic society by beating the competition by saying, "We have an exclusive," or "You heard it here first," or "We have the most extensive coverage."

For the next several days, true to the television announcers' words, there was all-day coverage. Every aspect of the senator's life was reviewed—the good and the bad, the beautiful and the ugly. All of it was laid bare. There were interviews with every conceivable personality—the rich and the poor, the high and the low. Every nationality, religious and political ideology was represented.

I remembered something Bishop F.D. Washington, High Prelate of the Churches of God in Christ, once said, "People lie on you when you're alive, and lie for you when you're dead." I want to offer a slight change: "People lie to you when you're alive, and make up lies for you and their relationship with you, when you're dead."

A Beloved Senator [7]

I really liked the senator. Not just for what he did, but who he was. I didn't really know him, was never close to him, but there was something about him that I liked. He gave me a good feeling when I saw him, especially in his later years. This is not to suggest that he was perfect, or that his relationship with people of African ancestry was impeccable. No. Indeed, he was all too human. As I thought about his life and times and my reasons for my affections, there were eight characteristics that came to my mind.

1. **His commitment to public service**. It seems he had a passion to serve. Jesus said to his disciples, and to all generations, "He that would be greatest should be the servant of all?" The greatness of Senator Kennedy and his family was their passion to serve and not to be served.

2. **He cared for society's least**. He had a deep concern for the "boats stuck at the bottom," to use Jesse Jackson's phrase. Among marks of authentic leadership, I look for where the

people deemed the least or the lowest in societies are placed in the order of concern. I learned that from Jesus, who began his first sermon with, "The Spirit of the Lord is upon me, because he hath anointed me to preach the gospel to the poor; he hath sent me to heal the brokenhearted, to preach deliverance to the captives, and recovering of sight to the blind, to set at liberty them that are bruised." Notice the order of concern: The first was the poor. Those who prioritize the least are exhibiting marks of a Christ-like spirit. A quote from President Kennedy represents this family's position: "A free nation that cannot help its poor, which are many, cannot save its rich, which are few."

3. **He embraced the right issues and causes.** He fought a good fight—civil rights, social and economic rights, and issues of justice, health care, minimum wage, and immigration, to name a few. Health care was one of his cardinal issues. For forty years, he kept the issue of quality health service for all Americans on the table. His last appearance, a year ago to the day he died, was at the 2008 Democratic Convention. His body was weak, but his voice was strong as it thundered across the packed arena: "Decent, quality health care for all Americans ought to be a right!"

4. **His courage.** He stood strong, and sometimes alone, against the pack, the majority, the powerful, for what he believed was right. He said the vote he was most proud of was opposition to the Senate resolution to support the Gulf War. He stood alone on that boat. A quote carved in a three-by-six-inch piece of wood on my desk brings certain people to my mind—Teddy among them. It reads, "Oh Lord, give me the courage not to give up on what I believe is right, although I believe is hopeless." It was against strong opposition and old allies that he courageously endorsed President Barack Obama. Among the many accolades, he can add that he played a significant role in the election of the first black President of the United States.

5. **His resiliency.** Few have been down so low and risen so high. Like the Phoenix bird of Greek mythology, from the ashes of degradation, indiscretion, and devastating loss and pain, he became the lion of the Senate—the personification of the best

of liberalism and compassion, and the patriarch of a proud, productive family.

6. **He was personable.** He was a friendly man who even knew how to work with his opponents. For days, the constant theme that ran through all the TV interviews was the nice things he did for people. How he remembered names, birthdays, and anniversaries. How he reached out to people in their hour of need. He really liked people, and you had to like him back.

7. **He loved and enjoyed life.** Like all great and secure people, he saw the lighter side of life. The Bible says, "A merry heart does good like a medicine."

8. **He radiated optimism and hope.** He lost some fights, but he was never a loser. His head blooded but never bowed. He reminded me of Bishop Desmond Tutu, who famously said, "I am addicted to hope," during the most brutal days of tyrannical apartheid South Africa. Senator Ted Kennedy was addicted to the hope that America could, and would, be better for all its people. He had a faith and hope, which was probably influenced by, or grounded in, his religion.

Even with a death sentence creeping in his head, if you had not been told, you would have never known it. At the aforementioned convention, he exuded vitality and confidence. His voice was strong and eloquent. His face was round, radiant, and cheerful. He was animated. Waving his arms and pointing his fingers, he said,

I'm glad I was fortunate enough to be at the 2008 Democratic Convention when he made his dramatic appearance and powerful speech. I'm glad I lived during the life and times of the Kennedy brothers. For all the reasons I've cited and more, we may never see their kind again. And I'm glad I played some infinitesimally small part in shaping the past fifty years in which the Kennedy's made their presence felt.

Endnotes

1   This is a version of an article that originally appeared in the April 6, 2011 edition of *The Daily Challenge*, published in Brooklyn, New York. Mr. Thomas Watkins, publisher.

2   See my book, *Traveling with Jesse Jackson*

3   This is a version of an article that originally appeared in the April 8, 2011 edition of *The Daily Challenge*, published in Brooklyn, New York. Mr. Thomas Watkins, publisher.

4   This is a version of an article that originally appeared in the January 14, 2009 edition of *The Daily Challenge*, published in Brooklyn, New York. Mr. Thomas Watkins, publisher.

5   Bernard Coard was released from prison on September 5, 2009.

6   This is a version of an article that originally appeared in the September 9, 2009 edition of *The Daily Challenge*, published in Brooklyn, New York. Mr. Thomas Watkins, publisher.

7   This is a version of an article that originally appeared in the September 11–13, 2009 edition of *The Daily Challenge*, published in Brooklyn, New York. Mr. Thomas Watkins, publisher.

9

Religious Leaders

Bishop Ralph E. Brower[1]

Sunset: December 11, 2010, Jersey City, New Jersey

A Prayer For a Bishop

At 10:17 a.m. on Saturday, December 11, 2010, I received a call from Mrs. Carolyn Oliver-Fair—a longtime resident of Jersey City, New Jersey, an excellent musician, and a founding member of our church in that town—informing me that Bishop Ralph E. Brower had passed away. I immediately called Bishop Brower's family and offered my prayers, condolences, and services.

I had known the Bishop since 1958. He was another "giant" I walked with.

Excerpts from his obituary tell some of his story:

Bishop Ralph E. Brower was born on April 28, 1921, to Walter and Monte Brower (deceased) in Robbins, North Carolina. At the age of 13, Bishop Brower attended Laurinburg Institute where he worked to maintain his living and received his high school diploma. His education achievements included a B.A. from Kittrell College in Kittrell, North Carolina, a M.A. from Kings College in Briarcliff Manor, New York, a M. Div. from Florida State

University, Fort Lauderdale, Florida; a Ph.D. from Grambling State University, and post-doctorate studies at Maryland Bible College and Seminary.

After completing his studies, Bishop Brower was ordained to the Christian ministry in 1954. Having served as a pastor for a short time at St. Paul's Reformed Methodist Church in Passaic, New Jersey, Bishop Brower was called to Jersey City to build the St. Michael Methodist Church. Having started with six members 56 years ago and being consecrated as Bishop on March 25, 2006, the Lord truly blessed his ministerial endeavors.

His professional and ministerial accomplishments included President of the Interdenominational Ministerial Alliance (I.M.A) for 25 years; Hudson County Chaplain for 25 years; Commissioner for the Jersey City Redevelopment Agency for five years; Deputy Mayor for the City of Jersey City for four years; Pastor of St. Michael Methodist Church for 56 years; and Bishop of St. Michael Methodist Church for four years.

Bishop Brower received numerous awards and recognitions, including the Dr. Martin Luther King Jr. Award, for his outstanding community involvement. In March of 1968, Bishop Brower, along with other clergy members, brought the late Dr. Martin Luther King Jr. to Jersey City to address civil rights issues. He was a dedicated advocate and supporter for the freedom of humanity, thus leading the way for St. Michael Methodist Church to become "The Black City Hall of Jersey City." He maintained an open-door policy for all civil, political, and community leadership. In 2003, he became the first living person in Jersey City to have a street named in his honor. Virginia Avenue was renamed Rev. Dr. Ralph E. Brower Drive.

I first met Bishop Brower over fifty summers ago, on a warm Sunday morning in August. Rev. Stan Smith, the father of Councilman Harvey Smith, introduced me to him. Stan and I started our spiritual journey together at the Hudson County Jail on Pavonia Avenue in Jersey City. I had my encounter with God through Jesus Christ about a week earlier at the police precinct on Montgomery Avenue in Jersey City.

After the usual greetings and niceties, Bishop Brower turned to me. In a stern and interrogative voice, he asked, "I heard that you are a preacher. Are you a preacher? Can you preach?"

I wasn't sure how to answer him. After all, I had been home from jail for only a few days. No one had ever asked me if I was a preacher and if I could preach. I can tell you this, many years later, when Muhammad Ali "The Greatest" asked me, "Can you preach?" I replied, "Can you fight? I preach like you fight." Shaking his head, he looked at me with a penetrating stare. He tightened his lips, and in the most forceful voice that he could summon, he said, "You are a preaching so-and-so."

I looked Bishop straight in the eye. I said proudly and assertively, "Yes, I am a preacher, and I can preach."

I wasn't ready for his next question.

"Well, do you want to preach?" he asked.

"Yes," I said, continuing with my bravado.

"Okay, you can preach today at my eleven a.m. worship service."

"Thank you," I replied, with much less bravado, trying to beat back fear and trembling. I uttered one of those desperation prayers when we don't have time to remember the old prayers we were taught by our parents or church leaders.

My subject was "As a Man Thinketh in His Heart, So is He." I don't remember anything else, but the congregation seemed to be pleased. I wasn't sure if it was out of politeness or sincere appreciation. The Bishop seemed satisfied, too. Maybe it was relief or something. I knew their reactions were encouraging. I didn't know whether or not I was preaching to the congregation, the Bishop, or myself. After all, I had just been released from prison. During my incarceration, I had written a grandiose plan on how I would convert the world to Jesus Christ. Well, here was my start. What was I going to do with it? I could falter and fail. I remember that I kept telling myself, *As I think, so I am.*

What Manner a Man is this?[2]

Long and often, I have thought about that summer day at St. Michael's Methodist Church in Jersey City, New Jersey, and the man named Bishop Ralph E. Brower. I asked myself, "What manner of man was this? Who would allow a person he didn't know, but had surely heard of his sinful past, to stand and preach in his pulpit?"

I was at Bishop Eddie Long's church in Atlanta, Georgia, for the funeral of Coretta Scott King. Yes, the Bishop is being accused of some awful things. Let me hasten to add that I don't know the man, nor have I ever been at his church prior to Mrs. King's funeral. However, I don't know whether he is guilty or innocent. If he is guilty, I pray for him. I don't cast in my lot with the rock throwers. I'm with the merciful and forgiving crowd. When I hear of people being accused, my mind goes digging in my past. I say, "Be merciful and forgive me, oh Lord." I am among those who received mercy, forgiveness, and healing, and I am ready to extend the same to others. I also pray for the healing and the happiness for those who might have been victimized.

At Mrs. King's funeral, I was standing in the pulpit and talking to Andy Young, one of Dr. King's trusted assistants, who had extraordinary achievements to his own credit—a man for whom I continue to have the highest admiration. Suddenly, an overbearing man with a mean and arrogant decorum appeared out of nowhere. Angrily, he told me to get off of the pulpit. Andy and I looked at each other, and then at the man. My immediate response was to resist. It wasn't what he said; it was the way he said it. There was contempt in his voice. After all, I was dressed in all of the symbols of my calling. Politeness should have been manifested. I said to myself, "He is simply following orders." I went away with some negative feelings about Eddie Long's church in Atlanta, Georgia.

What manner of man was Bishop Brower? What did his actions say to me? He was a man who was kind and profoundly empathetic. He was always helpful. He was thoughtful, courageous, and deeply secure in his faith. He was a strong man with a tender heart. Whenever I think of Bishop Brower, I remember the words of Antony in Shakespeare's Julius Caesar: "His life was gentle, and the elements / So mixed in him that / Nature might stand up. / And say to all the world, 'This was a man!'"

Above all, Bishop Brower was a man who was close to God. How else would he have known to trust me in his sacred place? Surely, God showed him something. He saw what only those close to God can see. Bishop Brower caught a glimpse of what I was to become. I know I have been called a troublemaker. I admitted to the accusations. I was, and still am, a troublemaker. I make trouble for those who unfairly victimize others. For them, I try to make a heap of trouble. I learned that from Jesus. However, I think I have put a few scribbles on the canvas of life that would qualify for universal approval. Surely, no small amount of the credit must go to Bishop Brower, who opened his door, gave his blessings to a former undesirable, and sent him encouragement and inspiration along the way.

Memories flooded my mind as I walked along Virginia Avenue to St. Michael's Methodist Church, where the funeral of Bishop Brower was to be held. It used to be Metropolitan African Methodist Episcopal (AME) Church, a white-framed structure. There was no connected mall in those days. On the northeast corner of Virginia Avenue and what used to be called Jackson Avenue (now Martin Luther King, Jr. Boulevard), sat Garner's Restaurant. In our youth, we gathered at Garner's to plan our devilment for the day while ordering scrambled two (eggs) and coffee or tea, for just twenty cents.

Out of the huge window of the restaurant, we watched the trolley cars run by electric lines at the top. When we didn't have anything else to do, which seemed to be most of the time, we pulled the cord that attaches the lines to its electrical connection, causing the trolley car to stop, then ran away before the conductor could disembark. We also put in our "numbers" for the day and discussed Bebop, the musical form of the time. We argued about sports. If it were winter, we argued about the Notre Dame, Army, and Navy teams. I rooted for Notre Dame when the incomparable "Springfield Rifle," Angelo Bertelli, quarterbacked the team. He went off to war, as did many of the good college players, leaving the Army and Navy to rule the Gridiron. In the summer, we argued about baseball: the New York Yankees, the Brooklyn Dodgers, and the New York Giants, which is now the San Francisco Giants. I was a Yankee fan until Jackie Robinson broke into the white major leagues in 1947. It was at the

Jersey City Roosevelt Stadium, now occupied by high-scaled condominiums, where I saw Jackie play in 1946.

Chief Apostle Carl E. Williams; Sr. D.D.[3]

Sunrise: March 7, 1918,
Sunset: September 27, 2007,

In the early 1960s, during the anti-poverty war, I first meet Bishop Carl Williams. Bishop Ithiel Clemmons, co-pastor at First Church of God in Christ in Brooklyn, and a preeminent community activist at the time, had organized a group of community leaders and clergy to avail ourselves of the resources to address the deteriorating social, economic, and political realities in our neighborhoods, particularly as it related to youth.

Bishop Williams was the center of attention. Surrounded by an enthralled audience, he told stories, made jokes, and kept us laughing.

Humor, laughter, and fun were characteristics that I was to learn were deeply ingrained in his makeup. It flowed in his blood. I liked that about him. We have come to learn that people with humor, contrary to the popular notion, are very intelligent. They are likable, personable, and winsome. Bishop Williams had these admirable qualities in abundance.

I like saints with smiling faces. We do not see them too much in our Black Pentecostal churches. We have sanctified sternness, stoicism. All too often, we make serving God burdensome and joyless. But Bishop Williams exemplified the biblical teachings that joy and happiness, in a life balanced with seriousness and solemnity, is part and parcel of our spiritual heritage. The scripture says, "The joy of the Lord is our strength," and "A merry heart doeth good like medicine."

Some saints are not so nice, and we really do not care to be around them. But God has some people who are what we call "sweetly saved." Bishop Williams was in this category.

There was another aspect to his character which showed during the years of the war on poverty: a love for the people. His compassion for the community drove him to do something about our situation. Keep in mind, it was turbulent times, with the Civil Rights Movement ending and the Black Power and Back-to-Africa-Movements on the rise. The country was in an upheaval. Most of our churches turned inward and became critical of those who were struggling to make the fervor of our faith applicable existing realities.

Bishop Williams was in the middle of it all. His huge, loving heart was big enough to embrace the church and the community. He was an active member of many community and religious organizations.

We were in the Holiness Ministers Alliance. Great men and women led the way—Bishops James Forbes, Sr., who was chairman; I. G. Glover; Itheil Clemmons; Nathanial Townsley; and F.D. Washington. I learned another quality about Bishop Williams—a rare quality, indeed: He did not have to be out front to lead. He could lead from anywhere. There is a saying, "Some are born to lead. Some are born to follow. Some are born to do neither. And some few are born to lead and to follow, and to know when to do either."

They asked me to do things: 1. Present a paper on Black Power and Pentecostal Power; and 2. Be the treasurer of the organization. Both were grave mistakes. In obedience to their request, I spoke on the subject: "Black Power and Pentecostal Power—Contradictory or Complementary?" I argued that the screams of Black Power were the cries of all self-respecting people demanding dignity and seeking empowerment to be all that they could be. Two bishops stood by me—Bishop Forbes, Sr., who wanted to publish the speech; and Bishop Williams, who did his usual, looked at me admiringly, put his lips out, starting with a smile which became laughter, and then an embrace and words, "Boy, you are something."

The second thing they did was to make me treasurer. They forgot what Bishop Glover had said: "You don't put a hungry dog to mind the meat house." I was a hungry dog. I confess for the first time, the $6.95 that was left in the treasury, as the organization declined, I did what David did when he ate the showbread off the altar, which he should not have done. I was hungry, and so it took $6.95 to buy bread.

Now, I hope that Bishop Williams and all the members of the Holiness Ministers Alliance, all deceased, don't organize a delegation and approach God about bringing me up there to heaven so they can forgive me and pray for me. I want their forgiveness and prayers, but I want them to pray that I might stay down here.

Things were hard in those days. We had a practice—I am not sure how it got started—that helped to sustain my salvation and my sanity. Bishop Williams and I started having early morning prayer meetings at the Institutional Church, where he was pastor. After which, we would go to Junior's Restaurant for breakfast. I do not want to leave the impression that I was driven to the prayer meeting because of holiness. I was driven by hunger. So during those prayer meetings we had, we prayed the shortest prayers on record. I couldn't wait until the prayer was completed to hear him say, "Let us go eat." Junior's should reserve a seat in the restaurant in memory of Bishop Carl E. Williams.

I kind of felt sorry for my wife. She had to stay home with the empty refrigerator and food closets. But due to the sensitivity and compassion of Bishop and Sister Williams, occasionally they would take us out —Sheepshead Bay, on the water—for a fresh fish dinner. It was, for us, about as close to heaven as you could get on this side of Jordan. And to top all of this off, Sister Williams honored us on occasions by bringing busloads of Institutional members to the youth programs at our church. They filled up our little church, which was then located at 1393 Pacific Street.

Then Bishop Williams invited me to conduct a revival at the Institutional Church. That was an unthinkable thing to do at the time because in church circles, I was a renegade to some of my colleagues, full of the devil to others, and too radical for most. They never thought of me in the role of an evangelist. Even then, I was preaching, teaching, and acting out the ministry to which God had call me. That ministry synthesized spirituality, Afrocentrism, and the struggle for human rights and self-determination.

I must say, one of the delightful satisfactions of my life, for which I am perpetually grateful to God, is I've lived to see the Gospel that I was preaching at that time—which is now called holistic gospel. Some of the ministers have been honest enough and bold enough to actually come to our church and confess that they were wrong. They really didn't understand what I was saying and doing.

But thank God for the encouragement and concrete support that He sent my way through men like Bishop Forbes and Bishop Williams.

I will always be grateful to Bishop Williams and his wife, Elvonia, and to his family for all that he did for me and for all of the people that he served so diligently, graciously, and sacrificially.

Years later, we felt it a special privilege to have in one of our day care centers his granddaughter, who grew up to become Evangelist Monique Walker, and who sang so beautifully at his funeral.

So long, Bishop. Thanks for everything. You fought a good fight. You finished your course. And there is laid up for you a crown of rightness.

Bishop Williams' funeral was held at Pilgrim Assemblies. Its pastor, the Archbishop Roy E. Brown, along with the Right Reverend Albert Jamison, pastor of Pleasant Grove Baptist Tabernacle, were the officiates. Professor I. ``Butch'' Heyward was the organist. Clergy appearing on the program in various capacities included Mother Gloria White, the Right Reverend Eric R. Figueroa, Bishop Huie Rogers, Overseer Robert L. Perry, Jr., the Right Reverend Carl E. Williams, Jr., the Right Reverend Jules Anderson. Musical contributions were performed by Evangelist Carolyn Johnson White and congregation; Evangelist Doreen Figueroa; the Institutional Radio Reunion Choir; Brother Alfred White; and Bishop's granddaughter, Evangelist Monique Walker. Deaconess Patricia Fulmore and Missionary Brenda Britt-Harris read the acknowledgements and obituary. The Most Reverend John C. White, Presiding Prelate, Church of God in Christ OGIC International, delivered the eulogy.

The following are excerpts from his obituary:

Chief Apostle Williams' secular career included teaching business courses at the Phyllis Wheatley School of Business in Winston Salem, North Carolina. This is where he met Elvonia Penn, his friend and sweetheart. After a short courtship, the couple was joined in holy matrimony on September 19, 1939. The newlyweds then moved to Brooklyn, New York, in 1940, and started their family. Born to this union are their two dear children, Carl Jr. and Amease.

Chief Apostle Carl E. Williams, Sr. was consecrated to office of Vice Presiding Bishop for the state of New York, and on August 22, 1976. A double honor was bestowed on him as he was appointed the Presiding Prelate of the Church of God in Christ International. He successfully guided this organization for 25 years, remaining faithful in this position until August 2001. He then released the helm of his ship into the hands of Bishop John C. White. Retiring was not an option for Chief Apostle Williams, for he still had much to offer the people of the world. During this interval in his life, the title of Chief Apostle was bestowed upon him and indeed it is a suitable, appropriate honor. We bless God for this innovator, Chief Apostle Carl E. Williams, who God has used to prove that "The last shall be first and first shall be last."

Chief Apostle Williams was the first pastor to charter a plane to transport his church and choir to Dallas, Texas, singing a Gospel concert in the airways and in the Dallas International Airport. He was also the first to rent major auditoriums like Carnegie Hall, Madison Square Garden, Lincoln Center, Avery Fisher Hall, Brooklyn Academy of Music, and Brooklyn College. All events produced full fledged sold-out Gospel concerts. Preaching two or three times each Sunday, Bishop Williams proved to be the anointed teacher that was commonplace for a man who was never tired of his obligation to God and God's people. We thank God for the precedent that the Chief Apostle has established for us all to follow. His faithfulness is certainly and undeniably untouchable. His desire to emulate Christ Jesus resulted in the anointing and power that was demonstrated everywhere he ministered.

On the faithful morning of Thursday, September 27th, at 4:41 a.m Chief Apostle Williams was changed from mortal to immortal. The Lord called His son home by saying, Well done, thy good and faithful servant. Enter thou into the joy of the Lord.

To God be the Glory! A great soldier has entered the pearly white gates. We will miss him, but we'll meet him again over in Zion.

The Rev. Dr. William Augustus Jones[4]

Sunrise: February 24, 1934, Louisville, Kentucky
Sunset: February 4, 2006, Brooklyn, New York

I do not recall where I first met the Rev. Dr. William "Bill" Augustus Jones. It might have been in the 1962–63 period, when they were struggling at the Downstate Hospital for jobs and better working conditions. Involved in that fight were some of the most prestigious religious leaders in Brooklyn. These leaders included Dr. Gardener Taylor, Concord Baptist Church; Dr. Sandy Ray, Cornerstone Baptist; Dr. Benjamin J. Lowry, Zion Baptist Church; and Dr. Milton Galamison, Siloam Presbyterian Church. Dr. Galamison later organized a successful boycott of New York City's racially segregated public schools, and also became the vice president of the city's Board of Education. I was not directly involved in that struggle, but I remember the leading role that Rev. Jones played.

We might have participated together in Youth in Action, one of the major community-based organizations in the so-called war on poverty, initiated by President Kennedy. Dr. Jones, at one point, was president of that program's board of directors. I was elected as the vice chairman. I am not sure if we served at the same time. However, it was in Operation Breadbasket where we became friends and commenced our many years of struggling together on many issues and in many places.

Operation Breadbasket was the economic arm of the Southern Christian Leadership Conference, and it was the brainchild of Dr. Martin Luther King Jr. Its purpose was to win greater economic opportunities for our people. The Rev. Jesse Jackson succeeded the Rev. Ralph Abernathy as the president. The Rev. Al Sharpton was our youth leader. Rev. Jones served as the Metro New York chairman, and I as the executive vice chairman.

At the Operation Breadbasket breakfast, I met the Rev. Dr. Wyatt Tee Walker, who had served as chief of staff for Dr. Martin Luther King Jr., and had recently been appointed pastor of Canaan Baptist Church in Harlem. We immediately became great friends and struggled together on many issues over many years. Dr. Jones was with us on most occasions. It was at the Saturday Operation Breadbasket breakfast that I met Rev. John Scott, who was hired as our executive director. And at the Operation Breadbasket breakfast, I learned from Bishop Edward Williams that the church at 415 Atlantic Avenue was for sale. Not long after, we purchased that church, and have been there since 1969.

During those years, we would meet every Saturday morning at Bethany Baptist Church for breakfast and strategizing. The composition of the organization was almost exclusively clergy. To achieve the purpose of economic opportunities, we would meet with the presidents of corporations. It was our undeviating policy to meet only with the president and whomever the president decided to bring with him or her.

The first session would be what Dr. Jones called a preaching session. In other words, we would educate the presidents regarding the conditions of our people and the legitimacy of our struggle. Then we would gather information regarding the hiring practices and the advertising budgets as they related to black media, deposits in Black banks, purchasing of Black products, the use of Black services—i.e., insurance, black business, and legal services—and develop demands. We returned to the church, studied the information, and then developed our demands.

At the second meeting, we would put forth our demands. Usually, it would require a study by the corporation. Thus, a third meeting would be necessary to hear a response from the business community. Then we would begin to negotiate. If there were an agreement, we would shake hands and put the agreement in writing. We would return to the church for a celebration and begin to widely disseminate the information. On the other hand, if the business community was unresponsive, we would begin a strategy of withdrawal of our business. We would inform our people not to shop at that establishment.

If the business's refusal continued, we would express our opposition in a demonstration in front of the store. These demonstrations provided opportunities to educate our people regarding our actions and to flex our collective muscle or considerable influence. If necessary, we would engage in civil disobedience. Usually, the corporations submitted to our demands. The most obstinate was the A&P

supermarket chain. In fact, we had to go to jail before they came to the table. We discovered that the A&P corporate headquarters was in the Graybar Building on Forty-Second Avenue and Lexington Street. We decided that we would take over the office. We gained entrance into the offices and stayed there until we were removed by the police. We were arrested and spent the night in jail. The next morning, we went before the judge. The judge sought to extract from us a promise that we would not do it again. Rev. Jones told the judge we could not make that commitment. In the face of an injustice, we reserved the right to choose the actions that served our purpose.

One of the memorable ironies of the movement is when Bethany Baptist Church opened Harvest Manor, a cafeteria-style restaurant, on St. John's Place between Brooklyn and Kingston Avenues where the A&P had been. Harvest Manor was a delightful place to dine. The food was delicious, the service was pleasant and efficient, and you could meet with relatives and old friends. Our church and our family had many functions there. After we were arrested, Rev. Jesse Jackson came to town to lend his support. Jesse was arrested, too. There is an unforgettable photo of Jesse being put in the back of the police vehicle.

(Years later, when the Downtown Brooklyn Neighborhood Alliance (DBNA), an organization I founded in 2004, negotiated with FCRC and later won an unprecedented legally binding community benefits agreement, we were doing what we had been doing for many years.)

In addition to addressing the economic situation, we also concerned ourselves with the social, political, and governmental realities. We would have what we called "accountability sessions." We would ask leaders of various institutions and organizations to give us an account of what Dr. Jones called "their stewardship."

Those were unforgettable times at Bethany Baptist Church. The community owes a great debt to the preachers and their churches who gave so much of their time, energy, and resources. For the most part, we labored in obscurity. I think I would be within the mark to say only a few people, outside of those who were the direct beneficiaries and our churches, knew what we were doing and what we were achieving. After the meeting with corporate leaders, we would usually go to McDonald's restaurant—not the fast-food chain, but the Black-owned restaurant on Macon and Stuyvesant, where you could run into almost any Black leader you were looking for. After long, tough meetings, Rev. Jones would say, "You know, fighting sin is a serious business. It wears you out. We must replenish ourselves with a hearty meal." We should never forget men like Rev. L.P. Taylor, Glover Memorial Baptist Church; Rev. Charles Nesbitt, Bethesda Baptist; Rev. Clarence Williams, Southern Baptist; Rev. Wharton, Charity Baptist Church; and Rev. Murray, Mt. Pisgah Baptist Church. All are deceased now, save Rev. Williams. They gave so much of themselves and asked for nothing in return.

It was a policy in Operation Breadbasket that we could not negotiate for ourselves. What we won was for others to receive.

Another place Rev. Jones and I worked together was in his candidacy for the borough president of Brooklyn in 1969. I was a member of a political group that had recently been organized for political empowerment. We called ourselves the Black Intellectual Political Organization. The membership included Attorney Clayton Jones (Bill's brother), Bill Strickland, Reverends Calvin Presley and Carl McCall. Carl McCall later became the president of the citywide anti-poverty council, the US associate ambassador to the United Nations, the head of New York State Corporation, and a candidate for governor of New York. We walked the streets of Brooklyn in a voter registration and education effort. That year, we supported Herman Badillo for mayor. Regretfully, Bill Jones lost the election.

Another place where we were active was in the South African anti-apartheid movement. Our churches, I think, were the only churches in Brooklyn that had purchased the anti-apartheid sign from Trans Africa. These six-by-three-feet signs attached to long polls were designed to conspicuously declare our opposition to the dehumanizing situation in South Africa.

Our churches were very much alike. We were the center of activism. The strategies to address the important issues of our community were usually formulated in our churches. Our churches were a haven to all who were under attack or needed a place of respite or inspiration.

A Mentor for us all[5]

In 1979, Bill founded National Black Pastors. I was one of the speakers for the second annual conference, October 6–10, 1980, in Chicago, Illinois. It was held at the Conrad Hotel, with workshops, music, and preaching. The theme of the conference was The Black Pastor: Prophet and Priest.

The friends and relatives of Tawana Brawley found a home at Bethany when they were being sought after and threatened with arrests. And there were many other issues that we fought, demonstrated, or spoke out against.

We were together in the fight for justice for Michael Stewart, a young Black man who was beaten to death by the police, and the racist attacks, the anti-Black, and anti-poor policies of Mayor Ed Koch. There were a few of us preachers who were always there for the people. In Queens, there was the Rev. Timmy Mitchell. The Bronx had the Rev. Wendell Foster. And Brooklyn had Reverends Cal Marshall, Herb Oliver, and Bill Jones. We were the activists. We sought to concretize the prophetic dimension of our ministry.

Dr. Jones remained consistent and true until the end. Some of the last words I heard him say were, "Bethany had never received anything from any governmental agency. Whatever Bethany had achieved, it had been done from Bethany's own resources."

Dr. Jones used to say, "If you eat the king's meat, eventually you will have to do the king's biddings." Of course, his position on receiving governmental assistance, along with assistance from outside sources, had been and is debatable. Sincere men and women of God have tried to get all they could from the government and anybody else, believing that whatever they got was owed to them anyway. Neither the government nor any other agency would be in existence had it not been for our labor, which built the country; our bodies, which were sold to enrich the country; and our blood, which was shed to protect the country. It is for this reason that most Black people believe that reparation is a legitimate demand. In a word, the country owes people of African ancestry a huge debt. But in any event, rejecting assistance from outside sources is what Dr. Jones believed, and many people shared his beliefs, and he kept that position until the end.

Rev. Jones was an extraordinary man. He was born February 24, 1934, in Louisville, Kentucky, the son and grandson of Baptist ministers. He had a deep love for our people. We would spend hours discussing and analyzing what he called the "pain predicament." He had this rare gift of being a scholar. He graduated with honors from the University of Kentucky. He received a Bachelor of Divinity degree from Crozer Theological Seminary in 1961. He received his doctorate from what is now Colgate Rochester Crozer Divinity School in New York. He also studied at the University of Lagos in Nigeria, and the University of Ghana.

We would all sit in his office and listen attentively and absorb the knowledge and experience that he had garnered from his travels, preaching, lectures, and pastorates. He was master of the succinct phrase. He used to say, "You don't have to be long-winded to be immortal." Several more of his memorable phrases that I recall, which he would say slowly, with carefully chosen words, "You know, I don't want to come to the end of my journey and discover that the Lord flunks me. I want to live a long time, but I don't want to outlive my mourners." And a classic for me was, "I don't want to die in shallow waters." And when we became frustrated and somewhat angry that the goodies we had won from corporations so often went into the pockets of those who didn't deserve it, he would say, "I'm tired of fattening frogs for snakes." He deserved to be named one of America's great preachers.

But in addition to being a scholar, he was also a student, which to me, is always a remarkable quality. He captured the literary giant, Ralph W. Emerson's practice, who said, "Every person I meet is my superior in some things. Therefore, I learn from them."

We worked together in the fight for community control of schools, particularly at PS 268 on Herkimer Street. The Rev. Herb Oliver, pastor of Bethany Presbyterian Church, was president of the Ocean Hill/Brownsville Board of Directors which gave direction to the struggle. The program was an experiment, or pilot project, in community control or parental participation funded by the Forward Foundation. Dr. R. McCoy was the supervisor.

The legitimate struggle for parental participation, or parental influence, over the school where their children attended was diverted by Albert Shanker, president of the United Federation of Teachers (UFT). He made it an anti-Semitic issue. Eventually, it was legislated that there be thirty-one school districts, with elections to choose officers in each district.

We were together on the historic occasion when Jesse Jackson came to Brooklyn to speak to Black leaders regarding his running for president. It was October 1983, at the House of the Lord Church.

The last time I saw Bill was at the magnificent retirement ceremony that Bethany prepared for him on September 17, 2005. After the ceremony, Dr. Gardener Taylor was the featured speaker. He was as eloquent then as he was later when he delivered the eulogy at the funeral. I went over to greet Bill. He was in a wheelchair. His body was slumped, so that his head seemed to be sunk into his shoulders. I leaned over and kissed his head.

He looked up, ever so slightly, and in words I could barely hear, he whispered, "Herb, it's so good to see you, buddy. Family doing well?"

"Everybody is doing great. I see your family is doing well."

Bill's family was at the ceremony. They had a special part where they honored their father. I wanted to linger. It took all of the strength I could summon to leave him there. But I didn't want to be selfish He was too weak for me to impose my feelings on him. And then, there were others around his chair eager to greet him. So I kissed his head again and whispered, "I'll see you later, old struggler." Almost the same words I had whispered to Sonny Carson the night before he made his transition. For Bill, I knew the next time I would see him alive would be on the other side of Jordan, in the promised paradise.

Amid the moving crowds from the capacity-filled celebration, and the regular flow of hotel customers, my wife and I made our way to our car and then homeward. As we traveled, we rehearsed our years of association with Bill. I even remembered that it was Bill who first made me health conscious. I went by his house one day. He, gracious as always, asked me what I wanted to eat or drink.

"A Coke," I said.

"Herb, I don't drink sodas anymore, and I feel so much better," he said.

"Is that right? Thank you very much, but I'll have that Coke now, if you have one."

I wasn't ready for the health message. Years later, I became a vegan. I remembered what Bill had told me about the sodas. He was right about that, as he was right about so many things. There is the saying, "When the student is ready, the teacher will appear." At the appropriate time, I was ready, and Dick Gregory's book *Cooking with Mother Nature* appeared. I read it, and it helped to turn my life around. Every time I see Dick Gregory, I shower upon him profuse praise. I thank him for saving my life.

They said at the retirement celebration that Bill was on his way to Atlanta so he could spend quality time with his family. Yes, I knew he was on his way home—not to any earthly home, but his home in heaven.

Rev. Joe L. Parker[6]

Sunrise: October 16, 1940
Sunset: July 29, 2007

It was 1:30 a.m., July 29, 2007, when the Rev. Allan Hand called to inform me that the Rev. Joe L. Parker had died an hour and a half earlier. It was not too unexpected. A few days before, we had discussed the severity of Rev. Parker's illness. But we are never altogether ready for the demise of loved ones.

As we pondered the condition of Rev. Parker, Rev. Hand counted seven other preachers who were seriously ill. My mind conjured up memories of friends who had "gone on to glory." These contemplations always send me into a swirling mixture of sadness and gratitude. Yes, sadness at the passing of old friends, but sadness, too, because in many instances, death, while coming at evening, was brought on by choices long before their night was to fall. Our eating culture, the absence of exercise or hobby or play, added to the stress and all the challenges that come with our calling. It is an invitation to the grim reaper to pay us a visit long before his scheduled due date.

"My people are destroyed for lack of knowledge," says the Bible. How true this is as it relates to our health habits. I am told that people of African Ancestry lead in all the major diseases. We who are ministers ought to be modeling lifestyles that lead to optimum health. Surely it is God's will that we should enjoy good health. The Bible says, "I would above all that you may prosper and be in good health, even as your soul prospers." Purposefulness or meaningfulness, health and spirituality are the birthrights of God's people, not poverty of life, paucity of health, and lack of spirituality. Regretfully, I have to admit, our churches, Black churches, have been unaccountably negligent in teaching and preaching health principles.

Mixed with my sadness and regret is gratitude. Daily, I thank God for wakening me to health consciousness. It was twenty-four years ago at age fifty-three when I heard the voice of God warning me that it was time to change my eating habits and to give greater attention to my health.

My family has a history of cardiovascular problems. My grandfather, the Rev. William Van Daughtry, had a stroke in the pulpit, from which he never recovered. My father, Bishop Alonzo Daughtry, died at fifty-two when obesity smothered his heart. Two brothers died six months apart, again due to cardiovascular complications. I often wonder if any of them associated their sickness with their lifestyles, particularly as it related to food consumption and the absence of exercise and positive play. I know that one of my brothers was told by the doctors he had inherited "bad tubes," meaning a bad heart condition, more specifically as it related to veins, arteries.

It was proverbial in my family that men did not live past sixty. About five years ago, I was hospitalized with arrhythmia—irregular heartbeat that causes blood to clot—thus the potential for sudden death if the clot reaches the heart, or paralysis should the clot reach the brain. I would have been dead if it were not for my health program. Even now, the possibility of this condition delivering a final blow is always with me. But I changed my lifestyle and became a vegan—the non-consumption of animal and animal products. This change substantially contributed to lengthening and enhancing the quality of my life.

At age 77, I enjoy playing basketball weekly with men who are much younger, stronger, and faster than I. 1 am full of energy and zeal. Most mornings, I do at least an hour of walking, running, and shadow boxing. If stay on my health program, I never get sick. I cannot say what will happen to me from day to day, but the time that God spoke to me, and I began to pursue optimum health principles, I have been blessed with vitality, health, and a zest for living. I believe God intended for us to live at least 120 years of quality, meaningful life, then die painless and peaceably.

A Man Concerned for the Community

I first met Rev. Parker in 1989, when we organized the African American Clergy and Elected Officials (AACRAO) to support Mr. David Dinkins run for the mayoralty seat. Dr. Gardner C. Taylor, Councilman Al Vann (then assemblyman) and I were the co-chairs. I resigned after five years, as chair. Rev. Parker was consistent, cooperative, and always friendly.

The last time I was with him was in City Council Speaker Christine Quinn's office. We had gone to see her to discuss the Sonny Carson Street naming. We thought we could find a way to encourage her to change her position. She opposed the street naming. Also, Rev. Clarence Norman Sr. was in the meeting. We were not successful. Ms. Quinn remained adamant.

The qualities I admired in Rev. Parker, in addition to his consistency and cooperativeness, were humility. He possessed that rare quality of knowing how to lead and how to follow—and knowing when to do either. I admired his concern for the community that manifested itself into a comprehensive ministry. He developed senior citizens programs, including housing. The sprawling complex of edifices that houses his church and other enterprises is a testimony to his creative vision. Under his leadership the blight, empty lots, and dilapidated buildings along Broadway in the Bedford-Stuyvesant area where his church is located began to come alive with new and renovated buildings, business ventures, and social programs.

He became the third chairperson of the AACAEO. He revived the organization as it began to decline. Everything Rev. Parker touched seem to blossom. He was personable and likable. He was always smiling or laughing. He had a refreshing since of humor. We will miss him very much. His kind does not come to the stage of life often. But thank God he made his contributions, and we have inspiring memories to cherish.

Pope John Paul II[7]

Sunrise: May 18, 1920, Wadowice, Poland
Sunset: April 2, 2005, Apostolic Palace, Vatican City

Reflections on Meeting the Pope

In 1985, I had the rare privilege of conferring with John Paul II at the Vatican. The Rev. Jesse Jackson called me one day and said he was going to see the Pope, and asked if I wanted to come along. Immediately, I said yes.

We departed New York on a Sunday night and arrived in Rome the next day. It is significant to relate here, that although you have an appointment with the Pope, the precise time is not given until you arrive. The fact that we had been given an appointment so soon upon our arrival (the day after we arrived) testifies to the esteem with which the Pope regarded us.

After meeting the Italian Prime Minister and American ambassador, the time came to meet the Pope. We drove up to the ancient rust-colored complex of buildings. We were guided past Swiss guards and through a maze of corridors, passing through buildings until we arrived at the anteroom next to the Pope's office. Here, all must wait until the Pope is ready to receive them. We were informed about the greats of the Earth who had sat where we were sitting, then given instructions regarding protocol.

It was a short wait. Soon, we were invited into a spacious room, which was the Pope's office. Everything about it—the art, the furniture, the architecture—spoke of antiquity. It was as if we had walked into the inner chambers of history.

The Pope was seated at a desk off to our right. He arose and warmly greeted us. Then we took our seats. Although we were told we had thirty minutes, our conversation must have lasted for at least forty-five minutes. During that time, Jesse gently but firmly pressed the anti-apartheid struggle in South Africa. He wanted the Pope to speak out more vigorously against apartheid in particular and racism in general. There were other world issues discussed—poverty, disease, and peace—but apartheid was the primary issue.

While the Pope didn't make firm commitments, we agreed that he was committed to ending apartheid in South Africa.

After our discussion, we prepared for photo ops. It was an informal, cordial atmosphere. The Pope smiled a lot as small talk and bantering occupied the time.

The Pope was so human, so down-to-earth. It had been his bearing throughout our conversation. He was completely without airs or ostentatious or an arrogant attitude. He seemed so humble. Yet you knew he was a man of prodigious intellect and deep spirituality.

He seemed to be enjoying himself with us. He gave us gifts, too. Then we were led back through the labyrinth of rooms and corridors, into the sunlight outside, where the press awaited.

What did I like about the Pope John Paul II, or what would be his lasting contributions? I liked his lobbying for peace. I liked his concern for the working class, especially the least in society. He seemed to be trying to embrace the world. To me, the highest human quality is to heal others while hurting. Down to the last, while his body was suffering debilitating pain, he was still trying to reach out to the people.

It was said of Jesus, "He was a wounded healer." It will be said of this Pope, "He loved the people till the end. He was a wounded healer."

The Rev. Dr. Earl Moore[8]

Sunrise: Unknown
Sunset: May 31, 2006

It was a beautiful morning as I drove to St. Paul Colored Baptist Church in Harlem, New York. The cars double-parked on West 132nd Street between Frederick Douglass and Adam Clayton Powell Boulevards. (Interesting how laws and rules can be flexible depending on the occasion). Police stood in a semi-circle in front of the church. People observed from the windows and stoops. Friends and relatives slapped backs, shook hands ,and greeted each other with smiles and sadness.

Inside, the church was filled to overflowing. It was a church crowd—clean, well-groomed, and churchly attired. Preachers were everywhere. There were elected officials and sundry movers and shakers. All had come to say wonderful things about, and to bid farewell to, the Rev. Dr. Earl J. Moore.

The first order of business was to rearrange the seating, which the Rev. Patricia Reeberg, the liturgist, did tenderly and expertly. Those in the front section, except for the participants, had to move to make room for the family. I was reminded of Jesus' admonition: When entering an assembly, always take the lower seat. It is better to be called up to the higher seat than to be removed to the lesser seat.

The program was readjusted to allow Congressman Charles Rangel and New York State assemblyman Keith Wright to speak on behalf of the civic leadership and to return to their legislative duties. There were those who spoke on behalf of the sons and daughters that Rev. Moore had assisted in the ministry, and Reverends Calvin Butts and James Forbes spoke on behalf of community churches. Rev. Butts spoke of his long friendship with Rev. Moore and the mentoring Rev. Moore provided. Rev. Forbes said Dr. Moore had conferred upon him the honorary degree of "Doctor of Friendship."

There were expressions from religious leadership, friends, and a family tribute. The eulogy was delivered by the Rev. Manuel Scott Jr. Rev. Reeberg made it known that Rev. Moore had arranged the funeral himself. Therefore, there would be no complaints about the program.

I met Rev. Moore more than thirty years ago. He had been pastoring St. Paul for about eight years. We immediately became friends. The Rev. Gloria Askew, one of the daughters in ministry, said Rev. Moore used to say, "I not only love you, but I like you. I am mandated by the Lord to love you. So I am mandated by the law to love everybody, but I don't have to like everybody."

I always felt I was one of the ones he liked. I know I liked him. Keith Wright, who sat next to me for a while, whispered to me, "I liked him. He really was a nice man. He was always trying to do some good things in the community." Rev. Moore's accomplishments were impressive. He was active in many civic and religious organizations. What I liked about him was his concern for the least in society, or the "boats stuck at the bottom," to quote Rev. Jesse Jackson. He was comfortable with the high and mighty, and he did marvelous things across the board. but he always had the left-out and the left-behind uppermost on his mind, and designed programs to benefit them.

It was this concern that brought him into the prison ministry. He made many changes in the New York State Department of Corrections. He was a commissioner for the Department of Corrections.

We shared a deep compassion for the incarcerated and their families, and a deep conviction that they could be redeemed and returned to the community to become law-abiding and productive citizens. Assemblyman Wright spoke movingly of Rev. Moore's family support program for incarcerated persons and their loved ones.

Rev. Moore prided himself on having the "All-American Family." He was married to Cora Lee Thornton on November 28, 1958. He had two children.

I was impressed with Rev. Moore's intellect. He had a brilliant mind. He graduated from Arkansas Baptist College with a bachelor's degree, received his Master of Divinity from Virginia Union University, and received his Doctorate in Divinity from New York Theological Seminary.

Rev. Moore emphasized the imperative for preachers to be prepared. Rev. Askew related that more than twenty-five years ago, when she, newly arrived from the South, announced her calling to the ministry, Rev. Moore told her to prepare herself. Then one day he drove her in his own car to New York Theological Seminary. He had her register in the seminary certificate program and New Rochelle College, and paid her tuition.

Perhaps the greatest testimony to his insistence on preparation was that he prepared his own funeral. He had learned to actualize the biblical injunction of "moderation in all things." He had achieved a balance in life as evidenced by his good humor. He liked to laugh. He could find humor in crisis. All too often, people, especially preachers, take life too seriously. Rev. Moore and I, even when we were seriously engaged in important issues and events, could still share some laughter.

Somewhere in glory, I fancy I see him standing with Dr. William Jones and Dr. Frederick Williams, laughing and saying, "Hey, Bill. I thought I'd come up here to be with you. We Baptists have got to stay together. Once Fred left, I had to follow quickly, because you know how these Episcopalians are. They got all the money and are still trying to take over everything. We can't let them take over heaven, too." And I can hear the boisterous laughter.

It's only a funny story. Some people may find it strange that we can be humorous at this time. But even Assemblyman Wright, in his public remark, commented upon the length of time Baptist churches devote to funerals, while he, a member of the "frozen chosen" Episcopal Church, doesn't spend as much time. Dr. Moore was ecumenical to the bone. We all shared good-natured exaggerated jesting about each other's churches when we were together. It was a sign that said, "I am comfortable with you. I like you."

I liked Earl. He was in a special class. We do not see his like often. So in conclusion, I say to Earl in the words of the Apostle Paul, "You've fought a good fight, you've finished the course, you've kept the faith. Therefore, there awaits you a crown of righteousness which the Lord himself shall give you. Have a great time! And give everyone my regards. And I know one day the bells will toll for me, and I will see you then."

The Rev. James Bullock[9]

I heard the news of the Rev. James Bullock's passing on Thursday, May 12, 2011. My daughter, Sharon Daughtry, and I were trying to decide if we should revive the National Religious Leaders of African Ancestry Concerned About Darfur (NRLAA), and were reviewing the organization's accomplishments. In light of the scheduled celebration of South Sudan's independence in July 2011, and the many other issues of the African people in the diaspora, we decided to resurrect the organization immediately. I commenced listing the founders and the most consistent members of NRLAA. The first to come to mind was Reverend James Bullock.

"I will call Reverend Bullock today," I said.

Sharon looked at me rather puzzled, then said, "Rev. Bullock is dead." Not wanting to put a finality on her statement, and reading the painful incredulity on my face, she added, "I think." Knowing that my next questions would be "When?" and "Why wasn't I informed?" she said, "I think he died right after your operation." Observing the deepening pain on my face, she said, "I think you should talk to Mommy. I think she attended the funeral."

I knew that there was no need to talk to anyone. Rev. Bullock was dead. "He was one of my dearest and most faithful friends," I mumbled, "He had stood by me when most of my colleagues were against me."

I thought back to the year 1991, when I chaired the Association of Brooklyn Clergy for Community Development (AB.CCD). I succeeded, with the help of Rev. Bullock and others, in expanding the organization from a storefront referral center with a part-time staff and a budget of $25,000, to a suite of offices, multiple staff members and volunteers, and a budget of more than $1 million. In addition to doing referral work, we developed more than five hundred units of new and renovated housing and an extensive AIDS/HIV program. We did all of this in one year.

Private and governmental sponsors, resource personnel, and consultants of every description were eager to help. They saw our potential to have a major impact on the life of Brooklyn and beyond. This was based on who we were and what we have had accomplished. Then the devil went to work. There were envy, resentment, and distrust among the members of ABCCD, which lead to false accusations and vindictiveness. The executive director proved to be incompetent. By the time I discovered his incompetence, we owed the federal government hundreds of thousands of dollars. The fiscal record was in shambles, and he had failed to deliver on goods and services.

Our sponsors and consultants insisted that he had to be terminated. This was a hard thing to do. He was a young brother just out of Harvard University. I hired and brought him to Brooklyn. I approached him with a plan in which he would become the program developer for a couple years, and we would hire a competent, ex-

perienced executive director. After two years, he could become an
executive director.

I thought it was an excellent plan, showing compassion for him
and still meeting the demands of the organization. I was surprised,
however, when the executive director resisted and aligned himself
with my enemies on the board of directors. Thus, it made life more
difficult for me. In addition, I had to find a way to pay the government, restore trust with our sponsors and supporters, and fulfill our
responsibilities. It was one of the most challenging times in my life.
My credibility and competence as a leader were on the line. Other
board members and I would be held accountable by the government
for indebtedness. Thus, our financial situation was threatened, and
I felt responsible for all of it. I had personally persuaded several
members to join the organization. On top of all of the above, I was
devastated by the petty meanness, schemes, and betrayals of the men
and women who called themselves ministers of Jesus Christ. It was
hard to believe that these men and women I had admired and trusted
could stoop to such Machiavellian behavior.

The tension became so intense that I decided to resign for the
good of the organization. However, I did not leave before the organization had succeeded in paying off the government, bringing
solvency to the organization, and rectifying the errors that had been
committed. In a word, with the help of my family and friends, we
put the organization back on sound footing. Through these stormy
times, there were two ministers who stayed with me: Rev. Richard
J. Lawson, pastor of New Canaan Baptist Church in Brooklyn, New
York; and Rev. James Bullock. I could always count on Rev. Bullock. Even when I did not seek his help, he took the initiative to be
by my side.

Counting on Rev. Bullock [10]

Somewhere along the way, my board membership was terminated
without notification. When I observed that I was no longer getting
correspondence from the organization, I inquired as to the reason. I
was informed that I was no longer a member of the board.

"How could that be?" I asked.

"You resigned," I was told.

"I did not resign from the board, but as the chairperson."

In fact, I reminded them that I continued attending the board meetings until I no longer received correspondence.

I took the matter to the New York State Attorney General, then Eliot Spitzer. The major reason I raised the issue with the attorney general was because the Black United Fund (BUF), of which I was a founding member, was being dismantled by Mr. Spitzer, with the installation of a board of directors of his choosing. Significantly, ABCCD was guilty of some of the same violations that Mr. Spitzer claimed to compel him to dismantle BUF. Mr. Spitzer never acted on my request for an investigation. At least, I never heard anything from him. Looking back, I guess Mr. Spitzer had something else on his mind.

I take no pleasure in discussing this piece of history, but it was necessary to show the kind of person Rev. Bullock was. To appreciate the depth of Rev. Bullock's courage, commitment, and affection for me, let us remember that he went against the ministers of his denomination. This meant that there were repercussions in his denominational conferences and churches.

During and after that time, my friendship with Rev. Bullock grew deeper. If it were not for him, I might have lost faith in some of my fellow ministers. It would have not been very disillusioning if these individuals were not ministers—men and women who were supposed to be paragons of moral and ethical behavior. It called to my mind a saying: "We can endure the evil that men do in the name of evil, but Lord save us from the evil that men do in the name of goodness."

My friendship with Rev. Bullock was as such that there was no action, plan, or important idea that I didn't share with him. He was included every time we organized. The many marches and demonstrations always had his blessings, although he couldn't physically participate in them. During the later years, even though his legs had become bent, and his mighty heart was failing, he would be at every meeting I organized. Sometimes we had to help him from the car, into the church and to his seat, and back again to the car.

He was there when we organized the African-American Clergy and Elected Officials. His wife, Sister Mary Bullock, told me, "He would fight to get to the meeting, and he would fight to get back home." Dr. Gardner Taylor, the venerable and retired pastor of Concord Baptist Church in Brooklyn, New York, initiated the call to former Assemblyman Al Vann and me to co-chair this clergy-politician effort to support the mayoral candidacy of David Dinkins.

When I conceived the idea of organizing NRLAA, Rev. Bullock was the first minister I thought of to include in the efforts. He was present at the creation, and he remained steadfast and loyal until he entered the hospital to come home no more. He brought wisdom, consistency, dependability, and integrity. He was very generous to me. It is worth noting, and perhaps carries a meaning that is deeper than I first thought, that Rev. Bullock died during the time of my operation and recovery. It may be that God intended to bring us home together. We had had many celebrative times, and it seemed right and proper to be together in the heavenly celebration that awaits all faithful servants of the Most High. For some reason, perhaps we will understand by and by, God changed the plan. It may be that God, in His infinite wisdom, concluded it wouldn't be wise for the two of us to enter heaven at the same time. The first thing Rev. Bullock and I would want to do is sit together, and we would probably find something to fix, criticize, or re-arrange.

I will miss Rev. James Bullock very much. It will be a long time before I get used to being in a meeting and not seeing him present, and not being greeted with his broad smile. I called him my big brother for that is what he was like to me. He was always present in the time of need. He always came to my defense. The lines of Lord Byron's narrative poem, "Childe Harold's Pilgrimage," come to mind:

What is the worst of woes that wait on age?
What stamps the wrinkle deeper on the brow?
To view each loved one blotted from life's page
And be alone on earth, as I am now.

The Rev. Lucius Walker, Jr.[11]

Sunrise: August 3, 1930, Roselle, New Jersey
Sunset: September 7, 2010, Demarest, New Jersey

An Activist with Vision and a Heart

"Intrepid, fearless, and integrity are three words that immediately characterize the Rev. Lucius Walker Jr. He was an adventurous, unrelenting pastor of peace, and a man whose words were his bond," wrote journalist Herb Boyd in the *Amsterdam News,* dated September 16–22, 2010.

As a result of his friendship with Cuba, Rev. Walker was able to assist many minority students with full scholarships to the Latin American School of Medicine (ELAM), starting in 1988.

I was supportive of Rev. Walker's Cuban efforts. When I headed the National Black United Front (NBUF). We also made annual trips to Cuba, and were able to negotiate scholarships in the early 1980s, and we negotiated a national recognition for Dr. Martin Luther King Jr. at one of our meetings with the Cuban leadership.

We had given the Cubans significant and diverse support and wanted some kind of reciprocity for our support. The scholarships were one of the suggestions, and another was to honor an African-American person. The Cubans agreed to both. When the question arose of which African-American individual to honor, the Cubans offered Dr. Martin Luther King Jr. It visibly startled members of our delegation, of which most considered themselves to be revolutionaries. The members of the delegation idolized Cuba as the model of the revolutionary spirit. They were certain that the Cubans would select Malcolm X as the person they wanted to recognize. After all, Malcolm X was a revolutionary as was the Cuban leadership. There was also the historic relationship between the Cuban Prime Minister Fidel Castro and Malcolm X that went back to the 1950s. Castro had visited the United States of America and stayed at the Theresa Hotel, where Malcolm X had an office.

When asked why they chose Dr. King, the Cubans said that Dr. King had more tendencies around him—meaning, Dr. King was a coalition-builder who could amass the widest representation of the human family. He was a master organizer. Malcolm X's appeal was limited. From the Cubans' standpoint, "If one is going to have a global impact, one has to have a global appeal," they said.

My relationship with Rev. Walker dated before his Cuban ventures. I met him when the issue of reparations had once again forced its way into public discussion. James Forman, who had gained prominence as a leader of the Student Non-Violent Coordinating Committee (SNCC) during the Civil Rights era, was the catalyst. He had demanded religious institutions to pay African Americans because of the institutions' participation in the transatlantic slave trade and the continuation of the discrimination and exploitation of African Americans. I, along with the Rev. Dr. Calvin Marshall, met with James Forman at the Interchurch Center at 475 Riverside Drive in New York City, in the early 1970s.

In 1967, Rev. Walker was appointed executive director of the Interreligious Foundation Community Organization (IFCO), which consisted of a group of progressive religious leaders and activists. In that position, Rev. Walker assisted hundreds of community organizations and public policy groups for more than four decades. IFCO provided technical assistance, trained organizers, made and administered grants, and used its global network of grassroots organizers, clergy, and others to advance the justice struggles of many people. Under Rev. Walker's leadership, IFCO became known as the first and one of the largest foundations controlled by people of color in the United States of America. At the time, it was the only foundation in the country to exclusively concentrate on community organizing. In terms of total grants, IFCO was one of the top two hundred foundations in the country.

His obituary outlined Rev. Walker's key accomplishments as the leader of IFCO:

In the early years, Rev. Walker steered IFCO to work in support of African liberation movements and the anti-apartheid struggle in South Africa. IFCO also provided support for hundreds of domestic grassroots organizations, from the American Indian Movement (AIM) and the Farm Labor Organizing Committee (FLOC) to the National Black United Fund (NBUF). Through IFCO, Rev. Walker was instrumental in helping to create a host of other organizations, including the National Anti-Klan Network (now known as the Center for Democratic Renewal) and the Ecumenical Minority Bail Bond Fund.

Minister and his Mission[12]

Rev. Walker was in the vanguard of the emerging radical and militant revolutionary wing of the Black Freedom Movement, which included the Black Theology movement spearheaded by Dr. James Cone of the Union Theological Seminary. Rev. Walker helped sponsor the Black Economic Development Corporation (BEDC) Conference in 1969. The conference was organized to give further study of the issue of reparations and its implementation. A major development at the conference was the Black Manifesto, which was developed and promulgated by James Forman. It spelled out the justifications for reparations and BEDC. According to Mr. Forman, Rev. Walker was forced to resign by the Interreligious Foundation for Community Organization (IFCO) board of directors upon his return to New York.

Rev. Walker also helped sponsor the Managua Conference in Managua, Nicaragua, in the 1980s. During the war in El Salvador, Rev. Walker put together a delegation to meet with the Salvadoran and Nicaraguan leaders who supported the Salvadoran Freedom Fighters. Attorney Michael Ratner, who is the brother of real estate developer Bruce Ratner, and the Rev. Dr. Jeremiah Wright attended the conference.

One of the reasons I support Forest City Ratner Company, which spearheads the $4.5 billion Atlantic Yards Project against formidable opposition, was because of Michael's relationship to Bruce Ratner. I knew Michael of his radicalism as evidenced in his support of the most radical causes such as the struggle for freedom in El Salvador. The support of the Salvadoran Rebels was in opposition to President Ronald Reagan's backing of the Contras. Along with Attorney William Kunstler, Michael also represented me in my victory over a television corporation that was guilty of defaming my character.

In 1988, Rev. Walker was shot by the US-supported Nicaraguan Contras as he led an IFCO delegation returning from the Nicaraguan coasts. He said that he spent that night praying for a response to the hit, which was paid for by my own government. The next morning, he announced the formation of IFCO's new program, Pastors for Peace. Since its founding, thousands of people have participated in more than forty Pastors for Peace caravans, which carried support materials to Mexico, Central America, Haiti, New Orleans, and the Gulf Coast after Katrina. The program also provided US–Cuba "Friendship-ment" caravans, which have delivered more than three thousand tons of humanitarian aid to Cuba.

During the funeral ceremony, as I looked across the crowded sanctuary of the Convent Avenue Baptist Church, I was deeply saddened. My sorrow for the passing of a friend and fellow struggler was enhanced by the absence of young people. I don't recall seeing one youthful person in his or her late teens or early twenties. We were all senior citizens. I was saddened by the contemplation that Rev. Walker did not reach the younger generation. There was a disconnection. Chances are, Rev. Walker's great contributions, sacrifices, commitment, and courage will go unnoticed by the following generation except by historians and writers of history.

It poses a challenge for all of us to remain relevant or in touch with our youth. For the knowledge we gain and the experience we accumulate to be taken to the grave will leave our people bereft of sorely needed help in the ongoing struggle of human rights and self-determination.

Between 1973 and 1978, Rev. Walker was an Associate General Secretary of the National Council of Churches of Christ in the US. In 1984, unwilling to resist his pastoral calling, he founded the Salvation Baptist Church in Brooklyn. On September 7, 2010, a massive heart attack did what external adversaries could not do—conquer him, stay at his feet, stop his mouth, squash his mind, and lay his body low. but only his body, and not his spirit. Rev. Walker still remains a conqueror and leaves us the hope that we shall meet again in the "sweet by and by." Jesus said in John 14:1–3, "Do not let your hearts be troubled. Trust in God; trust also in me. In my Father's house there are many rooms; if it were not so, I would have told you. I am going there to prepare a place for you. And if I go and prepare a place for you, I will come back and take you to be with me so that you also may be where I am."

The Rev. Calvin O. Pressley[13]

Sunrise: November 10, 1937, Harlem, New York City
Sunset: September 21, 2007, Boston, Massachusetts

A Quiet and Congenial Leader

I heard that the Rev. Calvin O. Pressley was dead on Thursday night, October 4, 2007. It was the same night I learned that Bishop Carl E. Williams had made his transition. It was a shock, like left-right punches. Two longtime friends, gone from the land of the living, almost at the same time. My mind raced from one to the other.

Somewhere a long time ago, I met Calvin. I think he was with former New York Comptroller Carl McCall. They were good friends. It might have been during the anti-poverty days of the early 1960s, or when Carl and others were organizing the Black Intellectual Political Movement in the 1970s, when we supported Herman Badillo for mayor. I remember we met in the Commodore Hotel in Manhattan with Mr. Badillo, who was expressing liberal views at that time.

Rev. Pressley was quiet and congenial with a ready smile. He was intelligent, compassionate, and committed to our struggle. He was of immense help to me. I'll share two memorable examples.

With the election of David Dinkins as the 105th, and first black, mayor of the City of New York, I knew I had a friend in City Hall. I decided to devote significant time to developing programs and services, particularly housing. Against the advice of family and friends, rather than create our own non-profit 501c3 corporation, I decided to join an organization already in existence—the Association of Brooklyn Clergy Community Development. The organization had a small storefront office, a couple of part-time staff persons, and primarily offered referral services. They had a $20,000- to $30,000-budget.

It was understood that by aborting my efforts to start a new organization, I would become chair of the clergy association and bring my considerable connections, credibility, and influence to develop and promote programs for the organization. In my mind, I was thinking I would need five to six years to achieve the results that we had formulated. I never sought permanent or longtime leadership in any organization. The only place I'd ever felt committed for longevity as pastor at my church.

We got off to a good start. With Rev. Pressley's help, they were able to reach a million-dollar budget in one year and moved to a suite of offices. We were able to build five hundred units of new and renovated housing in addition to other programs and services. The rapid enormous growth and inexperienced staff brought problems. When Rev. Pressley learned of our swiftly sinking situation, he dropped everything, flew in from Atlanta, Georgia, and took command. When he was finished, we were back to normal. Wish to God I could say we stayed that way. Due to staff incompetence and the board of director's lack of vigilance, we soon neared bankruptcy again. Aided by funders, friends, and again Rev. Pressley, I was able to bring the agency back to solvency.

In time, dissension arose, which I believe was due to jealousy and inordinate ambition among the board of directors, and I decided to resign as chair. For reasons beyond my understanding, I found myself no longer a member of the board of directors. I appealed to New York State Attorney General Elliot Spitzer [14] for assistance in understanding why I was put off the board and what was happening to the agency. At his direction, I met once with his office. I never heard another word.

In this context came the second time Rev. Pressley was helpful in a major way as director of the Institute of Church Administration and Management on the campus of the Interdenominational Theological Center (ITC) in Atlanta. For several consecutive years, he invited me to be the preacher-in-residence at the center. This entailed my staying several days and conducting workshops, for which I was substantially remunerated, plus room and board.

The position was near perfect for me. It gave me a chance to get away from the daily tensions of an activist pastor, be in an academic setting, and provided space for me to read, think, write, and interact with clergy, scholars, and community organizers. Plus, it was only 150 miles from Augusta, Georgia, where, as national minister of my church, I have to journey periodically. From ITC, I would go to Augusta. And on top of all that, I could bring my wife along. It was a refreshing and reinvigorating experience. I look forward to it each year.

Calvin knew this. I always felt he really was doing this to help me. Surely, there were those far more qualified than I, who would have jumped at the opportunity. While I was there, he would take us to dinner, to meetings with friends, and even to sporting events. He was a profoundly sensitive man.

I am certain my story could be repeated by many, many other people. He will be missed. But he earned his heavenly reward. So like all the giants of the human spirit, we hate to see them go, but we want what is best for them. And God is faithful, who will meet them and reward them on the other side.

Endnotes

1   This is a version of an article that originally appeared in the December 30, 2010, edition of *The Daily Challenge*, published in Brooklyn, New York. Mr. Thomas Watkins, publisher.

2   This is a version of an article that originally appeared in the December 31, 2010–January 2, 2011 weekend edition of *The Daily Challenge*, published in Brooklyn, New York. Mr. Thomas Watkins, publisher.

3   This is a re-edited version of the article "From Glory to Glory a Man of Great Faith, Power, Knowledge, Wisdom and Vision," which originally appeared in the November 9–12, 2007 edition of *The Daily Challenge*, published in Brooklyn, New York. Mr. Thomas Watkins, publisher.

4   This is a version of an article that originally appeared in the February 24–26, 2006 weekend edition of *The Daily Challenge*, published in Brooklyn, New York. Mr. Thomas Watkins, publisher.

5   This is a version of an article that originally appeared in the March 1, 2006 edition of *The Daily Challenge*, published in Brooklyn, New York. Mr. Thomas Watkins, publisher.

6   This is a re-edited version of an article that originally appeared in the August 10–12, 2007 weekend edition of *The Daily Challenge*, published in Brooklyn, New York. Mr. Thomas Watkins, publisher.

7   This is a re-edited version of an article that originally appeared in the

April 6, 2005 edition of *The Daily Challenge*, published in Brooklyn, New York. Mr. Thomas Watkins, publisher.

8   This is a version of an article that originally appeared in the June 14, 2006 edition of *The Daily Challenge*, published in Brooklyn, New York. Mr. Thomas Watkins, publisher.

9   This is a version of an article that originally appeared in the May 25, 2011 edition of *The Daily Challenge*, published in Brooklyn, New York. Mr. Thomas Watkins, publisher.

10   June 1, 2011

11   This is a version of an article that originally appeared in the September 29, 2010 edition of *The Daily Challenge*, published in Brooklyn, New York. Mr. Thomas Watkins, publisher.

12   This is a version of an article that originally appeared in the October 1–3, 2010 edition of *The Daily Challenge* newspaper, published in Brooklyn, New York. Mr. Thomas Watkins, publisher.

13   This is a re-edited version of an article that originally appeared in the November 2–4, 2007 weekend edition of *The Daily Challenge*, published in Brooklyn, New York. Mr. Thomas Watkins, publisher.

14   My primary reason for going to Mr. Spitzer, after much agonizing, was twofold. First, I thought I owed the people, who had invested time, energy, and money at my request a report regarding the agency's state of affairs. Similarly, the people for whom the resources were raised deserved to know what was happening to what was due them, i.e., the services and programs. I should say here, before I appealed to Spitzer, I requested in writing from ABCCD Board of Directors answers as to my termination from the board and a report on the state of the agency. I informed them that unless I heard from the board, I had no choice but to pursue a legal route. There was never a response.

Mr. Spitzer had wrecked or shifted control of the Black United Fund (BUF) away from those who started it to his own hand picked board of directors. BUF was competing with philanthropies for payroll deductions, which some people said was the real reason Mr. Spitzer shifted control of BUF.

In addition, Mr. Kermit Eddy, the founder and executive director of the clergy united was investing money in other ventures. I was a founding member; in fact, I was one of the first persons that Mr. Eddy talked to regarding his plan to start a BUF. He wanted to make sure there was no conflict between BUF and the Black United Front which

I chaired at that time. I stayed a member of the Board of Directors until the board was disbanded by Mr. Spitzer. Therefore, with that background, I wanted to see if Mr. Spitzer's office was fair, impartial in its investigation or was there a political agenda or ulterior motive. I never received any feedback regarding ABCCD.

10

The Law

Johnnie Cochran[1]

Sunrise: October 2, 1937, Shreveport, Louisiana
Sunset: March 29, 2005, Los Angeles, California

Jurist on a Journey for Justice

I can't remember when I first met Attorney Johnnie Cochran. It may have been at one of the National Action Network Saturday rallies. I do remember that when I put out my hand to introduce myself, he pushed it away and said, "Oh, Rev., I know who you are. I've been knowing of your work for years." We nodded at each other, acknowledging our appreciation for the work we had been doing. We had worked on many cases—Amadou Diallo, Abner Louima, Dandae Johnson, and more. He was a hardworking attorney with unusual empathy for those "boats stuck at the bottom." His mind was quicker than a mongoose and sharper than a two-edged sword. His legal erudition seemed boundless, and his courtroom decorum and skills were mesmerizing.

And running through all these admirable qualities, like the blood flowing through his body, was a love of his people and a determination to fight for their rights. His battlegrounds were in the courtrooms, in the streets, in the suites, anywhere and everywhere. He was a true warrior in the best sense of the term, always fighting, not for self, but for others—primarily the downtrodden. All the world knows of Mr. Cochran's courtroom demeanor and legal skills from the O.J. Simpson case. But before the Simpson case, Johnnie Cochran had already demonstrated his pit-bull tenacity, Job-like patience, undaunted courage, extraordinary legal knowledge and dexterity.

For twenty-seven years, he fought and eventually won freedom for Geronimo Pratt, a Vietnam War veteran who joined the Black Panther Party and became a target of the FBI's infamous COINTELPRO. I saw Mr. Pratt in Atlanta, Georgia, in 2004. I officiated the wedding of the sister of Tupac Shakur, and among the many well-wishers were several of the old Black Panthers, including Mr. Pratt. It was quite a reunion. During the reception, as Mr. Pratt and I talked about "the good old days," I couldn't help thinking, "Geronimo would still be confined if it were not for Johnnie." What O.J. Simpson is reported to have said, could be said by many others: "If it were not for Johnnie Cochran, I would be in jail."

Oddly enough, I think I really got to know Johnnie Cochran on a long funeral procession for famed musician Lionel Hampton. Following a horse-drawn caisson carrying the body, we talked and marched from the Cotton Club at 125th Street and 12th Avenue, to Riverside Church at 120th Street and Riverside Drive as renowned trumpeter Wynton Marsalis led a band in old Dixieland jazz.

Johnnie and I touched on many subjects: family, history, progress, the criminal justice system, war and peace, poverty, racism, religion, Black and white leaders. His interest and knowledge were deep and comprehensive.

Equally, he was an active listener. I'm convinced a person's knowledge and wisdom is in some way joined with how a person listens to others. How one listens says as much—or even more—about a person as how one talks.

I came away saying to myself, "This is a super brother—super in intellect and spirit, and equally super in sensitivity and caring. He was the first to make a substantial contribution when a tribute for me at the Brooklyn Academy of Music in January 2005.

We will miss him very much. There will never be another Johnnie Cochran. God made some people, then God threw away the model.

Judge Bruce McMarion Wright[2]

Sunrise: December 19, 1917, Baltimore, Maryland
Sunset: March 24, 2005, Old Saybrook, Connecticut

The Right Wright

Judge Bruce McMarion Wright died March 24, 2005. That was Holy Thursday on the Christian calendar, and significant for me since my most memorable recollection of Judge Wright was of an Easter Sunday at The House of the Lord Church.

Throughout the Black community, Judge Wright was admired and appreciated. His most notable acts related to his releasing accused persons on little or no bail. This infuriated many in the white community, particularly the Police Benevolent Association (PBA)—the union of New York City police officers. They were vicious and relentless in their attacks on Mr. Wright. They labeled him "Cut 'Em Loose Bruce." But all their venom didn't dissuade Judge Wright from applying what he believed was the Constitution of the United States of America.

Bail should not be used as a punitive whip. If it could be shown that the accused would show up in court at the appropriate time, why put a bail on him or her to say nothing of an exorbitant bail? Moreover, Judge Wright would vigorously argue that it was the indigenous and blacks and Latinos who suffered the most.

During those heated days with the PBA, Judge Wright never wavered. His Counter punches were well-timed and effective. At the height of the fracas, when Mr. Wright was under a furious assault by the PBA, I came up with a brilliant idea: Ask Bruce Wright to preach the Easter sermon. When I called him, he was surprised and amused. He liked the idea and said yes, he would be glad to deliver the Easter message. When Sunday arrived, the people started coming into the church early. By worship time at noon, the church was packed. All New York media was present, and some national press as well.

After the preliminaries—prayers, scripture, music, and offering—I introduced Mr. Wright as a fighter for justice who sought to protect the least in society, as Jesus had done.

Mr. Wright spoke for about thirty minutes. He was superb. He provided the constitutional basis for his actions. He vowed to continue doing what he believed was the right thing. But the best was yet to come.

Then I had a brainstorm: After the sermon, why not keep everybody in place and have a press conference right there in the sanctuary? Mr. Wright thought it was a great idea. I knew his competent, combative spirit would rise to the occasion.

We came out of the pulpit, had a table set up in front of the podium, and Mr. Wright, other leaders, and I sat down behind the table. I opened the press conference with instructions to the audience, who first cheered, then listened attentively as I spoke.

I said, "Here is your opportunity to see up close how the media behaves. Listen to the questions being asked, note who is asking the questions, mark Judge Wright's answers. Then when you watch the television or read the print media, notice how they report the event. What part of Mr. Wright's sermon or his answers are reported? Remember, Mr. Wright's entire sermon, and his full answers, are not going to be shown. There isn't enough time. So whatever is provided for the public is subjective. It will depend on the press's objectivity, life experiences, fairness, honesty, and skill—all those wonderful qualities. And since we are human—and therefore bound to err—the question then is, on which side will the media err?"

When I finished speaking, I invited the media to ask questions. The questions were as expected:

"Why did you release the accused?"

"Because the Constitution gave me the right to do so," Judge Wright replied.

"Aren't you afraid they're going to commit more crimes?" the media asked.

"They hadn't been convicted of any crime, although you in the media seem to have convicted them and want me to treat them as though they had been convicted. I refuse to use the bail as a punishing arm of the law, to treat the accused as though they have already been tried and convicted."

And so the Q & A went.

When one of the reporters asked him to respond to a derogatory comment by the PBA president, Mr. Wright gave this memorable response: "My father taught me never to get into a peeing contest with a skunk because you can't win."

The audience, who had been applauding Mr. Wright's every answer, now burst loose with laughter and thunderous applause, and that ended the press conference.

Judge Wright and I looked at each other, smiled, profoundly pleased and proud of the people and ourselves. We knew we had won this skirmish. We believed this would be the catalyst that would turn the "war" in our favor.

The next day, we marched with thousands of people to Center Street and held a rally in front of the jail and courthouse. We went to Judge Wright's office to encourage him to come out and greet his supporters. When we walked out into the open air, the crowd greeted Judge Wright with roaring cheers and applause, all of which reinforced our earlier feelings that, "The battle we were a-winning."

Judge Wright and I became great friends and mutual admirers of each other. He was a brilliant man, an artist, and a genius. He was more expansive than the judiciary system in which he was bound to move. His adventuresome, poetic juices flowing from his creative energy could never be chained by any one pursuit, especially something as stiff, staid, and imprecise as the system of law. And at the base of it all was a deep sensitivity to the human predicament, and a driving desire for justice tempered with mercy.

So since Judge Bruce Wright had had one of the greatest moments of his illustrious life on Easter, it seemed right that he should leave us during Holy Week.

Judge John Phillips

Sunrise: April 10, 1924,
Sunset: February 13, 2008,

Back in Georgia

While I was in Georgia, a request came for our church to be available for a funeral for Judge John L. Phillips. By the time I responded, arrangements had already been made. Judge Phillips died on February 13, 2008. The excerpts from his obituary read:

> *The Honorable John L. Phillips passed away unexpectedly on Saturday, February 16, 2008, from circumstances unknown. Phillips, known as the Kung-Fu Judge, for his habits of employing martial arts moves on the bench, was born April 10, 1924, to his beloved parents, John Sr. and Icie Mason. He grew up on a Kansas farm and lived in Ohio. He served in the Army Infantry during World War II but never saw combat.*

> *He worked his way through Wilberforce University, and later Akron Law College, where he obtained a law degree. An avid traveler, Phillips went to China and Japan, studying the martial arts, eventually developing his own school of combat, something he called the Gorilla-Gnat System of Scientific Movement and Defensive Fighting. He taught the style for 15 years in a dojo on Nostrand Avenue in Brooklyn, New York.*

> *His accomplishments were many. He was the first Black man admitted to the Montana State Bar and was a 10th degree black belt. He became a self-made millionaire buying up real estate in Bedford Stuyvesant, Brooklyn. He ran for judgeship in Brooklyn Civil Court in 1976, as the anti-machine candidate. He was first elected to the bench in 1977, without the support of Brooklyn's political machine. He served honorably for 17 years, before his retirement in 1994. In 2001, Judge Phillips, at age 77, announced he would challenge the incumbent Charles J. Hynes in the race for the District Attorney in Brooklyn.*

Judge Phillips's holdings included several apartment buildings and two movie theaters, both purchased in the 1980s. He named one, the Century-Regent, the Slave One Theater, "So that no one would ever forget our struggle." He called the other the Black Lady Theatre. Both metaphors of his love for his mother, Icie. Judge Phillips became more widely known, especially among the grassroots in the activities surrounding the Slave Theater. He had purchased the theater because his film work had been rejected by the movie world. The theater became a center for community meetings, forums, lectures, information sharing and organizing.

Sadly, the last days of Judge Phillips were spent in physical and mental deterioration. He was afflicted with Alzheimer's disease. Also, there was controversy regarding his wealth. There were accusations that unauthorized checks were written from his account. He is reported to have said, while in the hospital, "I've got to get out of here. They are stealing my money."

The wake was held at Woodard Funeral Home in Brooklyn. All levels of the community attended. All day long, starting at 2:00 p.m., they filed past the open coffin to see the Kung-Fu Judge. There were few people at the funeral on February 26, 2008, at the Church of the Open Door in Brooklyn. Family members occupied the first pew. Community activists and clergy and friends were scattered across the sanctuary. Everybody spoke highly of the judge's kindness, toughness, Afrocentrism, and community concern.

I confess that I had confused Judge Phillips with our first attorney in 1960, Mr. Phillip Roach. But the things I said, thinking I was speaking about Mr. Roach, are equally applicable to Judge Phillips. What will become of Judge Phillips's body we know. What will become of his wealth is uncertain. What will become of his spirit? Faith declares his spirit will return to the Creator.

Going from funeral to funeral, and remembering so many whose shadows crossed my path when they sojourned on this side of history, there came to my mind the words that I quoted before by Lord Byron: "What are the worst of woes that wait on age? What stamps the wrinkle deeper on the brow? To view each loved one blotted from life's page, and be alone on earth, as I am now."

I would make a slight modification on the reference to loved ones and insert acquaintances or contemporaries. And so, it would read, "To view each acquaintance or contemporary blotted from life's page…"

Surely, we who are among the aged or aging have a feeling of melancholy with the passing of anything we have been around or have known for many years, even inanimate things, such as old houses, shoes, clothes, trinkets, family heirlooms, neighborhoods. How much more do we mourn the passing of living members of the human family, especially those who were near and dear to us. How much more sadness do we feel with their passing.

Endnotes

1   This is a re-edited version of an article that originally appeared in the April 20, 2005 edition of *The Daily Challenge*, published in Brooklyn, New York. Mr. Thomas Watkins, publisher.

2   This is a re-edited version of an article that originally appeared in the April 13, 2005 edition of *The Daily Challenge*, published in Brooklyn, New York. Mr. Thomas Watkins, publisher.

Afterword

By Herb Boyd

Collected here is not only the *Passing of Giants* but a testament to the tireless devotion of Rev. Daughtry to chronicle the life and legacy of these noted and sometimes unknown personalities. How thankful they are that one of their ilk is still standing and dutifully making sure they are not forgotten. This is part of his calling to the good reverend, much like his commitment to the pulpit, anointing the dearly departed with eulogies, he often delivered or documented. Week after week, year after year, he found time in his busy mission to post an obituary in the *Daily Challenge*. As you will see, many of these appeared in the paper, and Rev. Daughtry extends his gratitude to the publisher Thomas Watkins for allowing him the space.

Those who could not keep up with his daily accounts of these words of compassion and commiseration are gathered here under several rubrics, and some resonate with particular agencies because the pastor knew them personally. The easy flow of information the minister delivered in *No Monopoly on Suffering* (Africa World Press, 1997) resumes here, and the individuals profiled, taken collectively, represent a veritable encyclopedia of memory and dedication. Rev. Daughtry has painstakingly researched and gathered data on the departed, several of whom presented a difficult challenge to completely fulfill. Even so, they are included and we hope their families and loved ones can appreciate the effort to make them immortal.

Readers should understand that Rev. Daughtry volunteered to do these obits, and I don't think he ever received any compensation, perhaps hoping that a mere thank you was sufficient. It was a pleasure to assist him in the completion of this project since much of what he has done has been part of my occupation, and to that extent, we have more in common than our names.

As we go to press, the reverend continues to record the names of the passing giants and will do so up until the moment he is one of them, but not too soon.